University of Michigan Studies

HUMANISTIC SERIES

VOLUME XXXVI

STAMPED AND INSCRIBED OBJECTS FROM SELEUCIA ON THE TIGRIS

STAMPED AND INSCRIBED OBJECTS FROM SELEUCIA ON THE TIGRIS

BY

ROBERT HARBOLD McDOWELL

ANN ARBOR
UNIVERSITY OF MICHIGAN PRESS
1935

Copyright, 1935,
By The University of Michigan
Set up and printed,
January, 1935

PRINTED IN THE UNITED STATES OF AMERICA
BY THE PLIMPTON PRESS • NORWOOD • MASS.

To
O. R. McD.
IN APPRECIATION OF LOYAL INTEREST
AND GREAT PATIENCE

PREFACE

The material upon which this volume is based was uncovered on the site of Seleucia on the Tigris. Excavations were conducted there during the seasons 1927/28 to 1931/32 by Professor Leroy Waterman, under the auspices of the University of Michigan, the Toledo Museum of Art and, during the last two seasons, the Cleveland Museum of Art.

A small proportion of the objects was found in trial trenches opened at various points on the mounds. One trench, No. 4, was extended as a vertical cut to water level. During the last three seasons the principal area of excavation comprised an entire city block occupied by a single residential structure. Here, too, a vertical cut was completed to water level, and the block has been cleared through three of its four principal phases of occupation. This building, which has been designated the Great House, formed part of a homogeneous system of rectangular city blocks covering the greater part of the complex of mounds. It lay in the third tier of blocks west of a street which led north from the principal city gate through the approximate center of the system. It was separated by one block from a canal which ran east through the northern portion of the system. This favorable location suggests that the Great House is representative of the upper-class residential section of the city. The three principal levels of occupation which have been completely excavated here correspond in time to the greater part of the period of Parthian occupation of Babylonia: Level I was occupied from between 115 and 120 A.D. to at least 198/99 A.D., Level II from about 43 A.D. to the inauguration of Level I, and Level III from about 141 B.C. to the inauguration of Level II. The earliest principal stratum of occupation in this section of the complex, Level IV, extended from a point in the reign of Seleucus I, probably shortly after 294 B.C., to about 141 B.C.; it was approximately coextensive, therefore, with the period of Seleucid rule in Babylonia.

It is a fact well known to archaeologists that objects of early periods are found in later levels, while numerous objects of all periods lie on the surface of an ancient site. These conditions are caused principally by building operations conducted by the successive occupants of the site and by the collecting instinct on the part of both adults and children in each generation. Objects passed along from level to level are in many cases finally exposed on the latest surface by the erosive action of wind and rain. Such surface objects comprise an important element in the body of material from Seleucia.

The greater part of the material included in this volume has been found in the small portions of Level IV of the Great House which have been revealed by the vertical cut and by the occasional clearing of foundation walls belonging to the level next above. The whole body of excavated material from this block, however, has come in large part from the three levels of the Parthian period.

Chapters I–VIII of this volume deal with impressions of seals and stamps most or all of which had been associated with documents or containers of a commercial or an official import belonging to the period of Seleucid control of Babylonia. Chapter IX is devoted to miscellaneous inscribed and stamped objects from both Seleucid and Parthian levels. Some of the seal impressions have been partly discussed by the present writer in two previous publications: "Bullae," *Preliminary Report upon the Excavations at Tel Umar, Iraq*, University of Michigan Press, 1931, pp. 26–42, and "The Bullae from Seleucia," Excursus III (pp. 98–111) in M. I. Rostovtzeff's "Seleucid Babylonia: Bullae and Seals of Clay with Greek Inscriptions," *Yale Classical Studies*, 3 (1932), 1–114.

The extent of my indebtedness to Professor M. I. Rostovtzeff's recent study of official seal impressions from Orchoi will be very evident to the reader. The material from that site is of a more limited character than that from Seleucia, but Professor Rostovtzeff has thoroughly covered the body of extant knowledge concerning the administration and the financial policy of the Seleucid Empire. His scholarly work has greatly simplified the task of preparation of the present volume, and from its inception his interest in the material has indeed been stimulating.

This volume has been prepared under the direction of the Institute of Archaeological Research of the University of Michigan, and to the members of the Institute I wish to express my appreciation that I have been enabled to study and publish the material. To individual members of the Institute I am indebted also for aid and encouragement in connection with numerous problems, in particular to Dr. F. E. Robbins, assistant to the President and secretary of the Institute, Professor Campbell Bonner, head of the Department of Greek, Professor A. E. R. Boak, chairman of the Department of History, who has been particularly generous of his time and counsel, and Professor Leroy Waterman, head of the Department of Oriental Languages and Literature and director of the excavations at Seleucia, under whom I had the pleasure of working during three seasons on the field. To the Executive Board of the Graduate School, under whose auspices this volume is published, I wish likewise to express my appreciation. Dr. Eugene S. McCartney, editor of the Graduate School Publications, and Mrs. Hilda J. Straw, assistant editor, have rendered very extensive and practical assistance in revision of the manuscript.

R. H. McD.

CONTENTS

CHAPTER		PAGE
	Preface	vii
	Bibliography	xv
I	Attached Sealings of the Seleucid Period. .	1

Definitions, 1; Bullae, 1–2; Appended sealings, 2–4; Interior and exterior versions and the appended sealings, 4–5; Bullae as evidence of registration, 5–6; Relationship of a bulla to its document, and its limitations, 6–9; Appended sealings used on containers, 9–10; Thumb-nail imprints as countermarks on seal impressions, 10; The archives of the Great House, 11–14; Analysis of the sealings; table, 14–24

II	Characteristics of Official Seals	25

Seals of the royal administration, 25; Size and shape as criteria, 25–26; Use of monograms, 26–28; Essential elements in the design of official seals; legends, 28–29; Royal portraits as seal types, 29–30; Representations of deities, 30–31; Types representing the general authority of government, 31–33; Types representing departments and subdivisions, 33–35

III	Catalog of Impressions	36

Synopsis of impressions, 36–39; Seals of departments of state and subdivisions, 39–48; Seals of controllers, 49–50; Stamps of collectors of taxes and other dues, 50–65; Seals of private agents of royalty, 65–73; Private seals, 74–126

IV	Impressions of Seals of Departments of State and Their Subdivisions.	127

An office of the treasury concerned with the issue of currency, 127–128; The bibliophylax, 128–131; The chreophylax, 131–138; Registration for appraisal, 138–141; The act of katagraphe, 141–148; Various acts of registration; evidence of a complex system of administration, 148–151; Controllers, 151–155

V	Stamps of Collectors of Taxes and Other Dues	156

Essential and common characteristics of the stamps, 156–157; The commercial calendar used in Seleucia, 157–161;

CHAPTER		PAGE
	The anchor as the emblem of the royal treasury, 161–163; Other symbols found on the stamps, 163–165; The status of the polis in the royal administration, 165–173; Port dues; the status of the port, 173–175; A tax on imported slaves, 175–179; The salt tax, 179–198	
VI	SEALS OF PRIVATE AGENTS OF ROYALTY	199
	Characteristics of the seals, 199–201; Stewards of royal estates, 201–202; Evidence concerning royal estates in Seleucid Babylonia, 202–206; Evidence concerning private agents of royal families, 206–208	
VII	NOTES ON THE ICONOGRAPHY OF THE IMPRESSIONS	209
	Portraits of Seleucus I; their value for a study of his apotheosis, 209–212; A portrait of Seleucus, son of Antiochus I, 213–214; Portraits assigned to Timarchus and Heracleides; the relation of Timarchus to Bactria, 214–220	
VIII	THE IMPRESSIONS OF PRIVATE SEALS	221
	Their value and limitations, 221–223; An analysis of the impressions, 223–225; The essentially Hellenic character of the seals, 226–228; The origins of the Greek settlers at Seleucia in the light of the quality of the seals, 228–230	
IX	MISCELLANEA	231
	Token sealings, 231–241; Models of Seleucid coins, 241–250; Monogram stamps on pottery, 250–252; Stamped jar handles, 252–253; A Greek stamp for bricks, 254–255; Inscribed objects for play, 255; An inscribed weight, 256–258; Stele fragments, 258–261	
X	CONCLUSION	262
	INDEXES	
	GREEK TERMS	267
	PROPER NAMES	267
	GENERAL INDEX	268

ILLUSTRATIONS

PLATES

(The plates are to be found at the end of the book)

- I Official seals, 1–12
- II Official seals, 13–23; seals of private agents of royalty, 24–32
- III Private seals, 33–57
- IV Private seals, 58–82
- V Private seals, 83–94; token sealings, 95–105
- VI Models of Seleucid coins, 106–116

FIGURES

Greek stamp for bricks	254
Inscriptions from fragments of stelae	258, 260

BIBLIOGRAPHY

ANDREADES, A., "Antimène de Rhodes et Cléomène de Naucrates," Bulletin de correspondance hellénique, 53 (1929), 1–18.
BABELON, E., Les Rois de Syrie, d'Arménie et de Commagène. Paris, 1890.
BELOCH, J. K., Griechische Geschichte. Second edition. Berlin, 1927.
BEVAN, E. R., The House of Seleucus. London, 1902.
BLÜMER, H., "Salz," Pauly-Wissowa Real-Encyclopädie der classischen Altertumswissenschaft. Zweite Reihe, I.
BOAK, A. E. R., "The Book of the Prefect," Journal of Economic and Business History, 1, (1929), 597–617.
BOUCHÉ-LECLERCQ, A., Histoire des Séleucides. Paris, 1914.
BREASTED, J. H., "Oriental Forerunners of Byzantine Paintings," The University of Chicago Oriental Institute Publications, I, 1922.
CARNEGIE, LADY HELENA, ed., Catalogue of the Southesk Collection of Antique Gems. London, 1908.
CAVAIGNAC, E., "La Chronologie des Séleucides," Revue d'Assyriologie, 28 (Sept., 1931), 73–79.
CHABOT, J. B., Choix d'inscriptions de Palmyre. Paris, 1922.
CUMONT, F., Fouilles de Doura-Europos. Paris, 1926.
DESSAU, H., "Der Steuertarif von Palmyre," Hermes, 19 (1884), 486–533.
DITTENBERGER, W., Orientis Graecae Inscriptiones Selectae. Leipzig, 1903–5.
DRIVER, G. R., "A New Seal in the Ashmolean Museum," The Journal of Hellenic Studies, 43 (1923), 55–56.
DUMONT, A., "Poids grec trouvé à Babylone," Revue archéologique, N. Sér. 20 (1869), 191–207.
EDGAR, C. C., "Notes from the Delta," Annales du Service des antiquités de l'Égypte, 8 (1907), 154–157.
FERGUSON, W. S., "The Leading Ideas of the New Period," The Cambridge Ancient History, VII, 1–40.
FURTWÄNGLER, A., Die antiken Gemmen. Leipzig, 1900.
GARDNER, P., Catalogue of Greek Coins, The Seleucid Kings of Syria. London, 1878.
GROSE, S. W., Catalogue of the McClean Collection of Greek Coins, Fitzwilliam Museum. Cambridge, 1929.
GUTSCHMID, ALFRED VON, Geschichte Irans. Tübingen, 1888.
HILL, G. F., Catalogue of the Greek Coins of Arabia, Mesopotamia and Persia. London, 1922.
HULTSCH, F., Griechische und römische Metrologie. Second edition. Berlin, 1882.
IMHOOF-BLUMER, F., Monnaies grecques. Paris, 1883.
—— Porträtköpfe auf antiken Munzen. Leipzig, 1885.

JASTROW, M., The Civilization of Babylonia and Assyria. Philadelphia, 1915.
JOHANSEN, K. FRIIS, "Tonbullen der Seleukidenzeit aus Warka," Acta Archaeologica, 1 (1930), 41–54.
JOHNSON, J., "The Dura Horoscope and the Seleucid Calendar," Dura Studies. Univ. of Penn., 1932, 1–15.
JORDAN, J., Uruk-Warka, Wissenschaftliche Veröffentlichungen der deutschen Orient-Gesellschaft. Leipzig, 1918.
—— Uruk-Warka, Nach den Ausgrabungen der deutschen Orient-Gesellschaft. Leipzig, 1928.
LANGDON, S. H., "Early Babylonia and Its Cities," The Cambridge Ancient History, I, 356–401.
LEHMANN-HAUPT, C. F., "Sprechsal: Noch einmal Kassû," Zeitschrift für Assyriologie, 7 (1892), 328–334.
—— "Hellenistische Forschungen," Klio, 3 (1903), 491–495.
MARSHALL, F. H., "Recent Acquisitions of the British Museum," The Journal of Hellenic Studies, 29 (1909), 151–167.
MECQUENEM, R. DE, "Inventoire de Cachets et Cylindres, Suse, 1925–26," Revue d'Assyriologie, 24 (1927), No. 1, 7–15.
MILNE, J. G., "Clay Sealings from the Fayoum," The Journal of Hellenic Studies, 26 (1906), 32–45.
—— "Ptolemaic Seal Impressions," *ibid.*, 36 (1916), 87–101.
MINNS, E. H., "Parchments of the Parthian Period from Avroman in Kurdistan," The Journal of Hellenic Studies, 35 (1915), 22–65.
POPE, W., Wörterbuch der griechischen Eigennamen. Braunschweig, 1911.
PREISIGKE, F., Namenbuch enthaltend alle . . . Menschen-namen, soweit sie in griechischen Urkunden . . . Ägyptens sich vorfinden. Heidelburg, 1922.
RAWLINSON, G., The Sixth Great Oriental Monarchy. London, 1873.
RICHTER, G. M. A., Catalogue of Engraved Gems in the Classical Style. Metropolitan Museum of Art, 1920.
ROSTOVTZEFF, M. I., "Ptolemaic Egypt," The Cambridge Ancient History, VII, 109–154.
—— "Syria and the East," *ibid.*, VII, 155–196.
—— "Pergamon," *ibid.*, VIII, 590–618.
—— "Seleucid Babylonia: Bullae and Seals of Clay with Greek Inscriptions," Yale Classical Studies, 3 (1932), 1–114.
—— AND C. B. WELLES, "A Parchment Contract of Loan from Doura-Europos on the Euphrates," *ibid.*, 2 (1930), 1–78.
SMITH, S., Babylonian Historical Texts. London, 1924.
SPELEERS, L., Catalogue des intailles et empreintes orientales des Musées royaux du Cinquantenaire. Brussels, 1917.
TARN, W., Hellenistic Civilisation. Second edition. London, 1930.
—— "Egypt against Syria and Macedonia," The Cambridge Ancient History, VII, 699–731.
—— "Parthia," *ibid.*, IX, 574–613.

TORREY, C., "Pehlevi Seal Inscriptions from Yale Collections," Journal of the American Oriental Society, 52 (1932), 201–207.
VOLKMANN, H., "Demetrius I. und Alexander I. von Syrien," Klio, 19 (1925), 373–412.
WEISS, E., Griechisches Privatrecht. Leipzig, 1923.
WESTERMANN, W., "Land Registers of Western Asia under the Seleucids," Classical Philology, 16 (1921), 12–19.
—— Upon Slavery in Ptolemaic Egypt. New York, 1929.
WILCKEN, U., Griechische Ostraka. Leipzig, 1899.
WROTH, W., Catalogue of the Coins of Parthia. London, 1903.

CHAPTER I

ATTACHED SEALINGS OF THE SELEUCID PERIOD

IN THIS volume the term "sealing" designates an object of clay or bitumen which has been impressed with one or more seals. The term "seal" is used only in reference to the original negative by which the positive impression is made. A particular form of seal employed by the Seleucid tax collectors is referred to as a "stamp."

The sealings recovered from the excavations at Seleucia comprise two general classes, distinguished by the uses to which they were put. There appear to be three principal purposes that may be served by sealings: (1) they invariably identify owners; (2) they may, in addition, record the nature of the object with which they are associated; and (3) they may prevent unwarranted access to a document or a container to which they have been attached. One class of sealings from the excavations simply identified owners and were not attached to other objects. These "token" sealings will be discussed in Chapter IX.[1] Chapters I–VIII are devoted to the principal class of sealings, those attached to documents or containers.

The essential characteristic that distinguishes the attached sealings is the presence on each of marks left by a cord. This class of sealings comprises two varieties which differ in the manner in which they were attached and in the purpose which they served. One variety has come to be known as "bullae"; the other is here designated "appended sealings." The term "bullae" is perhaps unfortunate in that the word is applied to a large group of sealings ranging in time from the Sumerian period to the Christian period. The uses to which these objects were put are only relatively analogous to that served by the bullae with which we are concerned.

This particular type of bulla was apparently a product of Babylonian culture in the Hellenistic period.[2] The Babylonians

[1] Pp. 231–241.
[2] Its genesis has been discussed by M. I. Rostovtzeff, "Seleucid Babylonia: Bullae and Seals of Clay with Greek Inscriptions," *Yale Classical Studies*, 3 (1932), 9–18.

had earlier developed clay envelopes for their tablets. The envelope served both to protect the tablet and to provide an accessible résumé of its contents. Since writing on parchment and papyrus superseded the use of clay tablets, the bulla appears to have been developed as an envelope for certain types of documents. The written sheet was rolled or folded and tied around several times with cord. A thick strip of soft clay or bitumen was then pressed over the cord to encircle the document completely. Rostovtzeff[3] has aptly compared this form to a napkin ring. While the material was still soft seals were impressed on its outer surface. A bulla as we find it, separated from its document, is, then, a spheroidal lump with a large tubelike hole through the center. The outer face is composed of a series of facets, each bearing a seal impression. The inner surface of the ring shows a series of grooves left by the now disintegrated cord. Since many of the bullae have survived only as fragments, it is largely the presence of these grooves that enables one to distinguish a bulla fragment from a flat appended sealing.[4] The size of a bulla was dependent upon two factors, the diameter of the rolled or folded document and the number of seals whose impressions were required. When the document was small and the number of seals were numerous, the walls of the ring were thickened to increase the outer surface.

We must now note a fact of prime importance for an appreciation of the purpose served by bullae. As the plastic material hardened, the cord which had been tied around the document became an integral part of the ring. It was entirely possible, therefore, to remove a document from its bulla and to replace it at will. That is, a bulla did not prevent unwarranted access to the document with which it was associated.

The appended sealings are distinguished primarily by the presence of a single small passage through the approximate center of the object from end to end. Such a sealing was formed by pressing a lump of plastic material completely around a section of loose-hanging cord composed of a single strand or of several strands that formed one unit. Its disintegration left the passage through the length of the sealing. That the cord had not been drawn taut is demonstrated by the fact that on all our

---

[3] *Ibid.*, p. 24.   [4] Whole and fragmentary bullae are illustrated on Plate I, Figs. 2, 6, 10, 11; Plate IV, Fig. 66; Plate II, Figs. 17–32.

examples the passage follows the center of the material with a more or less tortuous course. These sealings carry a single seal impression.

The appended sealings may be divided into two groups on the basis of form, which in turn implies a similar distinction in use. The individuals of one group have two faces: one bearing a seal impression is either plane or concave; the other is always convex and is smoothly finished. The faces are of a roughly oval outline. These forms are not the result of chance manipulation of the objects while the material was soft. The arcs of the concave and convex faces are regular. The hole left by the cord follows the lines of the arcs. This group of appended sealings is here termed "convex."[5] The following explanation of the reason for this form was suggested by a description of the well-known Avroman parchments and has been supported by actual experiments.

In describing these parchments Professor Minns explains that two versions of each document were written on a single sheet and were separated by a series of holes in the parchment.[6] The upper half of the sheet with one version was rolled or folded and cord was passed through the holes and tied around this roll. Small sealings were attached in some manner to this cord. The upper portion of the sheet with its version could then be opened only by cutting the cord or breaking the sealings. It is evident that the soft clay could not have been pressed *around* the strands that held the roll together; it could only have been pressed *over* cord that was held taut by the pressure of the roll. If the cord was encased within the sealings from Avroman, as is the case with those from Seleucia, it must be assumed that, after it had been passed through the holes and around the roll, it was tied and the sealings were pressed around the loose ends beyond the knots. No photographs of the Avroman rolls have been preserved, and the description by Minns does not elucidate this point. The circumstances with regard to the sealings from Seleucia, however, were determined by a simple experiment. A sheet of heavy paper was divided into two parts by a series of perforations. One part was rolled and tied with cord that had

---

[5] See Plate I, Fig. 12; Plate II, Fig. 16.

[6] E. H. Minns, "Parchments of the Parthian Period from Avroman in Kurdistan," *The Journal of Hellenic Studies*, 35 (1915), 22.

been passed through the holes. Small lumps of a heavy clay were pressed around the loose ends. The lower half of the sheet was then rolled around the inner portion with its sealings, and the whole was passed through a napkin ring. Later, when the roll was opened, the sealings were found to have assumed a concave-convex shape. The experiment was repeated with the inner portion of the sheet folded into a small compass rather than rolled. The outer portion was again rolled, and the sealings developed a plano-convex form.

On the basis of these observations it may be assumed that the convex sealings were always employed with bullae. The former prevented the unauthorized opening of a document; the latter served as labels to distinguish the nature of the contents. The simple sealings developed from Greek practice; the bullae, from the Babylonian. The combination was a product of the Graeco-Babylonian culture of the Seleucid Empire. This development, along with many other features of Seleucid administrative practice, appears to go back to the opening years of the third century B.C.

It must not be assumed that the documents with which the convex sealings were associated necessarily possessed "interior" and "exterior" versions. It is entirely possible that single versions were written on the upper part of a sheet and sealed in the manner suggested, and that the lower portion left blank was then rolled around the seals to protect them. Offices of registration had been developed in Seleucid Babylonia by the time of the death of Seleucus I. It is likely that such offices preserved abstracts of all documents registered.[7] The existence of these abstracts would to a degree remove the necessity for closed and open versions of contracts. Since, however, the evidence from Seleucia suggests that original contracts were not kept in the offices of registration and that each principal retained a copy in his own archives, it must be admitted that the retention of double versions would have facilitated reference to the details of the transactions in which each archive owner was interested, while at the same time it obviated all possibility of dispute regarding the terms of each contract. Though the government required registration in order to facilitate the collection of taxes, recourse to it as a measure of security was less frequent. In a

[7] See pp. 133-134.

large center such as Seleucia these two forms of registration were separated.[8] The presence of convex sealings in the remains of an archive may be said, therefore, to establish a probability that the documents to which these sealings were attached possessed both interior and exterior versions.

In this connection another question must be raised: Does the presence of a bulla imply the registration of the document to which it was attached? It has been shown that a bulla did not safeguard the contents of a document. As a label it bore the impressions of certain seals or official stamps that appeared on the document itself. If the bulla served simply to identify the document, the same purpose would have been satisfied by a notation on the outside of the roll. The preparation of a bulla in addition to the simple sealings that really protected the document represents a definite expenditure of effort. Business practice does not appear to afford a satisfactory explanation for the development of this form of sealing. What is known of the history of its use points to the same conclusion. Rostovtzeff has noted that no bullae have been found which may be assigned to the periods prior to or later than the Seleucid occupation of Babylonia.[9] Since the publication of his study bullae of the Sassanian period have come to light.[10] At Seleucia the major part of the excavations has been conducted in Parthian levels, but none of our bullae may be assigned to this period. They are first found toward the close of the reign of Seleucus I; they continue into that of Alexander Bala.[11] These limits within which bullae occur may be due to chance. They establish the basis for a presumption, however, that this form of sealing was developed under Seleucid rule. It appears to have been used again by the Sassanids. But its abrupt and apparently complete disappearance after the Parthian occupation of Babylonia points to a specific relation between this form and the Seleucid administrative regulations. Commerce under the Arsacid dynasty continued as before; if the use of bullae had formed a part of ordinary commercial practice, their discontinuance with the change

---

[8] See p. 36. [9] *Op. cit.*, p. 54.

[10] C. Torrey, "Pehlevi Seal Inscriptions from Yale Collections," *Journal of the American Oriental Society*, 52 (1932), 201. Although these sealings are not complete rings, they appear to have been employed in the same manner and for the same purpose as were the bullae of the Hellenistic period.

[11] See p. vii.

in government cannot be explained. On the other hand, it is quite possible that the extreme measure of control over the commerce of Seleucia exercised by the Seleucid kings was relaxed under their successors. Suggestive of such a change is the greater measure of real autonomy enjoyed by the city after the Parthian occupation. The circumstances of the use of bullae and of their occurrence in time can best be explained by an assumption that they were placed on documents as a part of the formality of registration, for fiscal purposes. Owing, however, to the somewhat incomplete character of the evidence it has been disregarded in later discussions concerning the regulation of individual classes of transactions with which our material deals. The circumstances connected with the employment of bullae and the apparently complete cessation of their use with the Parthian occupation have at least a certain value in any attempt to contrast the relations of the city of Seleucia with its successive overlords, the Seleucid and the Arsacid dynasties.

It should be noted further that the derivation of the form of sealing known as bulla from Babylonian practices suggests the influence of native elements in the early Seleucid administrative organization. For thousands of years the temples had been the depositories of documents; without doubt filing systems had been highly developed. Antiochus I, under whose direction there appears to have been constructed a complete administrative and fiscal organization that was continued by his successors, may well have had around him other priests besides the historian Berosus who were responsible for important elements in the structure.

The bullae from Seleucia may bear the impressions of one, two, four, or more seals. None were impressed with three seals. There can be no doubt as to the value of bullae having the impressions of four or more different seals; they encased documents that were contracts for which witnesses were required.[12] The documents represented by bullae bearing the impressions of one or of two seals may be unilateral statements that required some form of notarial registration. It will be suggested in a later paragraph that the seal of the person in whose archive a bulla was filed would not appear on the bulla. On this basis the two different seals on some bullae should represent the other principal

[12] See pp. 179 and 186–187.

to a contract and a single witness. The use in contracts of only one or two witnesses would constitute, however, an exceptional occurrence and is to be doubted. Bullae that bear the impressions of four or more seals form the great majority in the collection from Seleucia. A cursory examination of the large collection of bullae from Orchoi belonging to the Oriental Institute of the University of Chicago revealed a proportion at least as high.[13]

In order to visualize the exact relationship between each bulla and its document let us assume the conditions of the particular form of contract with which the bullae from Seleucia appear to have been chiefly concerned: a contract of sale in connection with which a tax was collected. We shall assume, further, that registration of the contract was required in order to facilitate control by the tax agents. These conditions would have necessitated the assembling of the principals, their witnesses, the tax collector, and an official of registration, meeting in the office of registration. Without doubt each of the persons present affixed his signature and seal to the contract. But for our purposes the important question is whether all the seals placed on the document were likewise impressed on the bulla within which the document was encased. If not, what seals were omitted? The greater part of the bullae from Seleucia were found in the remains of two archives that belonged to a single family. From one archive there have been recovered an almost unbroken annual series of bullae that extend over an entire generation.[14] They represent annual contracts to which the owner of the archive was a party. In no case, however, do we find the repetition of the impression of a particular private seal on a number of successive bullae. It cannot be presumed that the master of the archive changed each year the type of his seal. We must conclude, therefore, that the seal of the archive owner did not appear on the bullae filed within that archive. Another bulla, unrelated to the series mentioned above, bears the impressions of four seals of registration in addition to those of private seals.[15] One of these acts of registration served a juridical purpose, and the others must have been related to the collection of revenue

---

[13] The opportunity to inspect this important group of material was afforded by the courtesy of Dr. J. H. Breasted of the Oriental Institute.

[14] See p. 13.   [15] See pp. 149–150.

on the contract with which the bulla was concerned. But no stamp of a tax collector occurs on the sealing. We have here, then, another instance of the failure to reproduce on a bulla all the seal impressions that must have appeared on the document itself. In contrast with this illustration attention is directed again to the series of annual documents referred to above. The bullae in this series have all been stamped by a tax collector, but bear no impression of a seal of registration. Yet there are reasonable grounds for an assumption that these documents had been registered in connection with the tax payment.[16]

This failure to impress on the envelope all the seals that were placed on the document can be explained by reference to the purpose served by bullae. It has been shown that they were labels, probably to attest the registration of their inclosed documents, certainly to afford the archive owner an accessible résumé of the contents of the documents. In the latter capacity they may be compared to the folders in a modern filing cabinet. Such a folder bears the name of some other person, with whom the owner of the file is in communication; the name of the owner never appears on the folder. In addition to the name of the other party to a transaction a file container often gives explanatory terms such as "due" or "paid." The analogy is, I believe, justified. I assume that a bulla bore only such impressions as would facilitate reference to the contents of its document. Registration required the payment of a fee by one of two principals who submitted a contract. If payment of a tax accompanied the act of registration this also would be a charge on but one of the parties. By which of the principals these charges were met does not concern us here. The point is that whoever made a payment would wish to possess some form of accessible receipt. This purpose would have been served by impressing on the bulla to be retained by him the seal of registration or the stamp of the tax collector, depending upon which charge he had met. On the other hand, the principal who had not paid the fee or the tax would have had no interest in that particular impression. On the basis of these considerations it may be assumed that the series of bullae which have been stamped by a tax collector, but which do not bear the impression of a seal of registration, belonged to the one principal in a series of contracts who had paid

[16] See pp. 197–198.

the tax but not the registration fee. Similarly, the bulla that has been impressed with seals of registration but fails to show the stamp of a tax collector is evidence that the person to whom it belonged had been responsible for the various forms of registration but not for the tax. It is probable that bullae themselves attested the satisfaction of governmental requirements. In addition, when registration and tax payment were associated in one general act, the presence on a bulla of the seal impression of one of the two officials concerned implied the fulfillment of the double requirement. The impression on a single bulla of both the seal of registration and the stamp of the tax collector, a very rare occurrence, must be taken to prove that in this instance one party to a contract satisfied both the fee and the tax.[17]

If we assume again the conditions of a particular contract, it may be suggested that two copies were prepared in addition to a summary entered in the journal of the official of registration. On both documents would be affixed the seals of the principals, the witnesses, and the officials concerned. Each roll would be sealed with convex sealings, and a bulla would be placed around it. It is suggested further that each bulla would be impressed with the seals of one principal, of the witnesses, and of the official who had received a payment from the other principal, whether the amount of the tax or of the fee. The two principals would then exchange copies. On the bulla of the document to be retained by each of them would thus appear the information essential to his needs: the seal impression of the other party, those of the witnesses, and, as a receipt, that of the official to whom he had made a payment. This interpretation appears to fulfill in a satisfactory manner the requirements imposed by the arrangement on the bullae of the various classes of official and private seal impressions. The use of the bullae in an effort to reconstruct elements of the Seleucid administrative practice will lead to serious error unless one keeps in mind the limitations of these envelopes in relation to the original documents themselves.

It remains to discuss the second group of appended sealings.[18] It has been shown that the first group, the convex sealings, were

---

[17] This situation is illustrated by certain of the seal impressions from Orchoi. See Rostovtzeff, *op. cit.*, pp. 42–43, Nos. 63 and 64.   [18] See p. 3.

employed to seal individual documents within which they were rolled. The shapes that characterize the second group afford certain indications of the manner of their use. Some are simply irregular lumps of clay; others have finished faces that are always plane. It follows that they had been attached to loose ends of cord and had not been encased within documents.[19] A few are of small size, showing that single documents were rolled and tied around with cord, the ends of which, beyond the knot, were attached by such sealings. The greater number, however, are large and heavy. One must assume that they were attached to cord that fastened containers. They may have been employed on packages, on sacks, or on the doors of warehouses. This second group of appended sealings has been designated the "container" type.

Before proceeding further, attention must be called to a peculiar feature found on some sealings. Directly across the face of the seal impressions which they bear is an indentation that can have been produced only by the impression of the edge of a thumb nail. These impressions were made while the material was still soft, that is, immediately after the seals themselves had been impressed. They cannot have been intended to cancel a seal impression poorly made or impressed in error. Such mistakes would have been rectified by smoothing over the immediate surface, upon which another impression would have been placed. In the case of bullae with several impressions the thumb-nail mark is found only on the impression of one particular seal. The nail of the thumb was used at times in ancient Babylonia in place of a seal.[20] Although no reference in any period to a practice of countermarking seal impressions is known, no other explanation appears reasonable. It is suggested, therefore, that, if a seal was employed not by its owner directly but by an authorized agent, the latter crossed the seal impression with that of his thumb nail as evidence of his participation in place of the owner.[21]

The provenances of the bullae and the appended sealings are of importance for a study of the seal impressions they bear.

---

[19] Varieties of shape are illustrated on Plate I, Fig. 1; Plate II, Fig. 15.
[20] S. H. Langdon, "Early Babylonia and Its Cities," *The Cambridge Ancient History*, I, 384; cf. M. Jastrow, *The Civilization of Babylonia and Assyria*, p. 335.
[21] Countermarked impressions are illustrated on Plate III, Figs. 35, 41, 49.

On the basis of provenance they may be divided into three groups. The great bulk were found in two rooms of Level IV of the Great House.[22] The remainder come from the surface and from a variety of individual provenances.

The two rooms have been designated archives A and B and the sealings found in each, lots A and B, respectively. Archive A has not as yet been completely excavated; so far as it has been uncovered, the room itself shows no signs of a general conflagration. The sealings, however, found lying in a corner, had been thoroughly burned. In addition, many of them afford unmistakable evidence of having been maliciously broken beyond what would have been necessary in order to release the inclosed documents. On a number of them the seal impressions have been gouged out. The few that are whole and the fragments on which impressions have been preserved formed a small proportion of the total number of sealings which had composed the original lot. There can be no question but that the sealings and, presumably, the documents to which they had been attached were deliberately destroyed, not for purposes of cancellation but with hostile intent.

Archive B lay in a different part of the Great House, but the two rooms were contemporary. Since it has been entirely cleared some details regarding the room can be given. It was small. Along its eastern and western walls lay two platforms of beaten earth about seventy-five centimeters in height and one meter in width. The remains of the walls rose only a short distance above the platforms. The room was filled with débris, the remains of the upper part of the walls and of the ceiling. It was evident that the room had suffered a severe conflagration. The platforms were covered by a fine ash, with an average thickness of one and one-half to two centimeters, perhaps the residue of burned matting. The heat here had been sufficient to bake thoroughly the crude brick of the walls immediately above the platforms. The sealings were all found on the platforms directly in contact with the fine residue. With them were lying fragments of charred wood, not palm, so badly decomposed that it was not possible to form an idea of their original shape. Among these fragments lay iron nails and bronze straps. Some of these straps were perforated, and in the holes were iron nails. These

[22] See Preface, p. vii.

remains suggest shelves or chests; the shape of one of the straps makes the latter alternative the more likely. A whole bulla with its folds of string still unbroken affords evidence that documents had been burned with the sealings. No traces of writing material, however, could be distinguished. Since it was apparent that the upper portion of the walls and the ceiling had fallen upon the platforms after the contents of the latter had been burned, it does not seem possible that the remains of the burned documents could have preserved any recognizable shape. Scattered among the débris was a scant handful of charred small grain, not enough to suggest that grain had been stored in the room.[23] In addition, a few pieces of pottery were recovered from the platforms. The floor of the room between the two platforms did not show the layer of ash, nor were any objects recovered from it.

So far as it appears possible to form an idea of the contents of the room before its destruction, it is likely that the platforms supported chests, and that in the chests were filed documents to which the sealings had been attached. Since the sealings were found well distributed over the platforms and the chests, to judge from the number of the nails, were few, it is probable that the documents had been removed from the chests and scattered about before fire was applied. The sealings of Archive B have suffered less intentional breakage than those of Archive A, and the small fragments on which no impressions have been preserved form a slight proportion of the whole. That they were intentionally burned, however, and not simply destroyed as a result of a general conflagration is reasonably established by the fact that the inflammable contents of the platform had been reduced to ashes before the ceiling collapsed. It is always to be remarked in the burning of a house constructed of crude brick that the ceilings of the rooms tend to fall in at an early stage and that the mass of material thus brought down acts partly to preserve the contents of the rooms. Further evidence to establish the malicious destruction of the archive is afforded by the scattering of the contents of the chests before they were burned.

[23] It is worthy of note in this connection that the Avroman documents were found in a vessel that contained grain (see Minns, *op. cit.*, p. 22). Is it possible that grain was placed in the containers with documents to absorb excess moisture?

The date limits of the two archives can be established within a reasonably close range. Archive A had been opened as early as the closing years of the reign of Seleucus I, and had continued in use until some time in the reign of Demetrius II. The evidence for this dating is afforded by impressions that occur on the sealings from this archive. These impressions bear either royal portraits or dated legends. In spite of the destruction suffered by Archive A, sealings have been preserved that belong to the reigns of the following kings: Seleucus I, Antiochus I, Seleucus II, Antiochus, son of Seleucus III, Antiochus III, Antiochus IV, Demetrius I, Alexander Bala, and Demetrius II. The portrait of Seleucus I represents him as an elderly man.[24] The active commercial life of Seleucia appears to have been inaugurated during the period after 294 B.C., when Antiochus I was co-ruler in the east. It is to this period between 294 and 280 B.C. that we must assign the opening of Archive A. It is reasonable to assume that by 141 B.C. the archive had been closed.[25]

Since the greater part of the impressions on the sealings from Archive B have been preserved and since they contain an almost unbroken series of dated legends, it is possible to establish definite limits for the period in which this archive was in active use. It was opened about 188 B.C. and continued to receive accretions into the year 153/52 B.C.[26] Notwithstanding the fact that the special file was closed while Archive A continued in use, there is reason to believe that Archive B was destroyed only at the close of occupation of the level, at the same time as Archive A. This assumption is based on the fact that the room had been thoroughly gutted by the fire. If this fire had been limited to the one room and had occurred prior to the close of occupation of the level, the débris would have been cleared away and the room repaired. Since, on the contrary, the foundations of the succeeding level rest partly on the débris within Archive B, one is forced to assume that the fire marked the close of occupation. Some of the bullae bore a thin incrustation of light-colored clay similar in composition to that of which the crude brick was formed. I judge that the ruined room lay exposed to the winter

[24] See p. 65, No. IIA1a(1).

[25] The portrait of Demetrius II shows him bearded. Whether or not this is of significance for a close determination of the date of the sealing on which it occurs cannot be discussed in the present work.

[26] See pp. 55–64, Nos. IC1b(2) to IC1b(35).

rains, which seeped through the fallen walls to stain the bullae. The evidence of the fire in both archives and the clear-cut indications that the sealings in Archive A were maliciously broken link the destruction of both files with that of the house itself.

The attached sealings from Seleucia total two hundred and three. Of these one hundred and sixty-four, or just over eighty per cent, were recovered from the two archives. The impressions on these sealings belong, therefore, to the third century B.C. and the first half of the second, the period of Seleucid control of Babylonia. Of the remainder twenty-nine were found on the surface. Seventeen of the twenty-nine can be definitely assigned to the Seleucid period through the presence of dated legends, royal portraits, or other characteristic Seleucid emblems. The other twelve sealings bear impressions that represent motifs common to Greek artistic concept. The remaining ten were found in various provenances, for the most part from Parthian levels. Six of these bear impressions that represent either royal portraits or official seal types which identify them as of the Seleucid period. The remaining four have Greek motifs. Of the total of two hundred and three sealings only sixteen, less than eight per cent, are not directly connected through their impressions with the period of Seleucid rule; of these but two per cent are from Parthian levels. Merely two bullae, representing one per cent of the total number of sealings, were found in Parthian provenances. Since by far the greater part of the excavations at Seleucia have been carried on in Parthian levels, the fact that such a small proportion of the attached sealings has been found in these levels establishes a presumption that none of the specimens of this class should be assigned to the Parthian period. It is a well-known fact that successive occupations and rebuilding of an ancient site frequently carried along durable objects from earlier to later levels. The evidence afforded by the definite relationship of the class of attached sealings to the Seleucid period, therefore, more than counterbalances that of the provenance of the few sealings found in Parthian levels.

The accompanying table gives a list of the attached sealings from Seleucia according to the classification elaborated in the preceding paragraphs. In the table this classification has been expressed in terms of combined letter and numeral groups. The values of the elements in these groups are as follows:

A. The general class of attached sealings. (The letter B will be employed to denote the "token sealings" discussed in Chapter IX.)
   I. Bullae
      a. Single: bearing the impression of one seal
      b. Dual: bearing the impressions of two seals
      c. Multiple: bearing the impressions of four or more seals
      d. Indeterminate: fragments which because of their incompleteness cannot be assigned to one of the three preceding groups
   II. Appended sealings
      a. Convex
      b. Container type

TABLE OF ATTACHED SEALINGS

The serial group denoting each sealing is followed by a statement of its provenance. Under each sealing are listed the impressions that occur on it. Each impression is identified by the serial group employed in the catalog of impressions (pp. 39–126). The impression number is followed by a short description of its type.

Sealing number	Provenance	Impression number	Description of type
AIa			
(1)	Archive A	IIIA1a(2)	Private; Apollo
(2)	Archive A	IIIA1c(3)	Private; Athena
(3)	Archive A	IIIA1e(2)	Private; Nike
(4)	Archive A	IIIA3a(2)	Private; priest or worshiper
(5)	Archive A	IIIC1a(4)	Private; woman holding palm
AIb			
(1)	Archive A	IIA1a(1)	Private royal; portrait of Seleucus I
		IIIC3b(1)	Private; pastoral
(2)	Archive A	IIA2(4)	Private royal; portrait of a king, unidentified
		IIIA2a(2)	Private; Bust of Hermes
(3)	Archive A	IIIA1f(8)	Private; Tyche
		Another	Obscure
(4)	Archive A	IIIA1x(2)	Private; unidentified deity
		IIIE1b(1)	Private; bullock's head
AIc			
(1)	Archive B	IC1b(7)	Official; salt tax
		IIID3a(2)	Private; comic mask
		Two others	Obscure

Sealing number	Provenance	Impression number	Description of type
AIc			
(2)	Archive B	ICIb(8)	Official; salt tax
		IIIAIc(13)	Private; Athena head
		IIID2a(1)	Private; herm
		IIID3a(1)	Private; comic mask
(3)	Archive B	ICIb(11)	Official; salt tax
		IIIA2c(5)	Private; Psyche
		IIID3a(3)	Private; comic mask
		IIID4c(2)	Private; twin vessels inverted
(4)	Archive B	ICIb(13)	Official; salt tax
		IIID6a(2)	Private; palm tree
		Two others	Obscure
(5)	Archive B	ICIb(14)	Official; salt tax
		IIIBIa(1)	Private; Hercules
		IIID6a(3)	Private; palm tree
		Another	Obscure
(6)	Archive B	ICIb(17)	Official; salt tax
		IIIB2a(5)	Private; Medusa head
		Two others	Obscure
(7)	Archive B	ICIb(18)	Official; salt tax
		IIIAIf(10)	Private; Tyche
		Two others	Obscure
(8)	Archive B	ICIb(19)	Official; salt tax
		IIIA2c(6)	Private; Psyche
		IIID2b(1)	Private; herm
		Another	Obscure
(9)	Archive B	ICIb(20)	Official; salt tax
		IIIAIc(14)	Private; Athena head
		IIIA2d(1)	Private; Silenus head
		IIID3a(4)	Private; comic mask
(10)	Archive B	IB3(2)	Official; monogram (used unofficially by witness)
		ICIb(25)	Official; salt tax
		Two others	Obscure
(11)	Archive A	IAId(1)	Official; katagraphe
		IIAIq(1)	Private royal; portraits of Alexander I and Cleopatra Thea
		IIIAIx(3)	Private; unidentified deity
		Another	Obscure
(12)	Archive A	IAIb(1)	Official; chreophylax
		IA3a(1)	Official; portrait of Seleucus I as Zeus
		IA3c(1)	Official; portrait of Seleucus, son of Antiochus I

ATTACHED SEALINGS

Sealing number	Provenance	Impression number	Description of type
AIc			
(12)	Archive A	IA3u(2)	Official; Apollo head
		IIID1a(1)	Private; tripod
		IIID4c(5)	Private; twin vessels inverted
		Three others	Obscure
(13)	Archive A	IA1b(2)	Official; chreophylax
		IA1e(1)	Official; katagraphe
		IIID3c(1)	Private; multiple mask
		Two others	Obscure
(14)	Archive A	IIA1g(1)	Private royal; portrait of Antiochus, son of Seleucus III
		IIB1a(1)	Private royal; portrait of queen (wife of Seleucus III?)
		IIIA1d(6)	Private; Artemis head
		Two others	Obscure
(15)	Archive B	IIA2(7)	Private royal; portrait of unidentified king
		IIIA1a(1)	Private; Apollo
		Two others	Obscure
(16)	Archive A	IIB2(8)	Private royal; portrait of unidentified queen
		IIIA1b(6)	Private; Dionysus
		IIIA1c(5)	Private; Athena
		IIIA1c(6)	Private; Athena
		IIIA1c(7)	Private; Athena
		IIIC1a(2)	Private; woman holding palm
(17)	Archive A	IIIA2c(2)	Private; Psyche
		IIIA3a(1)	Private; priest or worshiper
		IIIB1b(1)	Private; Odysseus
		IIID5a(2)	Private; column
		IIIE1a(3)	Private; lion
(18)	Archive B	IIIA2b(2)	Private; Eros
		IIIA2b(10)	Private; Eros
		IIIA2d(3)	Private; Silenus
		IIIB3b(4)	Private; griffin
		IIIC2b(2)	Private; nude woman dancing
		IIIC2b(3)	Private; nude woman dancing
(19)	Archive B	IIIA2c(3)	Private; Psyche
		IIID4a(1)	Private; vessel
		Three others	Obscure
(20)	Archive B	IIIA2c(4)	Private; Psyche
		IIID4a(2)	Private; vessel
		Three others	Obscure
(21)	Archive A	IIID4c(1)	Private; twin vessels inverted

OBJECTS FROM SELEUCIA

Sealing number	Provenance	Impression number	Description of type
AIc			
(21)	Archive A	IIIE3a(1)	Private; insect
		Two others	Obscure
(22)	Archive A	IIIE1c(2)	Private; camel
		Three others	Obscure
(23)	Surface	IIIB1a(5)	Private; Hercules head
		IIIA2e(1)	Private; head of river god
		IIID3a(8)	Private; comic mask
		Two others	Obscure
(24)	Great House, Level III, Room 141 sub		
		IA3o(1)	Official; portrait of Timarchus
		IA3o(2)	Official; portrait of Heracleides
		IIIA1c(9)	Private; Athena
		IIIA1f(14)	Private; Tyche
		IIIB2a(2)	Private; Medusa head
		IIID4c(3)	Private; twin vessels inverted
(25)	Surface	IIIC2a(2)	Private; nude woman playing instrument.
		Three others	Obscure
(26)	Surface	IA3m(1)	Official; portrait of Antiochus IV
		IIIA2a(1)	Private; Bust of Hermes
		IIID3a(7)	Private; comic mask
		Two others	Obscure
AId			
(1)	Surface	IC1a(1)	Official; salt tax
(2)	Archive A	IC1a(2)	Official; salt tax
(3)	Surface	IC1a(3)	Official; salt tax
(4)	Archive A	IC1a(4)	Official; salt tax
		IIIA1e(3)	Private; Nike
(5)	Archive A	IC1a(6)	Official; salt tax
(6)	Surface	IC1a(7)	Official; salt tax
(7)	Surface	IC1a(8)	Official; salt tax
(8)	Surface	IC1a(10)	Official; salt tax
(9)	Archive A	IC1a(11)	Official; salt tax
(10)	Archive A	IC1a(12)	Official; salt tax
(11)	Archive B	IC1b(2)	Official; salt tax
		Another	Obscure
(12)	Archive B	IC1b(3)	Official; salt tax
		IIIA1f(7)	Private; Tyche
(13)	Archive B	IC1b(4)	Official; salt tax
		IIIC1a(3)	Private; woman holding palm
(14)	Archive B	IC1b(5)	Official; salt tax
		IIIB1a(2)	Private; Hercules
		IIID5a(1)	Private; column

ATTACHED SEALINGS

Sealing number	Provenance	Impression number	Description of type
AId			
(15)	Archive B	ICıb(6)	Official; salt tax
		Another	Obscure
(16)	Archive B	ICıb(9)	Official; salt tax
		Two others	Obscure
(17)	Archive B	ICıb(10)	Official; salt tax
		IIBıb(1)	Private royal; portrait of Laodice wife of Seleucus IV (?)
		IIIC2a(1)	Private; nude woman playing instrument
(18)	Archive B	ICıb(12)	Official; salt tax
		Another	Obscure
(19)	Archive B	ICıb(15)	Official; salt tax
(20)	Archive B	ICıb(16)	Official; salt tax
(21)	Archive B	ICıb(21)	Official; salt tax
		IIAım(1)	Private royal; portrait of Antiochus IV
(22)	Archive B	ICıb(22)	Official; salt tax
		Another	Obscure
(23)	Archive B	ICıb(23)	Official; salt tax
(24)	Archive B	ICıb(24)	Official; salt tax
		Two others	Obscure
(25)	Archive B	ICıb(26)	Official; salt tax
(26)	Archive B	ICıb(27)	Official; salt tax
(27)	Archive B	ICıb(28)	Official; salt tax
(28)	Archive B	ICıb(29)	Official; salt tax
		IIID3a(5)	Private; comic mask
(29)	Archive B	ICıb(30)	Official; salt tax
(30)	Archive B	ICıb(31)	Official; salt tax
(31)	Archive B	ICıb(32)	Official; salt tax
(32)	Archive B	ICıb(33)	Official; salt tax
(33)	Archive B	ICıb(34)	Official; salt tax
(34)	Archive B	ICıb(35)	Official; salt tax
(35)	Archive A	ICıc(1)	Official; slave tax
(36)	Archive A	IC2a(1)	Official; port dues
(37)	Archive A	IAıc(1)	Official; registration for assessment
(38)	Archive A	IA3f(1)	Official; portrait of Seleucus III
(39)	Archive A	IIAıg(2)	Private royal; portrait of Antiochus, son of Seleucus III
		IIBıa(2)	Private royal; portrait of queen (wife of Seleucus III?)
(40)	Archive A	IIAıi(1)	Private royal; portrait of Antiochus III

20   OBJECTS FROM SELEUCIA

Sealing number	Provenance	Impression number	Description of type
AId			
(41)	Archive A	IIA1p(1)	Private royal; portrait of Demetrius I
(42)	Archive A	IIA1s(2)	Private royal; portraits of Demetrius II and Cleopatra Thea
(43)	Archive B	IIA1k(1)	Private royal; portrait of Seleucus IV
(44)	Archive A	IIA2(2)	Private royal; portrait of unidentified king
(45)	Archive A	IIA2(3)	Private royal; portrait of unidentified king
(46)	Archive A	IIA2(5)	Private royal; portrait of unidentified king
		IIIA1f(11)	Private; Tyche
		IIIA3a(3)	Private; priest or worshiper
(47)	Archive A	IIB2(7)	Private royal; portrait of unidentified queen
(48)	Archive A	IIB2(3)	Private royal; portrait of unidentified queen
(49)	Archive A	IIB2(10)	Private royal; portrait of unidentified queen
(50)	Archive A	IIB2(4)	Private royal; portrait of unidentified queen
(51)	Archive A	IIB2(5)	Private royal; portrait of unidentified queen
(52)	Archive A	IIIA1a(3)	Private; Apollo
(53)	Surface	IIIA1b(1)	Private; Dionysus
		IIIA1d(5)	Private; Artemis
(54)	Surface	IIIA1b(5)	Private; Dionysus
		IIIB3b(2)	Private; Griffin
		Another	Obscure
(55)	Archive B	IIIA1c(1)	Private; Athena
(56)	Archive B	IIIA1c(2)	Private; Athena
(57)	Archive B	IIIA1c(4)	Private; Athena
(58)	Archive A	IIIA1c(11)	Private; Athena head
		IIIE1a(1)	Private; lion
		IIIE3b(1)	Private; crab or frog
(59)	Archive A	IIIA1c(12)	Private; Athena head
		IIIE1a(2)	Private; lion
		IIIE3b(2)	Private; crab or frog
(60)	Archive A	IIIA1d(1)	Private; Artemis
(61)	Archive A	IIIA1d(2)	Private; Artemis
(62)	Archive A	IIIA1d(3)	Private; Artemis

ATTACHED SEALINGS

Sealing number	Provenance	Impression number	Description of type
AId			
(63)	Archive A	IIIAId(4)	Private; Artemis
(64)	Archive A	IIIAIe(1)	Private; Nike
(65)	Archive A	IIIAIe(6)	Private; Nike
(66)	Archive B	IIIAIf(1)	Private; Tyche
(67)	Archive B	IIIAIf(2)	Private; Tyche
(68)	Archive B	IIIAIf(3)	Private; Tyche
(69)	Archive B	IIIAIf(4)	Private; Tyche
(70)	Archive A	IIIAIf(5)	Private; Tyche
		IIIB3b(1)	Private; Griffin
(71)	Surface	IIIAIf(6)	Private; Tyche
(72)	Archive A	IIIAIf(9)	Private; Tyche
		IIIA2b(9)	Private; Eros
(73)	Archive A	IIIAIf(12)	Private; Tyche
(74)	Archive B	IIIA2b(3)	Private; Eros
(75)	Archive B	IIIA2b(4)	Private; Eros
		Two others	Obscure
(76)	Archive A	IIIA2b(7)	Private; Eros
(77)	Archive A	IIIA2b(8)	Private; Eros
(78)	Archive A	IIIA2b(11)	Private; Eros
(79)	Archive A	IIIA2c(1)	Private; Psyche
(80)	Archive A	IIIBIb(2)	Private; Odysseus
(81)	Archive A	IIIBIb(3)	Private; Odysseus
(82)	Archive A	IIIBIb(4)	Private; Odysseus
(83)	Archive A	IIIBIb(5)	Private; Odysseus
(84)	Archive A	IIIBIb(6)	Private; Odysseus
(85)	Archive B	IIIB2a(1)	Private; Medusa head
(86)	Archive A	IIIB2a(4)	Private; Medusa head
(87)	Archive B	IIIBIa(4)	Private; Hercules head
		IIIC3a(2)	Private; warrior
		IIID5b(1)	Private; hand clasping object
(88)	Archive A	IIIB2b(1)	Private; Opheltes and the dragon
(89)	Archive A	IIIB3a(1)	Private; demon
(90)	Archive A	IIIB3a(2)	Private; demon
(91)	Archive A	IIICIb(2)	Private; woman holding lyre
		IIID6a(1)	Private; palm tree
(92)	Archive B	IIIC2b(1)	Private; nude woman dancing
(93)	Archive A	IIICIa(1)	Private; woman holding palm
(94)	Archive A	IIICIa(5)	Private; woman holding palm
(95)	Archive A	IIIC3a(1)	Private; warrior
(96)	Archive A	IIIC3c(1)	Private; convivial
(97)	Archive A	IIIDIe(1)	Private; ceremonial lamp
		IIIDIf(1)	Private; ceremonial standard

Sealing number	Provenance	Impression number	Description of type
AId			
(98)	Archive A	IIID4b(1)	Private; vessel
(99)	Archive A	IIID4b(2)	Private; vessels
(100)	Archive A	IIID4b(3)	Private; vessels
(101)	Archive A	IIID1c(1)	Private; star or sun
(102)	Archive A	IIA1s(1)	Private royal; portrait of Demetrius II
(103)	Archive B	IIIE2a(1)	Private; peacock
(104)	Archive B	IIIE2a(2)	Private; peacock
		Two others	Obscure
(105)	Archive A	IIIE2c(1)	Private; pheasant
(106)	Surface	IC1b(1)	Official; salt tax
(107)	Surface	IC1a(5)	Official; salt tax
(108)	Surface	IC1a(9)	Official; salt tax
(109)	Surface	IIIA2c(7)	Private; Psyche
(110)	Surface	IIIA2d(2)	Private; Silenus mask
(111)	Great House, Level III, Room 160		
		IIIA1e(4)	Private; Nike
(112)	Great House, Level III, Room 306		
		IIIA1x(4)	Private; unidentified deity
		IIIB1a(3)	Private; Hercules
(113)	Surface	IIIB3b(3)	Private; griffin
(114)	Surface	IIID6b(1)	Private; fruit on a branch
(115)	Surface	IIID1d(1)	Private; caduceus in obscure design
AIIa			
(1)	Great House, Level I, Room 130		
		IB3(1)	Official; monogram
(2)	Surface	IA3u(1)	Official; Apollo
(3)	Archive B	IIA2(1)	Private royal; portrait of unidentified king
(4)	Archive A	IIB2(6)	Private royal; portrait of unidentified queen
(5)	Archive B	IIB2(1)	Private royal; portrait of unidentified queen
(6)	Archive B	IIB2(2)	Private royal; portrait of unidentified queen
(7)	Archive B	IIB2(9)	Private royal; portrait of unidentified queen
(8)	Archive B	IIIA1f(13)	Private; Tyche
(9)	Archive A	IIIA1x(1)	Private; unidentified deity
(10)	Archive B	IIIA2b(1)	Private; Eros
(11)	Archive A	IIIB1c(1)	Private; Penelope
(12)	Archive B	IIIC1b(1)	Private; woman holding lyre

ATTACHED SEALINGS

Sealing number	Provenance	Impression number	Description of type
AIIa			
(13)	Archive B	IIIC2a(3)	Private; nude woman musician
(14)	Archive B	IIIC2c(1)	Private; nude woman
(15)	Archive B	IIIC2c(2)	Private; nude woman
(16)	Archive A	IIID3a(6)	Private; comic mask
(17)	Archive A	IIID3b(1)	Private; tragic mask
(18)	Archive A	IIIE1c(1)	Private; camel
(19)	Archive B	IIIE2b(1)	Private; dove
(20)	Surface	IB2a(1)	Official; monogram
(21)	Archive B	IIIA2b(6)	Private; Eros
(22)	Archive B	IIIA1b(4)	Private; Dionysus
(23)	Archive B	IIIB2a(3)	Private; Medusa head
(24)	Archive B	IIID6c(1)	Private; grain
(25)	Archive B	IIIA2b(5)	Private; Eros
(26)	Archive B	IIIA1c(15)	Private; Athena head
(27)	Archive B	IIIA1c(10)	Private; Athena head
(28)	Archive B	IIIA1b(2)	Private; Dionysus
(29)	Archive B	IIA10(1)	Private royal; portrait of Timarchus
(30)	Archive B	IIIA1b(3)	Private; Dionysus
(31)	Archive B	IIIA1c(8)	Private; Athena
(32)	Archive B	IIID1b(1)	Private; crescent and star in design
(33)	Archive B	IIIC3a(5)	Private; warrior
(34)	Archive B	IIIC3a(4)	Private; warrior
(35)	Archive B	IIIC3a(3)	Private; warrior
(36)	Great House, Level III, Room 14		
		IIID4c(4)	Private; twin vessels inverted
AIIb			
(1)	Trial Trench 4, D11		
		IA2a(1)	Official; anchor and horse's head
(2)	Surface	IA2a(2)	Official; anchor and horse's head
(3)	Surface	IA2a(3)	Official; anchor and horse's head
(4)	Great House, Level I, Room 38		
		IIIA1e(5)	Private; Nike
(5)	Surface	IIIE2d(1)	Private; eagle
(6)	Trial Trench 4, Level III		
		IIA2(6)	Private royal; portrait of unidentified king
(7)	Archive B	IIIA2b(12)	Private; Eros
(8)	Archive B	IIIA2b(13)	Private; Eros

Sealing number	Provenance	Impression number	Description of type
AIIb			
(9)	Archive A	IA1a(2)	Official; bybliophylax
(10)	Archive A	IA1a(1)	Official; bybliophylax
(11)	Surface	IA3u(3)	Official; Apollo
(12)	Surface	IA3v(1)	Official; Artemis head
(13)	Great House, Level III, Room 14		
		IA1b(3)	Official; chreophylax
(14)	Surface	IA1b(4)	Official; chreophylax
(15)	Great House, Level II, Room 260		
		IB1a(1)	Official; monogram
(16)	Surface	IA2a(4)	Official; anchor and horse's head
(17)	Surface	IIID1g (1)	Private; thunderbolt

CHAPTER II

CHARACTERISTICS OF OFFICIAL SEALS

The essential purpose of a seal is to identify the authority which it represents. That behind a private seal is single, representing the individual who owns and uses it. That behind an official seal is necessarily dual: it must identify the general authority of the government and, in addition, the particular subdivision of government which employs the seal. Official seals would fail to serve their purpose if they did not clearly distinguish a particular function of government as well as the general. Within the Seleucid Empire there existed seals of the royal government, of dependent principalities, and of the various city governments. These general groups in turn must have comprised categories of seals representing subdivisions of government. It is important to bear in mind that in a great center of administration such as was Seleucia the total number of offices and functions was large.

There is no question of the use in Seleucia of seals of a dependent principality.[1] For the time being it is assumed that all impressions of official seals with which we are concerned identify subdivisions of the royal government. The immediate problem is the determination of the characteristics that distinguish impressions of official seals from those of private seals, and that differentiate the various categories in the group of official seals. But little has been known of the administrative organization of the Seleucid Empire.[2] The seal impressions from Seleucia and Orchoi add considerably to this knowledge, especially as applied to Seleucid Babylonia. Owing to the necessarily incomplete evidence, deductions based on it regarding forms developed in this area may not be unduly stressed.

Characteristics possessed by every seal impression are shape

[1] Whether the polis of Seleucia is represented in any way among the impressions that have been found will be discussed in a later chapter.

[2] M. I. Rostovtzeff, "Syria and the East," *The Cambridge Ancient History*, VII, 166–167; W. Tarn, *Hellenistic Civilisation*², pp. 121–122.

and size and the details of the design. It will be found that a great many impressions do not reproduce all the characteristics of the seals by which they were made. Many were stamped in a careless manner; some have been overimpressed by other seals; and all have been subject to wear. In particular, legends, monograms, and symbols adjunct to the central type become obscure or are lost.

As a rule the shape of official seals does not appear to have possessed any significance. The one exception noted is furnished by the class of impressions that represents stamps of collectors of taxes and other dues.[3] These stamps, whatever the nature of the design, have a common shape, ovoid, with the short sides straight and the long sides very slightly curved. With few exceptions a uniform proportion between length and height is maintained. No impressions representing other classes of official seals or private seals appear to duplicate this shape.

It is generally assumed that official seals are larger than private ones. But in particular instances a writer, noting on a small seal a design that appears to have official characteristics, may classify the piece on the basis of design alone. With two definitely fixed exceptions there is no evidence from Seleucia or from other sites of Seleucid Babylonia that suggests the existence of official seals as small as the larger private seals, or of private seals comparable in size with the smaller official signets. One exception consists of a class of official seals that have monograms as types or as symbols; for the most part the impressions representing this class are small. As exceptions again must be noted a group of impressions whose designs do not suggest their official nature, but whose dimensions are greater than the average maintained by private seals. It is probable that such seals belonged to semipublic institutions such as temples. Since they possess no particular significance as a group and are limited in number, they have not been classified separately, but are listed under the various groups of impressions of private seals.

Reference has been made to a group of impressions that show monograms either as type or as adjunct to the type. One of these, impression No. IB1a(1), has the normal characteristics of an official seal; it is large and has as type a royal portrait. The monogram occupies a secondary position. The other three,

[3] See p. 156.

Nos. IB1b(1), IB2a(1), and IB2a(2), though larger than the average for private seals, have dimensions that fail to approximate those of the smaller official seals. The last two have monograms as types. The remaining impression is distinctive in that the monogram appears to have been incised on the gem as a subsequent addition to a motif that is characteristically private.[4] Superficially the four impressions appear to have little in common, though all but the first fail to display the elements that characterize normal official seals. The presence of monograms, however, appears to require their classification together as representative of a distinct form of official seal. One cannot defend the assumption that during the second and third centuries B.C. monograms were used at Seleucia as the type of, or other element in, private seals. Inspection of the catalogs of Greek and Roman gems shows practically no examples of the use of such a device. Dr. G. M. A. Richter, of the Metropolitan Museum of Art, has stated in this regard: "It would have been an alien thought to a Greek or Roman to use for his device merely his monogram, as we might nowadays. His name or initials might appear occasionally on the gem in a secondary place; but the principal design would be pictorial."[5] Monograms used alone or associated with a type figure would greatly facilitate the expression of individuality. It cannot be assumed that the idea did not occur to the Greeks, or that it was repugnant to them. Their failure to employ the monogram motif on their private seals would appear rather to have been due to the reservation of this class of design for a restricted purpose. Beginning with the fourth century B.C. monograms are found on coins, weights, and pottery. The first two groups are definitely official. It cannot be shown that monograms on pottery represented the maker. In some instances such a stamp denoted the genuine character of the ware; the monograms have, then, a value at least semiofficial.

Practical evidence that private citizens in Seleucia did not employ monograms as seal types is afforded by the proportion between the three small impressions that bear such a device and the total number of seal impressions of the Seleucid period recov-

---

[4] For the catalog description of these impressions see pages 49–50; a detailed discussion of their significance will be found on pages 151–155.

[5] *Catalogue of Engraved Gems in the Classical Style*, p. xxi.

ered, some three hundred. Of the many hundreds of contemporary seal impressions from other sites of Babylonia I know of none that have monograms as a part of the design. In groups such as those in Seleucia, which were obliged to share the small stock of familiar pictorial designs — the repetition of Athena types, Odysseus types, and so forth — would a design that afforded the individuality of which monograms are capable have appealed to but one individual of a hundred?

It is essentially the design engraved on a seal that identifies the authority behind the signet and distinguishes it from other seals. The design of a seal may consist of but one element, the type, or of a central type with which is associated a legend, monogram, or symbol. Variety of design may be attained in two ways: (1) by changing the type, or (2) by introducing new secondary elements in a common type. The great majority of the impressions of private seals from Seleucia show a design consisting of but one element. Variation was achieved largely in the manner of portrayal of a rather limited number of stock motifs.[6] No seal impression in our collection that by reason of size appears to be private bears a legend. All legends that occur on the impressions are definitely official in respect to their subject-matter. Legends on private seals are, of course, known from elsewhere. They consist for the most part of an ejaculation or of a name, that of the owner or that of the engraver.[7]

Although the occurrence of legends on the impressions from Seleucia is limited to those of an official character, not all official seals were inscribed. Impressions that on the basis of size and type appear to be official may be divided into three groups: those that have legends; those that bear symbols or monograms in place of legends; and those that are incomplete and show no legend, symbol, or monogram. This third category comprises impressions whose condition does not permit of the determination of the presence or absence on the original seals of one of

[6] The motifs common to private seals in Seleucia are discussed and compared in Chapter VIII (see p. 221).

[7] Professor Rostovtzeff has noted a fragmentary legend on a rather small seal impression from Orchoi. He takes this to be the impression of a private seal. Since, however, the legend appears to comprise the city name, an element not to be expected on the seal of a private individual, it is at least equally possible that we have here the signet of some minor municipal official. See Rostovtzeff, "Seleucid Babylonia: Bullae and Seals of Clay with Greek Inscriptions," *Yale Classical Studies*, 3 (1932), 21.

these subsidiary elements. The resolution of the individuals of this third class into one or the other of the first two groups is not, however, entirely impossible. To an extent, at least, the result may be attained by an analysis of the seal types. Bearing in mind that each official seal necessarily possessed a design that would distinguish it from all other official seals, one must inquire with regard to each of the incomplete impressions whether or not the type alone, without an associated legend or symbol, would serve to identify the particular office which it represented.

As the types of the impressions from Seleucia we find portrait heads and busts; representations of deities, heroes, and mythological persons and creatures; symbols and scenes of religious significance; scenes from daily life; animals and plants. In many the distinction between the designs of official and private seals is definite. At times, however, there is an overlapping; certain general types are common to both classes of seals. Though this tendency is superficially confusing, an analysis of the various type-groups reveals the existence of what apparently was a conscious effort on the part of the engravers to distinguish between the motifs of official and private seals. We do not know to what extent there may have been a formal regulation of seal cutters by the government for the protection of official emblems. There were apparently laws in Greece forbidding the unauthorized repetition of private seal types.[8] It is not necessary to presuppose the existence of statutes regulating the restriction of types for official use; social conventions may well have served as an adequate substitute.

The use of portraits is illustrative. Among the seal impressions are many representations of heads or busts that are clearly portraiture. They are thus to be distinguished from conventional portrayals of heroes and deities. Some of the portraits occur on impressions that by reason of size, the presence of a legend, and so forth, are clearly official. Others, however, are found as the type of small seals. Most of these represent men who through the presence of a diadem may be identified as kings. On some the portrait has become obscured, and the presence or absence of a diadem cannot be determined. A number, too, represent the portraits of women who display no attributes of

[8] Diogenes Laertius, i. 2. 9.

royalty.[9] Considered apart, it would appear reasonable to classify as private such small impressions as have for type a portrait of a man or woman without attributes of royalty. If, however, one takes into consideration the status of portraiture in the period with which we are dealing such an attribution cannot be supported. The exact date at which the employment of personal portraits as seal types on the part of private persons became common must have varied in each area of the ancient world in accordance with local conditions. Gems of the Roman period may have as type the portraits of men and women, but only after he became emperor did Augustus himself dare to adopt his own portrait as a seal design.[10] The use of royal portraits as coin types developed but slowly in the Hellenistic period. Even in the third century it was long associated with the deification of kings.[11] It would be unreasonable to assume, therefore, that in the third century and the first half of the second private persons in Seleucia had already begun to copy a style in sigillation which royalty had but recently and hesitantly adopted. Furthermore, there would surely have been no necessity for a formal regulation in this respect. As Dr. Richter has stated in regard to another point,[12] "It would have been an alien thought" at this period.

When we come to a consideration of types that represent deities and the symbols of deities, the situation is more confusing. These motifs occur on both official and private seals. It is obvious, however, that such a situation was not the result of popular imitation of official emblems. Rather, the dynasty in their choice of types for both coinage and seals of state drew in large measure on the store common to Greek culture. We find as exceptions the anchor and the horse's head, the personal emblems of Seleucus I, which became characteristic types for his successors as well. Other types such as the elephant drew attention to the far-flung power of the empire. Apollo and his cult furnished a significant proportion of the Seleucid official types, the result of the assimilation of Antiochus I to this deity in his apotheosis. As a rule, however, we find certain types

---

[9] For the catalog description of these impressions see pages 65–73; they are discussed on pages 199–208.   [10] Pliny, xxxvii. 1. 8.

[11] G. Macdonald, *Coin Types: Their Origin and Development* (Glasgow, 1905), pp. 150–152.   [12] See p. 27.

chosen to distinguish the coinage and seals of each reign, and these types are already familiar as the motifs of private seals. It is not possible, of course, to date any large body of private seals to a given reign, and consequently one cannot judge of the relation of strictly contemporary private and official types. However, if one examines the Seleucid coin types for the period covered by the seal impressions and compares the types of both coins and seal impressions, a fact of some importance emerges. On impressions which by reason of size and execution appear to be private every type that expresses a motif similar to those on coins and on what appear to be official seals is as a rule presented in a form or pose essentially distinct from that on the official monuments. The figure of Apollo leaning against his tripod or seated and holding a bow or arrows, both common types on coins, does not occur among the small impressions. He is shown, however, seated on the omphalos and holding a lyre.[13] Apollo Citharoedus constitutes, of course, a classical motif, but on the Seleucid coinage forms the type of but one limited issue under Antiochus I.[14] The tripod of Apollo on small seal impressions [15] is quite different from that on what are obviously impressions of official seals (see p. 39, Nos. IA1a(1) and IIIA1a(1)). The examples that may be drawn are sufficiently numerous to establish the presumption suggested above, that a conscious effort was made to distinguish between the manner of portrayal of similar concepts on impressions of official and of private seals. As the principal characteristics that distinguish private and official seals, therefore, we have the manner of portrayal of the motif as well as the execution of the engraving, the size of the seal, and, at times, the presence or absence of a legend or monogram.

We have now to consider the means used to distinguish the different categories of official seals so that each would serve to identify a particular office or function. It has already been stated that this might be accomplished by the use of a general official type accompanied by a legend, monogram, or symbol that would identify the individual function or official concerned. It is obvious that with this method the general type might be changed

---

[13] See p. 74, No. IIIA1a(1).
[14] E. Babelon, *Les Rois de Syrie, d'Arménie et de Commagène*, p. xlviii.
[15] See p. 112, No. IIID1a(1).

frequently in accordance with the desire of the reigning monarch. Illustrative of this is the long series of impressions from Orchoi, each identifying by means of a legend the office of the local chreophylax.[16] The types of these impressions may change not only with each reign but within a single reign. They represent the portraits of kings and the figures of deities. Types used in this general sense accompanied by a legend or monogram would not have been employed on other seals as the sole element. That is, a type could not be used in one instance to represent simply the general authority of the government, and, in another, to stand for a particular office or function as well as for the inclusive concept. If we bear in mind the considerable number of different official seals of which each administrative center stood in need, it is evident that such a procedure would have caused a confusion at variance with what we know of Hellenistic organization. Furthermore, the nature of these general types is hostile to such an assumption. It would have been highly unsuitable to use the portrait of the reigning monarch as the exclusive emblem of a particular office, or even of a department. On the other hand, as a general type employed simultaneously by a number of offices it could be supported by subsidiary elements for the identification of the particular local units concerned. I believe that the same conditions hold true for representations of Apollo or of Zeus, the deities so intimately associated with the Seleucid dynasty through the establishment and maintenance of the royal cults. In respect to other deities it does not seem possible to arrive at definite conclusions. Such of them as were represented on official seals accompanied by a legend or other subsidiary element would not have been used alone in the same area and in the same general period as the emblems of particular offices. After allowance is made for impressions that are incomplete and from which, therefore, a legend may have been lost, there is no evidence for the use in the Seleucid Empire of representations of deities, except possibly Apollo and Zeus, as the sole element in the design of official seals. The evidence, however, is insufficient definitely to establish the facts.

In brief, it is suggested that portraits of reigning monarchs and probably representations of those deities most closely associated with the dynasty were employed as the types of official

[16] Rostovtzeff, *op. cit.*, pp. 26–41.

seals only to express the general authority of the government and were, therefore, always accompanied by a legend, symbol, or monogram that identified a particular office or function within the government. In this connection one should note again the group of incomplete impressions of official seals. Of these, seven are portraits of rulers, three represent Apollo, and one appears to be an Artemis head. Whether or not this goddess furnished the exclusive type for the seal of a particular office cannot be proved. On the basis of the conclusions just reached, however, it is assumed that on the other ten impressions legends, symbols, or monograms, probably the first, should be understood. It is very possible that the same conclusions hold for the Artemis head.

That some departments of the government, however, did possess exclusive emblems or types appears to be demonstrated by certain impressions. The Seleucid anchor occurs on three forms of impressions. Represented with but one fluke and inverted it constitutes the regular type on stamps of all tax collectors both at Seleucia and at Orchoi.[17] The complete anchor accompanied by a vase-shaped vessel is the type of an impression that appears to represent an act of registration concerning slaves.[18] The complete anchor accompanied by a horse's head forms the design of four impressions from Seleucia and of one from Orchoi.[19] On the stamps of tax collectors and on the seal of registration legends formed part of the seal design. As to the third group of impressions, however, it is clear that neither legend nor monogram accompanied the type on the original seals. The horse's head, a characteristic Seleucid symbol, must be presumed to limit in some way the authority represented by the anchor. That is, in each of the three groups a general concept, that the anchor represents some form of the government's authority, is limited by legend or by symbol, so that the complete seal designs identify different individual offices or functions. The presence of the common element, the anchor, demonstrates that these offices formed units of one department. It will be shown in later discussions that this department was in all prob-

[17] Pp. 50–64, Nos. IC1a(1) to IC1c(1); Rostovtzeff, *op. cit.*, pp. 42–43, Nos. 62–64. The value of the half-anchor is discussed on pages 161–163.

[18] P. 41, No. IA1c(1). The impression is discussed on pages 138–141.

[19] Pp. 43 and 44, Nos. IA2a(1)–(4); Rostovtzeff, *op. cit.*, p. 47, No. 80. These impressions are discussed on pages 127–128.

ability the royal treasury. The use of the anchor on the Seleucid coinage is not opposed to this conclusion. The anchor appears as a coin type on early issues of Seleucus and Antiochus only prior to 280 B.C.; it occurs again, rarely, after 150 B.C. on coins of Alexander Bala and some of his successors.[20] The material from Seleucia points to Antiochus I as the great organizer of the Seleucid administrative system. It is perhaps significant, therefore, that the anchor which recurs so frequently on the coins of Seleucus I should have disappeared as a coin type upon the accession of the prince who probably was responsible for its reservation as the seal type of the treasury. The material is lacking for the determination of the significance of its readoption as coin type under the interloper, Alexander. As a symbol on Seleucid coins the anchor is of fairly common occurrence. To what extent, if any, this value may be related to its use as the emblem of the treasury depends upon a better understanding of the general significance of the Seleucid coin symbols than is now possible.

Although no examples have been recovered, there is no reason to doubt the existence of seals that identified various other principal divisions into which the Seleucid government was divided. It is probable that such seals were composed of a single element, the emblem of the departments concerned. This conclusion is based on the fact that the royal government does not appear to have possessed a permanent seal of state with a national emblem or a type that persisted over a number of reigns. In the absence of such a type the emblem of each department on its seal would serve a dual function as representative both of the general authority of the state and of that executed by the department. In the material from Seleucia there appears to be no impression that represents the seal of a department as opposed to seals of offices or functions within a department.

Those official impressions that are complete show in addition to the central type a legend, monogram, or symbol. The type may be general, as, for instance, a royal portrait. The presumption here is that the individual office or function represented by the subsidiary element of the design did not form a unit within a department, but was exercised directly under the authority of the executive official in each province or district. Again, the

[20] Babelon, *op. cit.*, pp. 8–10; also pp. xli, cxxx.

central type may identify the authority of the government as exercised through a department, and the particular office or function represented by the subsidiary element is thus shown as subordinate to the department. Illustrative of this form of administration are the impressions that show the anchor as a part of the seal design. There is no indication, however, that such departmental units were independent of the provincial executive. The incomplete impressions of official seals to which reference has been made appear to have possessed general types, and they must be presumed to have operated under the provincial or district governors without specific relation to a department.

In summary, the significance of the characteristics that distinguish the various categories of official seals may be determined within limits by the nature or form of the central type and by the presence or absence of a legend, monogram, or symbol. In turn, the presence or absence of these subsidiary elements on the original seals, the extant impressions of which are incomplete, may frequently be judged by the form of the central type. It has been shown that distinctions between private and official seals and between various classes of official seals involve the application of several criteria. The basing of identification upon one characteristic while ignoring others has frequently resulted in error. Shape, size, the nature of the type, the manner of its portrayal, and the use of legends and other subsidiary elements must all be taken into account, and the value of each compared with that of the others.

CHAPTER III

CATALOG OF IMPRESSIONS

A SATISFACTORY classification of the impressions which occur on the attached sealings from Seleucia is rendered somewhat difficult by the breakage and the wear to which they have been subjected. In some instances it has been impossible to determine the significance of the types and in others the identification offered is tentative. In formulating a system of serial numbers and letters by which to distinguish variations in the design of the impressions the possibility has been kept in mind that further excavation may add to the classes and subclasses which have been recognized. As a result, some gaps will be noted in the natural sequence of numerals and letters.

In the catalog the description of the design on each impression is preceded by a statement giving the shape, the dimensions, and the quality of execution, and is followed by the serial number of the sealing on which the impression occurs and its provenance. The terms used to express the quality of execution — "good," "fair," "mediocre," "crude," and "obscure" — and the cultural relationship of the motifs — "Greek," "Oriental," and "general" — are discussed in Chapter VIII, page 224. To avoid confusion it is important to note that the term "Greek," as applied to the motif of an impression is used in a special and restricted sense. By checking the sealing number for each impression in the Table at the close of Chapter I (pp. 15–24) a comparison can be made of the various impressions which may be found associated on individual sealings.

SYNOPSIS OF IMPRESSIONS

I. Impressions of Official Seals

A. SEALS OF DEPARTMENTS OF STATE AND THEIR SUBDIVISIONS

1. With a principal type and a secondary legend
    a. Bybliophylax
    b. Chreophylax
    c. Registration of slaves, perhaps for assessment

CATALOG OF IMPRESSIONS

   d. Registration of slaves, apparently the act of katagraphe
   e. Katagraphe
2. With a principal type and a secondary symbol
   a. Anchor and horse's head
3. With a principal type and no legend or symbol visible, but incompletely impressed and belonging, therefore, to either class No. 1 or class No. 2
   a. Portrait of Seleucus I
   c. Portrait of Seleucus, son of Antiochus I
   f. Portrait of Seleucus III
   m. Portrait of Antiochus IV
   o. Portraits of Timarchus and Heracleides
   u. Apollo types
   v. Artemis type

B. SEALS OF SPECIAL CONTROLLERS

1. With a type representing the general authority of the state
   a. Royal portrait as type
2. With the type of a private seal
   a. Deity figure as type
3. With a monogram as type

C. STAMPS OF COLLECTORS OF TAXES AND OTHER DUES

1. With a type representing the general authority of the state
   a. A tax on salt
   b. Exemption from the salt tax
   c. A tax on imported slaves
2. Special stamps having no type representing a general authority
   a. A form of port dues

II. SEALS OF PRIVATE AGENTS OF ROYALTY

A. PORTRAITS OF KINGS, ALONE AND JUGATE

1. Identified
   a. Seleucus I
   g. Antiochus, son of Seleucus III
   i. Antiochus III
   k. Seleucus IV
   m. Antiochus IV
   o. Timarchus
   p. Demetrius I
   q. Alexander I (with Cleopatra Thea)
   s. Demetrius II
2. Unidentified

B. PORTRAITS OF QUEENS

1. Identified
   a. Wife of Seleucus III (?)
   b. Laodice, wife of Seleucus IV (?)
2. Unidentified

III. Impressions of Private Seals

A. With a Significance Probably Religious

1. Representations of principal deities
   a. Apollo
   b. Dionysus
   c. Athena
   d. Artemis
   e. Nike
   f. Tyche
   x. Deity types not identified

2. Representations of minor deities
   a. Hermes
   b. Eros
   c. Psyche
   d. Silenus
   e. River god

3. Representations of acts of religious observance
   a. Priests or worshipers

B. Representations of Heroes, Mythological Personages, and Fanciful Figures

1. Heroes
   a. Hercules
   b. Odysseus
   c. Penelope

2. Mythological personages
   a. Medusa
   b. Opheltes and the dragon

3. Fanciful figures
   a. Winged demon
   b. Griffin

C. Representations of Mortals

1. Draped women in formal pose (religious connotation ?)
   a. Holding palms
   b. Holding lyres

2. Nude women
   a. Musician
   b. Dancer
   c. Posed informally

3. Various representations of men
   a. Warrior
   b. Pastoral
   c. Convivial

D. Representations of Symbols and Objects

1. Of religious significance
   a. Tripod
   b. Crescent and star as parts of design
   c. Star or sun as design
   d. Caduceus as part of design
   e. Ceremonial lamp (?)
   f. Ceremonial standard (?)
   g. Thunderbolt

2. Herms
   a. With crescent
   b. Alone

3. Masks
   a. Comic
   b. Tragic
   c. Multiple

4. Vessels
 a. Amphora
 b. Jar or urn
 c. Twin jars inverted
5. Miscellaneous
 a. Column
 b. Hand clasping an object

6. Plant life
 a. Palm tree
 b. Fruit on a branch
 c. Grain

E. REPRESENTATIONS OF ANIMAL LIFE

1. Quadrupeds
 a. Lion
 b. Bullock's head
 c. Camel

2. Birds
 a. Peacock
 b. Dove
 c. Pheasant
 d. Eagle

3. Miscellaneous
 a. Insect
 b. Crab or frog

CATALOG

(In this catalog several works are referred to by the names of the authors only; the titles of a few publications are given in condensed form. Full titles may be found in the Bibliography on pages xv–xvii.)

I. IMPRESSIONS OF OFFICIAL SEALS

A. SEALS OF DEPARTMENTS OF STATE AND THEIR SUBDIVISIONS

1. *With a principal type and a secondary legend*

a. Bybliophylax

(1) Oval; 25 × 16 mm.; somewhat worn; execution very good. Pl. I, Fig. 1.

Type: Tripod-lebes.

Legend, to the right and reading down: [β]υβλιοφυλακικός. The legend is discussed on pages 128–129.

Sealing No. AIIb(10), appended; container type; bitumen. Archive A.

(2) Oval; incompletely impressed at the bottom; 14⁺ × 12 mm.; execution fair.

Type: Tripod-lebes. The form differs from that of No. (1).

Legend, to the right and reading down: βυβ[λιοφυλακικός].

Though the two impressions represent the same office of government, they were made by different seals and, therefore, are probably not contemporary. It should be noted that the sealings on which the two impressions occur are of similar form but of different material.

Sealing No. AIIb(9), appended; container type; clay. Archive A.

b. Chreophylax

(1) Oval; broken at the top and incompletely impressed at the sides; 22⁺ × 25⁺ mm.; execution very good. Pl. I, Fig. 2.

Type: Portrait head of Antiochus I, right.

Legend, to the left and reading up: [χρε]οφυλάκων.

The portrait is very characteristic, but varies in detail from those on his coins. It most closely approximates the portrait on a tetradrachm in the British Museum (Gardner, *The Seleucid Kings of Syria*, Pl. III, 4), described as a "middle-aged portrait of Antiochus." It is to be noted that the king is shown wearing the diadem without attributes of deity. The possible values that may attach to the use of royal portraits as types of official seals are discussed on pages 31–33. The proposed restoration of the legend is based on the space available for the initial characters and on analogy with the frequent occurrence of the form at Orchoi. Its significance is treated on pages 131–138. Impression No. (2), below, has as type a portrait of Antiochus. On the basis of detail measurements I am convinced that the two impressions were made by a single seal. Both are incompletely impressed, especially the right side of No. (1) and the left side of No. (2). On the latter, therefore, the legend cannot be discerned, but the complete impression of its right side demonstrates that the original seal bore but the one line of legend.

Sealing No. AIc(12), a bulla complete in two pieces; multiple; bitumen. Archive A.

(2) A duplicate impression of No. (1), above. Pl. I, Fig. 3.
Sealing No. AIc(13), a bulla fragment; multiple; bitumen. Archive A.

(3) Oval; very incompletely impressed at the sides, badly worn; 26 × 17⁺ mm.; execution seemingly good.

Type: Portrait head of Antiochus I right, apparently as on No. (1).

Legend: Owing to incomplete impression the presence or absence of a legend on the original seal cannot be determined by an examination of the specimen. So far as it is possible to judge from a comparison of this impression with Nos. (1) and (2), it appears that the three impressions were made by a single seal. Because of the condition of the piece, however, we cannot exclude the equal possibility that the impressions were made by two different seals representing the same office but not contemporary. The close agreement between such details of the three impressions as are visible does not permit an assumption that they represent different offices.

Sealing No. AIIb(13), appended; container type; bitumen (?). Great House, Level III, Room 14.

(4) Oval; incompletely impressed and broken, worn; 21+ × 18+ mm.; execution good.

Type: Portrait head of Antiochus I right, apparently as on No. (1).

Legend: Not visible. See under No. (3). By reason of the close similarity in the type figures this impression is considered to be that of a seal of the chreophylax in Seleucia of the period of Antiochus I, but whether it was made by the same seal as was No. (1) or No. (3) cannot be determined.

Sealing No. AIIb(14), appended; container type; bitumen (?). Surface.

c. Registration of slaves, perhaps for assessment

(1) Apparently rectangular; incompletely impressed at bottom; 19+ × 15+ mm.; execution fair. Pl. I, Fig. 4.

Type: Complete anchor and to left a slender vase or other vessel.

Legend, above, left to right: [ἀν]δραποδικῆς; below, left to right, [ἐ]πιιη[or [ἐ]πιφη[.

The type symbols and the legend are discussed on pages 138–141. The reading of the second line must remain somewhat doubtful pending the recovery of other impressions of similar seals. Severe abrasion as well as incomplete impression has rendered it very obscure. The group ΠΙΦΗ (or ΠΙΙΗ) is reasonably certain. Before the pi there is room for but one letter, and epsilon is a reasonable conjecture. Either iota or phi is possible. Traces of other characters may be seen after the eta, and there is room for a word of at least nine letters.

Sealing No. AId(37), a bulla fragment; indeterminate; clay. Archive A.

d. Registration of slaves, apparently the act of katagraphe

(1) Since all but one side of the impression has been broken off, and one extremity of what remains has been incompletely impressed, it is not possible to determine the shape or the dimensions of the original seal. One of the dimensions was at least 19 mm.

Type: Traces only of the type may be seen along the edge of the break. Though it cannot be identified, there is no question but that the type of this impression differs from that of the one preceding, the anchor and vase.

Legend: [ἀν]δραποδικ|ῆs.

The position held by the word in relation to the type figure cannot be determined. The legend and the question whether it consisted of one or of two words are treated on pages 146–148.

Sealing No. AIc(11), a bulla fragment; multiple; bitumen. Archive A.

e. Katagraphe

(1) Since a very incomplete fragment of the impression has been preserved, it is not possible to determine the shape or the dimensions of the seal.

Type: Entirely destroyed.

Legend: καταγραφῆ[s].

Sufficient space has been preserved below the first part of this word to indicate that it was not followed immediately by a second word. There is no doubt that the center of the field was occupied by a principal type figure. Whether there may have been a second line of legend below the type figure on the original seal cannot be determined from the impression itself. The known values of the term καταγραφή, however, appear to require the assumption that it was accompanied by a second modifying term (see pp. 141–146). The impression occurs on the same bulla with that of the seal of the chreophylax of the reign of Antiochus I (No. IA1b(2)), and is to be dated, therefore, to the reign of this king.

Sealing No. AIc(13), a bulla fragment; multiple; bitumen. Archive A.

2. *With a principal type and a secondary symbol*

a. Anchor and horse's head

(1) Oval; incompletely impressed; 16+ × 13+ mm.; execution fair. Pl. I, Fig. 5.

Type: Anchor *not inverted*, and to left a horse's head, left. Though the impression is not complete, an examination of the object makes it evident that no legend formed a part of the original seal. It must be presumed, therefore, that the type with its secondary symbol identified the particular subdivision of government which the seal represented. There is evidence that warrants an assumption that the Seleucid anchor became the exclusive emblem of the royal treasury. The associated symbol, the horse's head, must be taken to represent a subdivision of the treasury. The evidence is discussed on page 127, where it is suggested that the particular form of sealings on which alone this type of impression occurs was used to seal bags of currency issued by the treasury for circulation. It has not been possible to assign a date to this impression or to the other similar impressions which follow. The fact that the anchor and the horse's head were the personal emblems of Seleucus I cannot be accepted as evidence that the sealings should be assigned to his reign. Both emblems used separately are found as coin types or symbols in the reigns of many of his successors. Their use together as the design of the seal of a government office suggests, however, that the designs were adopted at an early date. It will develop in the course of the discussion that Antiochus I appears to have been responsible for the organization of the greater part of the Seleucid administrative system in Babylonia. It is possible, therefore, that both the choice of the designs and the office which they represent may be dated to his reign. To what reign the four sealings under consideration belong cannot be determined. Impression No. (2), below, appears to have been made by the same seal as was No. (1). No. (3) shows slight differences in detail measurements. It was made, therefore, by a different seal representing the same office and presumably was not contemporary with Nos. (1) and (2). With regard to No. (4) I have been unable to determine whether it is a duplicate of one of those preceding, or whether it was made by a third seal of the one office.

Sealing No. AIIb(1), appended; container type; clay. Trial trench 4, D 11, 3 m.

(2) A duplicate of No. (1), above.

Sealing No. AIIb(2), similar in form to No. AIIb(1), above. Surface.

(3) Similar in design, size, and execution to No. (1), but differing from it in detail measurements.

Sealing No. AIIb(3), similar in form to No. AIIb(1). Surface.

(4) Similar in design, size, and execution to No. (1). Whether it was impressed by the same seal as were Nos. (1) and (2) or as was No. (3) cannot be determined.

Sealing No. AIIb(16), similar in form to No. AIIb(1). Surface.

3. *With a principal type and no legend or symbol visible, but incompletely impressed and belonging, therefore, to either class No. 1 or class No. 2*

a.[1] Portrait of Seleucus I as Zeus

(1) Oval; the left half overimpressed by another seal, the bottom abraded; l. 24 mm.; execution good. Pl. I, Fig. 6.

Type: Head right, with mustache and beard. Owing to overimpression, only the face from the ears forward has been preserved. The coiffure cannot be distinguished. The impression distinctly represents a portrait, not an idealization. The argument for the identification of the portrait as that of Seleucus I requires considerable space and is discussed below on pages 209–212. The conclusion reached is that the impression represents the features of Seleucus but as assimilated to Zeus. The possible character of the office represented by the impression is discussed on pages 148–151.

Sealing No. AIc(12), a bulla complete in two pieces; multiple; bitumen. Archive A.

c. Portrait of Seleucus, son of Antiochus I

(1) Oval; incompletely impressed at the sides, partly obscured by finger marks; 19+ × 19+ mm.; execution good. Pl. I, Fig. 7.

[1] The sequence of the index letters follows the complete Seleucid dynastic list rather than the incomplete list at present represented by our impressions.

Type: Head right, male, the portrait of a young man or a youth. The details of the headdress are obscured by finger marks, and the presence or absence of a diadem cannot be determined. On the basis of evidence that is discussed on pages 213–214 the portrait is identified as that of Seleucus, a son of Antiochus I, older than Antiochus II, who died before his father. This impression and the other impressions of official seals found on the same bulla are discussed again on pages 148–151, in connection with an estimate of the functions or offices of government which they may be presumed to represent.

Sealing No. AIc(12), a bulla complete in two pieces; multiple; bitumen. Archive A.

f. Portrait of Seleucus III

(1) Oval; incompletely impressed, lower portion broken off, abraded in part; 18+ × 19+ mm.; execution probably good. Pl. I, Fig. 8.

Type: Head right, male, with diadem. The ribbons of the diadem are shown divided, one bent upward, the other hanging down. A slight forelock of hair may be distinguished. The features are youthful without being childish. The details of diadem, hair, and features more closely approximate the portrait of Seleucus III, as known from his coins, than that of any other Seleucid king (see Babelon, Pl. VIII, 10, 11). The impression is, therefore, assigned to his reign. It is not possible to determine the office which it represents.

Sealing No. AId(38), a bulla fragment; indeterminate; bitumen. Archive A.

m. Portrait of Antiochus IV

(1) Probably oval; incompletely impressed on three sides; 18+ × 17+ mm.; execution good. Pl. I, Fig. 9.

Type: Head right, male, with traces that suggest a radiate headdress. The details of eye, nose, and chin approximate those on a portrait of Antiochus IV represented on his coinage (Babelon, Pl. XII, 3). On the particular coin cited the king is wearing the diadem rather than a headdress with rays, but the radiate crown is very characteristic of other representations of Antiochus on his coins (Babelon, Pl. XIII, 2 ff.). The details of our impression, including the radiate headdress, approximate closely those of a portrait of this king found on sealings from Orchoi (Rostovtzeff, "Seleucid Babylonia," p. 28, No. 6; p. 44, No. 67). Confirmation of the identification is afforded by another impression associated with that under discussion on the same bulla, No. IIID3a(7), described on page 117. The impressions from Orchoi that bear the portrait of Antiochus IV are all of seals of the chreophylax of that city. It is possible, therefore, that our impression represents the seal of the corresponding official at Seleucia, but definite proof is lacking.

Sealing No. AIc(26), a bulla fragment; multiple; clay. Surface.

o. Portraits of Timarchus and Heracleides

(1) Probably oval; very incomplete at the top and the bottom, slightly so at the right; 21+ × 24+ mm.; execution very good. Pl. I, Fig. 10.

Type: Head left, male, Greek features, wearing a petasos-like hat or kausia but no diadem. This impression and No. (2), below, from the same bulla are the largest in our collection. The execution of the two portraits is superior to that displayed by the other impressions of official seals. There can be no doubt that this impression together with its companion is of an official character. But neither of the personages represented is shown wearing the insignia of royalty, and on both impressions the heads are turned left, a feature not found on the other impressions of official seals. Owing to the space required the discussion of the identification of the two portraits has been postponed to a later chapter (see pp. 214–220). On the basis of evidence largely indirect it is there suggested that No. (1) is a representation of Timarchus and No. (2), below, of his brother, Heracleides. Since the two impressions occur on one bulla, the seals with which they were impressed represent two different offices or functions of government. To define these, however, is not possible.

Sealing No. AIc(24), a whole bulla; multiple; clay. Great House, Level III, Room 141 sub.

(2) Probably oval; very incompletely impressed on all sides, cracked at the center, and partly defaced by finger marks; 19+ × 19+ mm.; execution excellent. Pl. I, Fig. 11.

Type: Head left, male, uncovered, without diadem. There appears to be a fine, very close beard and mustache, executed in a style found on Roman gems (Furtwängler, Pl. XLVIII, 25). Though the quality of execution of both Nos. (1) and (2) is superior, in respect to individualized portraiture, the latter surpasses the former. The identification of this portrait as that of Heracleides depends upon the attribution of that on No. (1) to Timarchus.

Sealing No. AIc(24) described under No. (1), above.

u. Apollo types

(1) Oval; incompletely impressed at the left, broken at the top and bottom; 20+ × 13+ mm.; execution good. Pl. I, Fig. 12.

Type: Figure standing right, male, nude. The details of the headdress are obscured by a break. The figure holds in the left hand a bow; in the right, an arrow pointing diagonally down. The representation is of Apollo, but this particular pose is not one found on the Seleucid coins. The motif is somewhat akin to that of a gem of the Graeco-Roman period shown by Furtwängler (Pl. XXXIX, 15). For other representations of Apollo on the sealings see page 74. It is not possible to assign a date to the impression.

Sealing No. AIIa(2), appended; convex; bitumen. Surface.

(2) Oval; incompletely impressed at the top, bottom and left; 24+ × 15+ mm.; execution very good. Pl. II, Fig. 13.

Type: Head right, apparently male, although the features are fine, almost feminine. The details of the headdress have been obscured. It does not appear that a portrait was intended, but rather an idealization. It must be presumed, therefore, that the representation is of deity. The characteristics of the face strongly suggest portrayals of Apollo on Seleucid coins (Babelon, Pls. V, 3–5; X, 12, 15), and to a greater degree those on gems of the Hellenistic and Roman periods (Furtwängler, Pls. XL, 5, 49; LXI, 67). By the association on the same bulla of impressions with portraits of Antiochus I and of the deified Seleucus this impression may be dated to the reign of the first Antiochus.

Sealing No. AIc(12), a bulla complete in two pieces; multiple; bitumen. Archive A.

(3) Probably oval; incompletely impressed at the top, bottom and left; 25+ × 15+ mm.; done in high relief, execution very good.

Type: Head right, of which only the face has been preserved. The features closely approximate those of No. (2), above, and I consider this also to be a representation of Apollo. It is quite possible that the two seals by which the impressions were made were the work of a single engraver. There is no direct evidence that serves to date the piece. If, however, the two impressions are the work of one hand, the second head should belong either to the reign of Antiochus I, as does the first, or to that of Antiochus II, his successor. There is no evidence to suggest that any of the impressions of official seals found at Seleucia should be assigned to the reign of Seleucus I prior to 293 B.C., when Antiochus became co-ruler with his father.

Sealing AIIb(11), appended; container type; bitumen. Surface.

v. Artemis type

(1) Shape obscure; incompletely impressed at the top, bottom and right; 19+ × 12+ mm.; done in high relief, execution good. Pl. II, Fig. 14.

Type: Head left, female, with diadem. The features are conventional and do not appear to indicate portraiture. I assume, therefore, that the representation is of deity. The head of Artemis, diademed, is found as a Seleucid coin type in the reigns of Seleucus IV and of Demetrius I (Babelon, Pls. XI, 18; XVI, 5). On the coins the quiver and bow are usually associated with the head or bust. Since our piece has been incompletely impressed, it is possible that on the seal with which it was made these or other attributes of Artemis were present. So far as I know, the diadem is not employed on representations of female deities other than Artemis. On these grounds the type of the impression is assigned to her. Since Artemis first appears as a coin type in the reign of Seleucus II, it is not unreasonable to assume that the impression should not be dated prior to this reign. Other than this I should not venture to suggest date limits for this type.

Sealing No. AIIb(12), appended; container type; clay. Surface.

B. SEALS OF SPECIAL CONTROLLERS

1. *With a type representing the general authority of the state*

a. Royal portrait as type

(1) Rectangular; with broad border, broken at the bottom; 27+ × 26+ mm.; execution good. Pl. II, Fig. 15.

Type: Head right, male. Traces of a diadem can be distinguished. The details of the features approximate those of Demetrius I on some coins (Gardner, *Syria*, Pl. XV, 2, and especially Imhoof-Blumer, *Porträtköpfe*, Pl. III, 23), and I assign the impression to his reign with little hesitation.

Monogram: ✻. For a discussion of the value of monograms see pages 151–155.

Sealing No. AIIb(15), appended; container type; bitumen. Great House, Level II, Room 260.

2. *With the type of a private seal*

a. Deity figure as type

(1) Oval; incompletely impressed at the left; 16.5 × 10+ mm.; execution good. Pl. II, Fig. 16.

Type: Figure standing facing, head turned left. It appears to be nude and to bear a wreath on the head. No characteristics definitely indicative of the sex of the figure can be remarked, but the build of the body is masculine to a degree. On the left wrist is a bracelet. On the left shoulder is supported a vessel having a squat body, a long slender neck, and two handles. The form of the vessel is such that it must be presumed to have been made of metal rather than of clay. What appear to be ribbons are suspended from the vessel. The right hand of the figure, dropped at the side, rests on an obscure object that may be a thymiaterion. I am somewhat at a loss to explain the figure. The vessel carried on the shoulder and the bracelet give the impression that the figure represents a young girl. On the other hand, the lines and the proportions of the trunk and the limbs are not only masculine but mature. It appears that the figure must be taken to be male and the vessel regarded as symbolic. The general build and the pose, aside from the position of the vessel on the shoulder, suggest Dionysus. The wreath on the head supports such an identification of the figure. Against such an identification, however, are both the form of the vessel and its position on the shoulder. Accepting the vessel as symbolic and bearing in mind the general pose of the body and the presence of a wreath, I tentatively assume that the representation is of Dionysus.

Monogram: ⌘.

Sealing AIIa(20), appended; convex; clay. Surface.

3. *With a monogram as type*

(1) Oval; 13 × 7.5 mm.; execution fair.

Type: Monogram ⌘. The use of a monogram as the type of an official seal is somewhat analogous to its occurrence as the type of some autonomous coins of Seleucia. For further discussion see pages 151–155.

Sealing No. AIIa(1), appended; convex; clay. Great House, Level I, Room 130.

(2) Oval; broken at the right; 15 × 10+ mm.; execution fair.

Type: Monogram ⌘. Note the reference under No. (1) to the general discussion of the values of monograms. This impression occurs on a bulla in connection with an impression attesting the satisfaction of the tax on salt. As will be seen in the discussion of this tax, the owner of the monogram seal must have been associated with the transaction in a non-official capacity, probably as witness. The date of the impression is fixed by that of the tax stamp, which is of the year 163/62 B.C. in the reign of Antiochus IV.

Sealing No. AIc(10), a bulla complete in two pieces; multiple; bitumen. Archive B.

C. STAMPS OF COLLECTORS OF TAXES AND OTHER DUES

1. *With a type representing the general authority of the state*

a. A tax on salt

(1) Ovoid; with the short sides straight; slightly broken at the right and bottom, very worn; 16+ × 12+ mm. Pl. II, Fig. 17.

Legend: ἁλικῆς | ΣΚ | Σελευκεία[ς].

Type: Half-anchor reversed, alone at the right edge of the face.

Date: 26 A.S., 286/85 B.C., reign of Seleucus I with Antiochus I associated.[2] The bottom of the impression has been broken off, but the legend appears to have been composed originally of three lines only, not of four, as on the later impressions. The basis for this supposition is the fact that relatively wide spaces separated the lines of the legend, the top edge of the impression from the first word, and the last word from the edge of the break at the left bottom. In these respects the impression differs from the arrangement of those having four lines of legend. If a fourth line is restored, the proportion between the length and the height of the impression would become definitely unlike that found on other impressions having four lines of legend. The significance of the distinction between the form of this impression and that of the impressions which follow is discussed on page 194. The value of the type, the half-anchor, is treated on page 162. With one exception, No. (2), this type is common to all stamps that attest the satisfaction of a general tax. The Greek words of the legend are discussed on pages 179–182.

Sealing No. AId(1), a bulla fragment; indeterminate; clay. Surface.

(2) Shape, like No. (1); broken at the lower right; 15+ × 14+ mm. Pl. II, Fig. 18.

Legend: ἁλικῆς | Σελευκείας | ΓΠ | ἐπιτε[λῶν].

Type: Winged figure advancing right, fully draped. The right hand is advanced, holding what appears to be a wreath. Beneath the wreath and at the edge of the break appear rays which I take to form a part of a representation of the head of Helios such as appears as a symbol on coins of Seleucus I (Babelon,

---

[2] Rostovtzeff ("Seleucid Babylonia," p. 51, note 2a) has called in question my reading of this date. It should be observed that in the dates on all our impressions there is evidence of an attempt to space the numerals in relation to the center of the face. When a date is composed of two numerals, they appear close together at the center; if three numerals are required, they are separated by wider spaces, with the second numeral at the approximate center. I have repeatedly examined this impression under varying conditions of light and with the surface dampened. There can be no possibility here of three numerals. As for the second numeral the perpendicular bar and the upper diagonal stroke of the kappa are unmistakable. The form of the numeral kappa is that of the letter in the preceding word, ἁλικῆς, but, of course, larger. There is no possibility that the cross stroke was connected with the upright to form the character rho. I have read the first numeral as stigma, formed as on a number of our impressions to be seen below, but a rectangular epsilon is a possibility.

Pl. I, 6). The winged figure is without doubt Nike. This is the sole occurrence of Nike as the type on a stamp of a tax collector. Its significance is discussed on page 163.

Date: 83 A.S., 229/28 B.C., reign of Seleucus II.

Sealing No. AId(2), a bulla fragment; indeterminate; bitumen over clay. Archive A.

(3) Shape, like No. (1); incompletely impressed, worn; 19⁺ × 15⁺ mm.

Legend: ἁλικῆς | Σελευκεία[ς] | Η? | [ἐπι]τελῶν.

Type: Half-anchor, as on No. (1).

Date: 98 A.S., 214/13 B.C., reign of Antiochus III. The restoration of the fourth line of the legend as ἐπιτελῶν rather than ἀτελῶν, the only alternative, is based on the following considerations. We have another impression, dated in the same year, on which ἀτελῶν may be plainly read (see p. 55, No. ICIb(1)). That the two impressions were not made by one stamp is demonstrated by a difference in the forms of the second numeral of the date, and by variations in the relative positions of the letters of the legend on the faces of the impressions. If, then, the last line should be restored as ἀτελῶν, it would be necessary to assume that in Seleucia during the same year there were in existence two different seals having a common type and legend and representing a single act. It would follow that Seleucia was divided into two or more tax districts. The occurrence on each impression of the city name without qualification is hostile to an assumption that there was such a subdivision for fiscal purposes. The extant evidence, therefore, requires the restoration ἐπιτελῶν.

Sealing No. AId(3), a bulla fragment; indeterminate; pink clay. Surface.

(4) Shape, like No. (1); incompletely impressed at the right; 16⁺ × 13 mm. Pl. II, Fig. 19.

Legend: ἁλικῆς | ΔΡ | Σελευκεία[ς] | ἐπιτελῶ[ν].

Type: Half-anchor, as on No. (1).

Date: 104 A.S., 208/07 B.C., reign of Antiochus III.

Sealing No. AId(4), a bulla fragment; indeterminate; bitumen. Archive A.

CATALOG OF IMPRESSIONS 53

(5) Shape, like No. (1); incompletely impressed at the right; $13^+ \times 12^+$ mm.

Legend: ἁλικῆς | ΘΡ | Σελευκ[είας] | ἐπιτε[λῶν].

Type: Owing to incomplete impression the type does not appear. Presumably it was the usual half-anchor (cf. p. 162).

Date: 109 A.S., 203/02 B.C., reign of Antiochus III.

Sealing No. AId(107), a bulla fragment; indeterminate; clay. Surface.

(6) Shape, like No. (1); broken around the edges; 17×12 mm.

Legend: ἁλικῆς | Σελευκείας | ΕΙΡ | ἐπιτελῶν.

Type: Half-anchor, as on No. (1). The impression occurs in duplicate on parts of a single bulla.

Date: 115 A.S., 197/96 B.C., reign of Antiochus III. The epsilon of the date is rectangular, a shape rarely found on our impressions.

Sealing No. AId(5), a bulla fragment in three pieces; indeterminate; bitumen. Archive A.

(7) Shape, like No. (1); incompletely impressed at the right; $17^+ \times 14$ mm.

Legend: ἁλικῆς | Σελευκεία[ς] | ϹΙΡ | ἐπιτελῶν.

Type: Half-anchor, as on No. (1).

Date: 116 A.S., 196/95 B.C., reign of Antiochus III.

Sealing No. AId(6), a bulla fragment; indeterminate; clay. Surface.

(8) Shape, like No. (1); incompletely impressed at the right; $14^+ \times 11$ mm.

Legend: ἁλικῆς | Σελευκεία[ς] | ΘΙΡ | ἐπιτελῶ[ν].

Type: Owing to incomplete impression the type does not appear.

Date: 119 A.S., 193/92 B.C., reign of Antiochus III. This impression and No. (9), below, have been made by the same stamp, but they occur on parts of two bullae recovered from different areas of the surface.

Sealing No. AId(7), a bulla fragment; indeterminate; clay. Surface.

(9) A duplicate impression of No. (8). Owing to incomplete impression the type does not appear.

Sealing No. AId(108), a bulla fragment; indeterminate; pink clay. Surface.

(10) Shape, like No. (1); incompletely impressed at the left and right; abraded; 16+ × 13 mm.

Legend: ἁλικῆς | Σελευκεί[α] | ς ΚΡ | ἐπιτελῶ[ν].

Type: Half-anchor, as on No. (1).

Date: 120 A.S., 192/91 B.C., reign of Antiochus III. The reading of the third line of legend presents some difficulties. This line contains the date and shows three characters. The first has been partly destroyed by a nick, and at first glance may be taken for either a zeta reversed or a sigma. I read sigma for the reasons that the fragmentary character more closely resembles the forms of this letter on our impressions than those of zeta and that a date of two numerals is more to be expected here than one of three. As a general rule, on the impressions the date is well centered in reference to the impression as a whole; when the date consists of two numerals, these are written closely together at about the center of the face; when of three, the characters are spaced some distance apart. On this impression we find the three characters placed closely together and occupying more of the left side of the face than of the right. The second and third characters taken alone have a position normal in respect to a date consisting of two numerals. On AId(17) (No. IC1b(10)), below, the final two letters of the city name have been brought down to form the initial characters on the date line. I assume that in the present instance either one or two characters of the city name were relegated to the beginning of the third line, and that the date is composed of kappa rho.

Sealing No. AId(8), a bulla fragment; indeterminate; clay. Surface.

(11) Shape, like No. (1); incompletely impressed at the right; 16+ × 12 mm.

Legend: ἁλικῆς | Σελευκεία[ς] | ΑΚΡ | ἐπιτελῶν.

Type: Half-anchor, as on No. (1).

Date: 121 A.S., 191/90 B.C., reign of Antiochus III.

Sealing No. AId(9), a bulla fragment; indeterminate; clay. Archive A.

(12) Shape, like No. (1); almost entirely destroyed by gouging; 18 × 17 mm.

Legend: [ἀλικ]ῆς | [Σελε]υκεία[ς] | — — — | [ἐπιτελ]ῶν.

The type and the date have been destroyed. A possible alternative to the restoration of the first word as ἀλικῆς is furnished by ἀνδραποδικῆς, which appears on another impression of a tax stamp in Archive A (cf. No. ICIc(1), below). The restoration of a word of twelve characters, however, is made improbable by the position of the surviving letters of the first line in respect to those of the second line, which is composed of ten characters. The restoration of the last line as ἐπιτελῶν, rather than as ἀτελῶν, is suggested by two considerations. The last two letters appear close to the right edge of the impression under the final surviving letters of the city name; if these two letters had completed the short form ἀτελῶν, they normally would have appeared farther to the left. In the second place, the impression under consideration formed a part of Archive A, which contained no impressions on which ἀτελῶν may be read. The latter group comprised a special file, Archive B (cf. p. 182).

Sealing No. AId(10), a bulla fragment; indeterminate; clay. Archive A.

b. Exemption from the salt tax

(1) Owing to breakage and incomplete impression the original shape and dimensions of the impression cannot be determined.

Legend: ἀλικ[ῆς] | [Σ]ελευ[κείας] | HϘ | ἀτε[λῶν].

The form of the type has not been preserved. I assume that it was the half-anchor as found on the other impressions with similar legends.

Date: 98 A.S., 214/13 B.C., reign of Antiochus III. This impression constitutes the earliest single occurrence of the formula ἀλικῆς | ἀτελῶν. The new term is discussed on page 180.

Sealing No. AId(106), a bulla fragment; indeterminate; clay. Surface.

(2) Ovoid, with short sides straight; slightly abraded; 18 × 14 mm.

Legend: ἁλικῆ[ς] | Σελευκείας | ΔΚΡ | ἀτελῶν.

Type: Half-anchor reversed, as on No. ICia(1), above.

Date: 124 A.S., 188/87 B.C., reign of Antiochus III. This is the earliest occurrence of the formula ἁλικῆς | ἀτελῶν on a sealing from Archive B. The impression occurs in duplicate on two parts of a single bulla.

Sealing No. AId(11), a bulla fragment in two pieces; indeterminate; clay. Archive B.

(3) Shape, like No. (2); 17 × 14 mm.

Legend: ἁλικῆς | ΕΚΡ | Σελευκεία[ς] | ἀτελῶν.

Type: Half-anchor, as on No. (2).

Date: 125 A.S., 187/86 B.C., marking the death of Antiochus III and the accession of Seleucus IV. The impression occurs in duplicate on parts of a single bulla.

Sealing No. AId(12), a bulla fragment in two pieces; indeterminate. Archive B.

(4) Shape, like No. (2); incompletely impressed at the right, broken at the bottom, abraded; 15⁺ × 11.5 mm.

Legend: ἁλικῆς | Σελευκ[είας] | ΖΚ[Ρ] | [ἀτελῶν].

Type: Owing to incomplete impression the type does not appear.

Date: 127 A.S., 185/84 B.C., reign of Seleucus IV. The initial numeral of the date is incomplete. I read it as zeta, reversed as it appears on No. (23), below. A similar form of the numeral zeta occurs on a Parthian coin from Seleucia, dated 46/47 A.D.

Sealing No. AId(13), a bulla fragment; indeterminate; clay. Archive B.

(5) Shape, like No. (2); badly abraded in part; 19 × 14 mm.

Legend: ἁλικῆς | Σελευκεία[ς] | ΗΚ[Ρ] | ἀτελῶν.

Type: Owing to abrasion no type may be distinguished.

Date: 128 A.S., 184/83 B.C., reign of Seleucus IV.

Sealing No. AId(14), a bulla fragment; indeterminate; clay. Archive B.

CATALOG OF IMPRESSIONS

(6) Shape, like No. (2); worn; 18 × 13 mm.

Legend: ΘΚΡ | ἁλικῆς | Σελευκείας | ἀτελῶν.

Type: Half-anchor, as on No. (2).

Date: 129 A.S., 183/82 B.C., reign of Seleucus IV. Note the position of the date as the first line of the legend found only on this impression, which occurs in duplicate on two parts of a single bulla.

Sealing No. AId(15), a bulla fragment in two pieces; indeterminate; clay. Archive B.

(7) Shape, like No. (2); incompletely impressed; 16⁺ × 13 mm.

Legend: ἁλικῆ[ς] | Σελευκεία[ς] | ΛΡ | ἀτελῶν.

Type: Owing to incomplete impression the type does not appear.

Date: 130 A.S., 182/81 B.C., reign of Seleucus IV. The impression occurs in duplicate on two parts of a single bulla.

Sealing No. AIc(1), a bulla practically complete in two pieces; multiple; clay. Archive B.

(8) Shape, like No. (2); 17⁺ × 13 mm.

Legend: ἁλικῆς | Σελευκεία[ς] | ΑΛΡ | ἀτελῶν.

Type: Half-anchor, as on No. (2).

Date: 131 A.S., 181/80 B.C., reign of Seleucus IV. The impression occurs in duplicate on a single bulla.

Sealing No. AIc(2), a bulla complete in two pieces; multiple; clay. Archive B.

(9) Shape, like No. (2); 18 × 16 mm.

Legend: ἁλικῆς | Σελευκείας | ΒΛΡ | ἀτελῶν.

Type: Half-anchor, as on No. (2).

Date: 132 A.S., 180/79 B.C., reign of Seleucus IV. The impression occurs in duplicate on two parts of a single bulla.

Sealing No. AId(16), a bulla fragment in two pieces; indeterminate; clay. Archive B.

(10) Shape, like No. (2); incompletely impressed; 15⁺ × 13 mm.

Legend: ἁλικῆς | Σελευκεί|ας ΓΛΡ | ἀτελῶν.

Type: Owing to incomplete impression the type does not appear.

Date: 133 A.S., 179/78 B.C., reign of Seleucus IV. Note that the final two letters of the city name have been written as the initial characters of the line next below. The impression occurs in duplicate on two parts of a single bulla.

Sealing No. AId(17), a bulla fragment in two pieces; multiple; clay. Archive B.

(11) Shape, like No. (2); incompletely impressed at the right, the left, and the bottom; 15⁺ × 10⁺ mm.

Legend: [ἁ]λικῆς | [Σε]λευκείας | ΔΛΡ | [ἀτε]λῶν.

Type: Half-anchor, as on No. (2).

Date: 134 A.S., 178/77 B.C., reign of Seleucus IV. The right-hand diagonal stroke of the first numeral of the date can just be distinguished. The impression occurs in duplicate on a bulla that is whole as well as complete.

Sealing No. AIc(3), a whole bulla; multiple; clay. Archive B.

(12) Shape, like No. (2); 16 × 13 mm.

Legend: ἁλικῆς | Σελευκεία[ς] | ΕΛΡ | ἀτελῶν.

Type: Half-anchor, as on No. (2).

Date: 135 A.S., 177/76 B.C., reign of Seleucus IV. The impression occurs in duplicate on two parts of a single bulla.

Sealing No. AId(18), a bulla fragment in two pieces; indeterminate; bitumen. Archive B.

(13) Shape, like No. (2); 19 × 11 mm.

Legend: ἁλικῆς | Σελευκείας | ϚΛΡ | ἀτελῶν.

Type: Half-anchor, as on No. (2).

Date: 136 A.S., 176/75 B.C., reign of Seleucus IV. The impression occurs in duplicate on two parts of a single bulla.

Sealing No. AIc(4), a bulla, nearly complete in two pieces; multiple; clay. Archive B.

(14) Shape, like No. (2); incompletely impressed; 17⁺ × 13 mm.

Legend: ἁλικῆς | Σελευκεί[ας] | ΖΛΡ | ἀτελῶν.

Type: Owing to incomplete impression the type cannot be distinguished.

Date: 137 A.S., 175/74 B.C., reign of Seleucus IV. The impression occurs in duplicate on two parts of a single bulla.

Sealing No. AIc(5), a complete bulla in two pieces; multiple; clay. Archive B.

(15) Shape, like No. (2); incompletely impressed; 18+ × 15 mm.

Legend: ἁλικῆς | Σελευκε[ίας] | ΗΛΡ | ἀτελῶν.

Type: Half-anchor, as on No. (2).

Date: 138 A.S., 174/73 B.C., close of reign of Seleucus IV, accession of Antiochus IV.

Sealing No. AId(19), a bulla fragment; indeterminate; clay. Archive B.

(16) Shape, like No. (2); incompletely impressed, abraded; 18+ × 12 mm.

Legend: ἁλικ[ῆς] | Σελευκε[ίας] | ΘΛ[Ρ] | ἀτε[λῶν].

Type: Half-anchor, as on No. (2).

Date: 139 A.S., 173/72 B.C., reign of Antiochus IV. The impression occurs in duplicate on two parts of a single bulla.

Sealing No. AId(20), a bulla fragment in two pieces; indeterminate; clay. Archive B.

(17) Shape, like No. (2); incompletely impressed; 15+ × 11 mm.

Legend: ἁλικῆς | Σελευκε[ίας] | ΜΡ | ἀτελῶ[ν].

Type: Half-anchor, as on No. (2).

Date: 140 A.S., 172/71 B.C., reign of Antiochus IV. The impression occurs in duplicate on two parts of a single bulla.

Sealing No. AIc(6), a complete bulla in two pieces; multiple; clay. Archive B.

(18) Shape, like No. (2); incompletely impressed; 19+ × 13+ mm.

Legend: ἁλικῆς | Σελυκεία[ς] | ΒΜΡ | [ἀ]τελῶν.

Type: Half-anchor, as on No. (2).

Date: 142 A.S., 170/69 B.C., reign of Antiochus IV. The impression occurs in duplicate on two parts of a single bulla.

Sealing No. AIc(7), a bulla practically complete in two pieces; multiple; bitumen (?). Archive B.

(19) Shape, like No. (2); 19 × 14 mm. Pl. II, Fig. 20.

Legend: ἁλικῆς | Σελευκείας | ΓΜΡ | ἀτελῶν.

Type: Half-anchor, as on No. (2), followed by a second symbol, probably a caduceus. This form of type is discussed on page 163.

Date: 143 A.S., 169/68 B.C., reign of Antiochus IV. The impression occurs in duplicate on two parts of a single bulla.

Sealing No. AIc(8), a bulla practically complete in two pieces; multiple; bitumen. Archive B.

(20) Shape, like No. (2); incompletely impressed at the left; 21+ × 15 mm.

Legend: [ἁ]λικῆς | Σελευκείας | ΔΜΡ | ἀτελῶν.

Type: Half-anchor, as on No. (2), followed by a star with seven rays. The form is treated on page 163.

Date: 144 A.S., 168/67 B.C., reign of Antiochus IV. The impression occurs in duplicate on two parts of a single bulla.

Sealing No. AIc(9), a bulla complete in two pieces; multiple; bitumen. Archive B.

(21) Shape, like No. (2); incompletely impressed; 20+ × 14 mm.

Legend: ἁλικῆς | Σελευκε[ίας] | ΕΜΡ | ἀτελῶν.

Type: Half-anchor, as on No. (2).

Date: 145 A.S., 167/66 B.C., reign of Antiochus IV. The impression occurs in duplicate on two parts of a single bulla.

Sealing No. AId(21), a bulla practically complete in two pieces; indeterminate; bitumen (?). Archive B.

(22) Shape, like No. (2); incompletely impressed; 19+ × 14.5 mm.

Legend: ἁλικῆς | Σελευκεία[ς] | ϛΜΡ | ἀτελῶ[ν].

Type: Owing to incomplete impression the type does not appear.

Date: 146 A.S., 166/65 B.C., reign of Antiochus IV. The type occurs in duplicate on two parts of a single bulla.

Sealing No. AId(22), a bulla fragment in two pieces; indeterminate; bitumen. Archive B.

(23) Shape, like No. (2); incompletely impressed; 17⁺ × 16⁺ mm.

Legend: [ἁ]λικῆς | Σελευκεία[s] | ΣΜΡ | ἀτελῶν.

Type: Half-anchor, as on No. (2).

Date: 147 A.S., 165/64 B.C., reign of Antiochus IV. (The zeta of the numeral is reversed.) The impression occurs in duplicate on two parts of a single bulla.

Sealing No. AId(23), a bulla fragment in two pieces; indeterminate; bitumen. Archive B.

(24) Shape, like No. (2); damaged by rubbing; 18.5 × 12 mm.

Legend: ἁλικῆς | Σελευκε[ίας] | ΗΜΡ | ἀτελῶν.

Type: Half-anchor, as on No. (2).

Date: 148 A.S., 164/63 B.C., reign of Antiochus IV. The impression occurs in duplicate on two parts of a single bulla.

Sealing No. AId(24), a bulla fragment in two pieces; indeterminate; bitumen. Archive B.

(25) Shape, like No. (2); 22.5 × 14 mm.

Legend: ἁλικῆς | Σελευκεία[s] | ΘΜΡ | ἀτελῶν.

Type: Half-anchor, as on No. (2).

Date: 149 A.S., 163/62 B.C., close of reign of Antiochus IV. The impression occurs in duplicate on two parts of a single bulla.

Sealing No. AIc(10), a bulla complete in two pieces; multiple; bitumen. Archive B.

(26) Shape, like No. (2); worn; 20.5 × 14.5 mm.

Legend: ἁλικῆς | Σελευκεία[s] | Ν[Ρ] | ἀτελῶν.

Type: Half-anchor followed by a star, as on No. ICib(20), above.

Date: 150 A.S., 162/61 B.C., the period of the revolt of Timarchus.

Sealing No. AId(25), a bulla fragment; indeterminate; bitumen. Archive B.

(27) Shape, like No. (2); 19.5 × 13 mm.

Legend: ἁλικῆς | Σελευκεία[s] | ΑΝΡ | ἀτελῶν.

Type: Half-anchor, as on No. (2).

Date: 151 A.S., 161/60 B.C., reign of Demetrius I. The impression occurs in duplicate on two parts of a single bulla. On one of the impressions the first numeral of the date has been destroyed, but a comparison of the relative positions of the letters on the different lines of legend indicates that both impressions were made by one seal.
Sealing No. AId(26), a bulla fragment in two pieces; indeterminate; bitumen. Archive B.

(28) Shape, like No. (2); 20 × 13.5 mm.
Legend: ἁλικῆs | Σελευκείας | BNP | ἀτελῶν.
Type: Half-anchor, as on No. (2).
Date: 152 A.S., 160/59 B.C., reign of Demetrius I. The impression occurs in duplicate on two parts of a single bulla.
Sealing No. AId(27), a bulla fragment in two pieces; indeterminate; clay. Archive B.

(29) Shape, like No. (2); incompletely impressed, badly worn; 17⁺ × 14 mm.
Legend: ἁλικῆ[s] | Σελευκε[ίας] | ΓNP | ἀτελῶ[ν].
Type: Half-anchor, as on No. (2).
Date: 153 A.S., 159/58 B.C., reign of Demetrius I. The impression occurs in duplicate on two parts of a single bulla. On one of the impressions the second numeral of the date has been entirely obscured by wear. In other respects, including the relative positions occupied by the letters of the different lines of legend, the impressions are alike. In addition, it should be noted that the duplicate impressions for the years ΓΛΡ and ΓΜΡ are complete, and the series of ΚΡ dates are all impressed on light-colored clay instead of bitumen, as are these impressions. There appears to be no question, therefore, that the two impressions were made by one seal, and that they formed parts of a single bulla.
Sealing No. AId(28), a bulla fragment in two pieces; indeterminate; bitumen. Archive B.

(30) Shape, like No. (2); broken off around the edges; 19⁺ × 14⁺ mm.
Legend: ἁλικ[ῆs] | Σελευκείας | ΔNP | ἀτελῶ[ν].
Type: Half-anchor, as on No. (2).

Date: 154 A.S., 158/57 B.C., reign of Demetrius I. The impression occurs in duplicate on two parts of a single bulla.

Sealing No. AId(29), a bulla fragment in two pieces; indeterminate; bitumen. Archive B.

(31) Shape, like No. (2); broken at the left edge; 18⁺ × 15 mm.

Legend: [ἀλ]ικῆς | Σελευκείας | ϵΝΡ | [ἀ]τελῶν.

Type: Half-anchor, as on No. (2).

Date: 155 A.S., 157/56 B.C., reign of Demetrius I.

Sealing No. AId(30), a bulla fragment; indeterminate; bitumen (?). Archive B.

(32) Shape, like No. (2); incompletely impressed at the right; 17⁺ × 12 mm.

Legend: ἀλικῆς | Σελευκεία[s] | ϚΝΡ | ἀτελῶ[ν].

Type: Owing to incomplete impression the type cannot be distinguished.

Date: 156 A.S., 156/55 B.C., reign of Demetrius I. The second numeral of the date is somewhat obscure, but the reading nu appears to be required.

Sealing No. AId(31), a bulla fragment; indeterminate; clay. Archive B.

(33) Shape, like No. (2); 19 × 14 mm.

Legend: ἀλικῆς | Σελευκείας | ΖΝΡ | ἀτελῶν.

Type: Half-anchor, as on No. (2).

Date: 157 A.S., 155/54 B.C., reign of Demetrius I. The impression occurs in duplicate on two parts of a single bulla.

Sealing No. AId(32), a bulla fragment; indeterminate; clay. Archive B.

(34) Shape, like No. (2); 19 × 14 mm.

Legend: ἀλικῆς | Σελευκείας | ΗΝΡ | ἀτελῶν.

Type: Half-anchor, as on No. (2).

Date: 158 A.S., 154/53 B.C., reign of Demetrius I. The impression occurs in duplicate on two parts of a single bulla.

Sealing No. AId(33), a bulla fragment in two pieces; indeterminate; clay. Archive B.

(35) Shape, like No. (2); incompletely impressed at the top and the right; 16⁺ × 14⁺ mm. Pl. II, Fig. 21.

Legend: ἁλικῆs | Σελευκεί[as] | ΘΝΡ | ἀτελῶν.

Type: Half-anchor, as on No. (2).

Date: 159 A.S., 153/52 B.C., reign of Demetrius I, opening of the revolt of Alexander Bala.

Sealing No. AId(34), a bulla fragment; indeterminate; clay. Archive B.

c. A tax on imported slaves

(1) Shape, like Nos. ICia(1) and ICib(1); incompletely impressed; 14⁺ × 14 mm. Pl. II, Fig. 22.

Legend: ἀνδραπ[οδικῆs] | Σελευκε[ίας] | ΒΚΡ | εἰσαγω[γικῶν].

Type: Half-anchor, as above.

Date: 122 A.S., 190/89 B.C., reign of Antiochus III. The first line of the legend has been completed by reference to Nos. IAic(1) and IAid(1). The new Greek terms are discussed on pages 175–177.

Sealing No. AId(35), a bulla fragment; indeterminate; bitumen. Archive A.

2. Special stamps having no type representing a general authority

a. A form of port dues

(1) Ovoid; the precise shape cannot be determined, owing to incomplete impression and to distortion as a result of subjection to heat; 15⁺ × 11 mm. Pl. II, Fig. 23.

Legend: λιμένο[s] | ΣΜΡ |]α[.

No type appears. The extent of blank space on the second line between the last numeral of the date and the edge of the impression is sufficient to show that a type emblem did not form a part of the original seal. Note that the city name has been omitted from the legend. The first character of the second line may be either a zeta reversed, as on No. ICib(23), above, or a badly made sigma. If a sigma, it must be read as the final letter of the preceding word brought down to the lower line, as was done with the final letters of the city name in No. ICib(10), above. This character is noticeably larger than the two which follow it and is rather crudely made. It has been stated above that the numerals of dates on our impressions are as a rule well centered, and that dates composed of two numerals are compactly placed, whereas those of three numerals are spaced out. The mu and the rho thus form a normally placed date. The large size of the first character makes more difficult its reading as the final sigma of the preceding line than as the initial numeral zeta of the date. The characteristics and the position of the letter on the face suggest that it may have been engraved on the stamp as an alteration of the original date. That is to say, the stamp originally bore the date 140 A.S., and it was later changed to read 147 A.S., equivalent to 165/64 B.C., in the reign of Antiochus IV.

The third line is in a very unsatisfactory condition, a result of distortion by heat. Remains of a number of characters can be distinguished. The second letter is without doubt alpha. It is probable that the first is tau. However, as it appears on the extreme left edge of the face, one may not disregard a possibility that the character was pi and that only its right portion has been impressed. I have tentatively read the next character as mu. Alternatively the strokes may be taken to form lambda and iota written close together. The first reading is the more probable. The following character is very faint, but it appears to be iota. Farther to the right occur indistinct traces of other letters. There is room on the impression for a word of seven or eight letters. In view of the apparent significance of the legend as a whole, one is tempted to restore the line as ταμιείου. The evidence, however, is insufficient (see below, pp. 173–175).

Sealing No. AId(36), a bulla fragment; indeterminate; bitumen. Archive A.

II. SEALS OF PRIVATE AGENTS OF ROYALTY

A. PORTRAITS OF KINGS, ALONE AND JUGATE

1. *Identified*

a.[3] Seleucus I

(1) Oval; incompletely impressed; 12+ × 9 mm.; execution fair. Pl. II, Fig. 24.

Type: Head right, with mustache and beard. The head is encircled with a diadem. The engraving is distinctly portraiture,

[3] See page 44, note 1.

not an idealized representation. The features are those of an aged man. The bases for the identification as Seleucus are given on pages 209–210 in connection with the discussion of another representation of Seleucus, No. IA3a(1).

Sealing No. AIb(1), a bulla nearly complete; dual; clay. Archive A.

g. Antiochus, son of Seleucus III

(1) Oval; incompletely impressed; broken at the top; w. 12 mm.; execution fair. Pl. II, Fig. 25.

Type: Head right, male, with diadem; distinctly a portrait. The nose is short and somewhat *retroussé*. The features are decidedly youthful. The identification is definitely established by comparison with Seleucid coins (Babelon, Pl. VIII, 17). This Antiochus reigned in the year 222/21 B.C. Another impression of the same seal on a different fragment is No. (2), below.

Sealing No. AIc(14), a bulla fragment; multiple; bitumen. Archive A.

(2) A duplicate impression of No. (1), above.

Sealing No. AId(39), a bulla fragment; indeterminate; bitumen. Archive A.

i. Antiochus III

(1) Oval; worn; 13 × 9 mm.; execution fair. Pl. II, Fig. 26.

Type: Bust right, male, with diadem; a portrait. The features approximate those of Antiochus the Great as found on certain coins (cf. Babelon, Pl. IX, 15). The identification is made with some reserve.

Sealing No. AId(40), a bulla fragment; indeterminate; clay. Archive A.

k. Seleucus IV

(1) Oval; incompletely impressed at the bottom, badly abraded; 15+ × 12.5 mm.; execution good. Pl. II, Fig. 27.

Type: Bust right, male, with diadem; clearly a portrait. Owing to the abrasion identification is difficult. A definite relationship may be noted, however, between the features of the impression and those on certain coins of Seleucus IV (Babelon, Pl. XI, 13–15).

Sealing No. AId(43), a bulla fragment; indeterminate; clay. Archive B.

m. Antiochus IV

(1) Oval; badly chipped; 13 × 11 mm.; execution obscure but probably good.

Type: Head right, male; a portrait. There are traces which perhaps represent a diadem. Though the features are very obscure, one can note the straight line of the forehead and nose in profile characteristic of some coins of Antiochus IV (Babelon, Pl. XIII, 16, 17). Another impression on the same bulla concerned with the salt tax is dated in the year 167/66 B.C., in the reign of Antiochus. The identification appears to be reasonably certain.

Sealing No. AId(21), a bulla nearly complete in two pieces; indeterminate; bitumen (?). Archive B.

o. Timarchus

(1) The shape cannot be determined, since only the center of the impression has been preserved; execution fairly good. Pl. II, Fig. 28.

Type: Head right, male, wearing either a kausia or a helmet shaped like a kausia. The outline of the features appears to relate the portrait to that of Timarchus as reproduced on the impression of an official seal and on a coin model (p. 46, No. IA30(1); p. 249, No. 7a(1)). The attribution of these two pieces to Timarchus is defended on pages 214–220, where the significance of the kausia form of headdress is also discussed. In respect to the impression with which we are now concerned the similarity of features and the Bactrian relationship of the headdress both require the identification proposed.

Sealing No. AIIa(29), appended; convex; clay. Archive B.

p. Demetrius I

(1) Oval; chipped; 12 × 9 mm.; execution good. Pl. II, Fig. 29.

Type: Head right, male; a portrait. Definite traces of the diadem may be observed. Over the forehead is a pronounced lock of hair; the nose and the chin are strong. There is a distinct resemblance to the portrait of Demetrius on his coins (Babelon, Pl. XVI, 9, 14, and 16).

Sealing No. AId(41), a bulla fragment; indeterminate; bitumen. Archive A.

q. Alexander I (with Cleopatra Thea)

(1) Probably oval; but very incompletely impressed and broken at the bottom; execution fair. Pl. II, Fig. 30.

Type: Jugate heads right; in the background the king with diadem, in the foreground the queen. Owing to the incomplete impression and to breakage details of the features cannot be determined. The identification of the portraits is made possible by the position occupied by the figure in the foreground. Cleopatra is so shown on coins of Alexander Bala and of Antiochus VIII, the son of Cleopatra (Babelon, Pls. XVIII, 20, 21; XXIV, 1, 5). By 125 B.C., when Antiochus VIII was reigning with his mother, all Babylonia was definitely under Parthian rule. A representation of this king would not occur in the archives from Seleucia. On some coins of Demetrius I, Laodice, his wife, is portrayed with him, but in the background. The unusual pre-eminence attained by Cleopatra Thea was due in part, of course, to her own masterful character as well as to the influence of her father, Ptolemy Philometor. But of greater importance was the fact that Alexander was a usurper with no established position. Another impression below appears to represent the jugate heads of Cleopatra and Demetrius II, who became her husband after the defeat and death of Alexander. Here the queen is shown in the background, an arrangement to be expected in view of the position of Demetrius as the legitimate claimant to the Seleucid throne.

Sealing No. AIc(11), a bulla fragment; multiple; bitumen. Archive A.

s. Demetrius II

(1) Oval; broken, 12+ × 7 mm.; execution good. Pl. II, Fig. 31.

Type: Head right, male, in elephant scalp headdress, a portrait. Both Alexander the Great and Demetrius II are portrayed on coins with this style of headdress. It cannot be assumed that a private individual would adopt this style for his personal portrait, or that such a person would employ a representation of Alexander the Great as his personal seal motif. The features, especially the line of the forehead and nose, are not unlike those of Demetrius II as found on his coins, and I assign the portrait to him.

Sealing No. AId(102), a bulla fragment, indeterminate; clay. Archive A.

(2) Oval; broken at the top; 12+ × 11 mm.; execution good. Pl. II, Fig. 32.

Type: Jugate busts right; in the background the queen, in the foreground the king with diadem and a beard. As has been stated in the description of No. IIA1q(1), the only queens of the Seleucid line to be represented on coins alongside the reigning kings are Laodice, wife of Demetrius I, and Cleopatra Thea, wife in turn of Alexander Bala, Demetrius II, and Antiochus VII, and mother of Antiochus VIII. The only Seleucid kings shown on coins as bearded are Seleucus II and Demetrius II. The representation on our impression depicts the king as a man, not a god. It is definitely portraiture. The features indicate no relation to the known portrayals of Seleucus II. The nose and the line of the profile, however, do resemble the "beardless" features of Demetrius II on his coins (Babelon, Pl. XIX, 1, 17), although on the coins he is much younger. On his "bearded" coins Demetrius is shown with a slight growth of whiskers (Babelon, Pl. XIX, 15) and again with a full, rather long beard (*idem*, Pl. XXII, 9 ff.). The style on our impressions is between these two extremes. There appears to be no question that the representation is of Demetrius II with Cleopatra. The possible significance of the presence of the beard in relation to the exact date of the impression cannot be discussed.

Sealing No. AId(42), a bulla fragment; indeterminate; bitumen. Archive A.

2. *Unidentified*

(1) Oval; with short sides straight; badly worn; 11.5 × 7 mm. Execution obscure.

Type: Head right, male, diademed; apparently a portrait. The features show some resemblance to those of Demetrius I, but owing to the poor condition of the piece I prefer to make no identification.

Sealing No. AIIa(3), appended; convex; clay. Archive B.

(2) Oval; cracked and worn; 10⁺ × 8 mm.; execution fair.

Type: Head right, male, diademed; evidently a portrait. The features are not sufficiently clear to warrant an attempt at identification.

Sealing No. AId(44), a bulla fragment; indeterminate; bitumen. Archive A.

(3) Oval; incompletely impressed at bottom, worn; 9⁺ × 7 mm.; execution obscure.

Type: Head right, male, apparently diademed; definitely a portrait. I have not been able to identify the representation.

Sealing No. AId(45), a bulla fragment; indeterminate; clay. Archive A.

(4) Oval; incompletely impressed; badly cracked; 12⁺ × 8⁺ mm.; execution fair.

Type: Bust right, male, diademed; evidently a portrait. Owing to the poor condition of the impression it is not possible to make an identification.

Sealing No. AIb(2), a whole bulla; dual; clay. Archive A.

(5) Oval; the right edge broken off, worn; 10 × 7⁺ mm.; execution obscure.

Type: Head right, male, diademed. The greater part of the face has been obscured by the break, and no identification is possible.

Sealing No. AId(46), a bulla fragment; indeterminate; clay. Archive A.

(6) Oval; badly worn; 16 × 14 mm.; execution probably fair. Across the face of the impression is an indentation caused apparently by the impression of a thumb nail. (See p. 10.)

Type: Head right, male, apparently diademed. The impression is very obscure. It appears to represent a royal personage, but beyond such an assumption it is impossible to go.

Sealing No. AIIb(6), an appended sealing; clay. Trial trench 4, Level III.

(7) Oval; broken and badly worn; 11 × 9 mm.; execution perhaps good.

Type: Head right, male. There are traces that indicate either a diadem or a wreath. The representation may be either a portrait or an idealization. On the basis of general comparison, however, its classification here may be warranted.

Sealing No. AIc(15), a bulla fragment; multiple; clay. Archive B.

B. PORTRAITS OF QUEENS

1. *Identified*

a. Wife of Seleucus III (?)

(1) Oval; the lower part broken off; 8+ × 7 mm.; execution fair.

Type: Head left, female; probably a portrait. The hair is done in a knot at the back of the head and is bound with a fillet. On the same bulla occurs a similar impression representing the portrait of the youthful king Antiochus, son of Seleucus III. It is probable, therefore, that the royal lady of this impression is the mother of Antiochus, the wife of Seleucus. Another impression of the same seal is No. (2), below.

Sealing No. AIc(14), a bulla fragment; multiple; bitumen. Archive A.

(2) A duplicate impression of No. (1).

Sealing No. AId(39), a bulla fragment; indeterminate; bitumen. Archive A.

b. Laodice, wife of Seleucus IV (?)

(1) Oval; the edges slightly broken; 10 × 8 mm.; execution fair.

Type: Bust right, female; apparently a portrait. The hair is rolled into a knot behind and bound with a fillet. On the same fragment is an impression dated in 179/78 B.C., in the reign of Seleucus IV. On the assumption which forms the basis for the classification of these impressions of portraits, that they represent members of the Seleucid royal family (see pp. 199–208), the present impression must be taken as the portrayal of a royal lady who was the contemporary of Seleucus IV. Since this king married his sister, Laodice (Appian, *Syriaca*, iv), the portrait should probably be assigned to her.

Sealing No. AId(17), a bulla fragment in two pieces; indeterminate; clay. Archive B.

2. *Unidentified*

(1) Oval: incompletely impressed; 11 × 7+ mm.; execution good.

Type: Bust right, female; apparently a portrait. The shoulders are draped; the hair is rolled in front and drawn into a knot at the back of the head. Another impression of the same seal is No. (2), below.

Sealing No. AIIa(5), an appended sealing, convex; bitumen. Archive B.

(2) A duplicate impression of No. (1).

Sealing No. AIIa(6), appended; convex; bitumen. Archive B.

(3) Oval; badly worn; 14 × 9 mm.; execution apparently good.

Type: Bust right, female; apparently a portrait. The hair is bound with a double fillet, but is not drawn into a knot. The neck is long and rather slender, but the effect is graceful. Note the similar style on an impression of the Parthian period on which the tendency has become exaggerated (p. 236, No. BId(1)).

Sealing No. AId(48), a bulla fragment; indeterminate; clay. Archive A.

(4) Oval; worn; 12 × 8 mm.; execution fair.

Type: Bust right, female; apparently a portrait. The shoulders are draped. The hair is bound with a fillet that is very pronounced; it appears to end under the large knot of hair at the back. Another impression of the same seal is No. (5), below.

Sealing No. AId(50), a bulla fragment; indeterminate; clay. Archive A.

CATALOG OF IMPRESSIONS

(5) A duplicate impression of No. (4).
Sealing No. AId(51), a bulla fragment; indeterminate; clay. Archive A. The two fragments, AId(50) and (51), are not parts of a single bulla.

(6) Oval; 12 × 10 mm.; crossed by thumb-nail impression (see p. 10). Execution fair.
Type: Head right, female; apparently a portrait. The hair is rolled in front and done in a knot behind. The impression just below is very similar, but the two have not been made by one seal.
Sealing No. AIIa(4), appended; convex; bitumen. Archive A.

(7) Oval; 12 × 10 mm.; execution fair.
Type: Head right, female; apparently a portrait. The details approximate those of No. (6). It is probable that both impressions represent one subject, although produced by different seals.
Sealing No. AId(47), a bulla fragment; indeterminate; bitumen. Archive A.

(8) Oval; cracked; 13 × 11 mm.; execution rather good.
Type: Head right, female; probably a portrait. The hair is bound with a fillet and is drawn into a knot at the back of the head.
Sealing No. AIc(16), a whole bulla; multiple; clay. Archive A.

(9) Oval; incompletely impressed; 10+ × 6.5 mm.; execution rather good.
Type: Head right, female; apparently a portrait. The hair is bound with a double fillet and is drawn into a knot at the back of the head.
Sealing No. AIIa(7), appended; convex; clay. Archive B.

(10) Oval: very worn; 11 × 9 mm.; execution obscure.
Type: Head right, female; probably a portrait. The hair is rolled in front and drawn into a knot at the back.
Sealing No. AId(49), a bulla fragment; indeterminate; clay. Archive A.

III. IMPRESSIONS OF PRIVATE SEALS

A. WITH A SIGNIFICANCE PROBABLY RELIGIOUS

1. *Representations of principal deities*

a. Apollo

(1) Oval; cracked and worn; 13 × 11 mm.; execution good. Pl. III, Fig. 33.

Type: Figure, male, partly draped, seated right on omphalos. The hair is rolled into a large bunch on the top of the head. The right arm hangs down with the hand resting on the omphalos. The right foot is advanced; the left, drawn back. The left arm holds an object which rests on the lap. Although somewhat obscure the object appears to represent a lyre. The omphalos is egg-shaped. The details of its covering are distinctly traced. This pose of Apollo is not one exactly reproduced on Seleucid coins. Babelon (Pl. V, 15) shows a coin of Antiochus I with Apollo seated on the omphalos and holding a lyre, but the head is turned front and a tripod stands behind. The motif of our impression has more in common with the Apollo of Delphos than with the Apollo of Antioch, a common type for the Seleucid coinage. On the other hand, the lack of emphasis on the drapery suggests Syrian influence. It has been related that a statue of Apollo was carried away from Seleucia to Rome by Avidius Cassius in 166/67 A.D. (Ammianus Marcellinus, xxiii. 6. 23). No details of its characteristics are known. The motif is of course Greek.[4]

Sealing No. AIc(15), a bulla fragment; multiple; clay. Archive B.

(2) Oval; short sides straight; 12 × 7 mm.; execution fair.
Type: Figure, male, nude, standing facing with head turned left. The hair is rolled in a bunch at the back of the head. The left elbow rests on a tripod; the right hand holds an arrow pointed diagonally down. The general motif is one common to Seleucid coins, especially in the reign of Seleucus II (Babelon, Pl. VII, 4-7). The impression, however, differs from the coins in certain details: the position of the body, the treatment of the hair, the

---

[4] This term is defined on page 224.

shape of the tripod, etc. The motif is Greek. The impression occurs in duplicate on two parts of a single bulla.

Sealing No. AIa(1), a bulla complete in two pieces; single; clay. Archive A.

(3) Oval; the lower half broken off; w. 9.5 mm.; execution fair.

Type: Figure, male, nude, standing facing with head turned left. The hair is drawn into a knot behind and is encircled with a wreath. The left elbow rests on a tripod which appears to have an extension that reaches up to the level of the head. The right hand holds an arrow pointed diagonally down. The pose is very similar to that on No. (2), but there are slight variations. The two representations of Apollo may well derive from a common original, but the two seals are the product of different engravers.

Sealing No. AId(52), a bulla fragment; indeterminate; clay. Archive A.

b. Dionysus

(1) Oval; incompletely impressed, worn; 20+ × 15+ mm.; execution fair. Pl. III, Fig. 34.

Type: Figure, male, nude, standing facing with head turned left. The head is very obscure, but there appear to be traces of a wreath. The left arm rests on a long stafflike object the top of which has not been impressed. This may be a thyrsos. What is apparently a chlamys is draped over this arm. The right arm hangs down with the hand extended. In the hand is an obscure object. The impression somewhat resembles a representation of Dionysus on a coin of Antiochus VI (Babelon, Pl. XX, 12). On the coin the object held in the right hand is a kantharos, and the god is clad in a chiton. Furtwängler (Pl. LXV, 32; cf. Pl. XXXIV, 22) shows intaglios of the Hellenistic period representing Dionysus with attributes and a pose which approximate those of our impression except that the head is facing rather than turned left. Although the cult of Dionysus was widespread in Asia, the motif here appears to be Greek. The impression is larger than the average private seal; it is possible that it represents the seal of some semipublic institution such as a temple. The impression occurs in duplicate on the one fragment.

Sealing No. AId(53), a bulla fragment; indeterminate; clay. Surface.

(2) Oval; badly worn; 14 × 8 mm.; execution fair.
Type: Figure, male, standing right. The trunk is apparently nude; the lower limbs are draped. The head is obscure but is bearded and crowned with a wreath or garland. The figure holds, in front, a vessel that is rather obscure. Furtwängler (Pl. XXV, 23) shows a somewhat similar representation of Dionysus where the god holds in addition a thyrsos. Such an object cannot be distinguished on the impression, but it is possible that this is due to wear. The figure appears to be Dionysus, and his representation on this impression with a beard must be set off against the three impressions on which he is shown clean-shaven. Two other impressions of the one seal are Nos. (3) and (4), below. Whatever the identification of the figure, the undraped trunk and the wreath suggest Greek rather than Oriental associations.
Sealing No. AIIa(28), appended; convex; clay. Archive B.

(3) A duplicate of No. (2).
Sealing No. AIIa(30), appended; convex; clay. Archive B.

(4) A duplicate of No. (2).
Sealing No. AIIa(22), appended; convex; clay. Archive B.

(5) Oval; very badly worn; 24 × 18 mm.; execution obscure.
Type: Figure, male, nude, standing right. The impression is very obscure. No details of the headdress may be distinguished. The weight of the figure appears to be resting on the left foot while the right foot is set on an obscure object of no great height. This serves to throw the right knee forward. The right elbow is bent, but there are no traces to indicate that drapery was suspended from this arm or that the elbow was supported by a short column. The left arm is outstretched in front and holds an object which has a long shaft. On the lower extremity of this object is a small knob; the upper extremity has been entirely obscured. The object is not held diagonally, as is the arrow in portrayals of Apollo. I am convinced that the figure represents deity; to judge by the lines and the style, the choice appears to be limited to Apollo or Dionysus. The object held in the

left hand can best be identified as a thyrsos, an attribute of Dionysus. The position of the right arm suggests that drapery was suspended from it, an arrangement characteristic of the same deity. It is very possible that all traces of the garments have been worn away. For these reasons I tentatively assign the impression to Dionysus. The large size of the impression makes possible an assumption that the seal with which it was made represented a semipublic institution. The motif is Greek.

Sealing No. AId(54), a bulla fragment; indeterminate; clay. Surface.

(6) Oval; incompletely impressed, badly worn; 16+ × 10 mm.; execution obscure.

Type: Figure, male, clothed, standing right. The details of the headdress are obscure, but there are traces that suggest a wreath. The clothing appears to be limited to a tunic. In the outstretched right hand is a vessel, apparently a kantharos. Held diagonally under the left arm is a wand with streamers attached, suggesting a thyrsos. Comparable to this is a representation of Dionysus on an Italic seal shown by Furtwängler (Pl. XXIV, 42). The god here holds a similar thyrsos in the same position and in the other hand a kantharos, but he is bearded and is clothed in a long robe. The assignment of the impression to Dionysus appears to be reasonable. The motif is Greek.

Sealing No. AIc(16), a whole bulla; multiple; clay. Archive A.

c. Athena

(1) Oval; incompletely impressed, broken at the bottom, cracked, and counter-impressed with thumb nail (cf. p. 10); 19.5 × 14+ mm.; execution apparently very good. Pl. III, Fig. 35.

Type: Figure, female, fully draped, advancing right. The figure wears a high-crested helmet, and holds a shield advanced on the left arm. The right arm held above and slightly behind the shoulders prepares to hurl a thunderbolt. The pose shows vigorous movement; the weight of the body rests on the left foot with the right foot about to be brought forward. This is a beautiful representation of Athena Alkis. The goddess of the thunderbolt is a type common to the coinages of a number of the Hellenistic rulers; among the Seleucid kings it is found on the coins of Seleucus I, Antiochus I, Antiochus IV, and Alexander

Bala (Babelon, Pls. III, 7; V, 1; XV, 8; and p. 112, No. 883). On the coins, however, the goddess is standing rather than advancing, a pose that harmonizes little with the position of the arm. The concept and the workmanship represented by the impression are superior to those of the coin types. Athena the Thunderer was especially venerated by the Macedonians (Babelon, p. xxvi). The motif, therefore, may be said to be not only Greek but Macedonian. Another impression of the same seal is No. (2), below. Nos. (3), (4), and (5) show slightly variant representations of Athena Alkis.

Sealing No. AId(55), a bulla fragment; indeterminate; clay. Archive B.

(2) A duplicate of No. (1).

Sealing No. AId(56), a bulla fragment; indeterminate; clay. Archive B. It is probable that sealings Nos. AId(55) and (56) are parts of a single bulla.

(3) Apparently rectangular; slightly broken at the bottom; 11+ × 8.5 mm.; execution good.

Type: Athena Alkis, as above, except that the type is smaller and the left knee is somewhat more advanced. The chlamys is shown hanging from the shoulders, as on the coins. This feature cannot be discerned on impressions (1) and (2). The impression occurs in duplicate on two parts of a single bulla.

Sealing No. AIa(2), a bulla complete in two pieces; single; bitumen. Archive A.

(4) Oval; 9.5 × 8 mm.; execution crude. Pl. III, Fig. 36.

Type: Athena Alkis, as on Nos. (1) to (3), but very crude and stiff. The shield is held in an unnatural position almost parallel with the ground. The chlamys appears to be hanging from the waist and is of exaggerated size. The trunk is disproportionately small as compared with the limbs and arms. The helmet has been obscured.

Sealing No. AId(57), a bulla fragment; indeterminate; clay. Archive B.

(5) Oval; cracked and marred by a flaw in the seal; 13 × 11 mm.; execution fair.

Type: Athena Alkis, as on Nos. (1) to (3), but standing rather than advancing. This type approximates the representations of the goddess on the coins rather more closely than do the other impressions. The seals with which the five impressions were made appear to have been the work of at least three different engravers.

Sealing No. AIc(16), a whole bulla; multiple; clay. Archive A.

(6) Oval; incompletely impressed, worn; $14^+ \times 12^+$ mm.; execution rather obscure but at least fair.

Type: Figure, female, fully draped, standing left. The head bears a crested helmet; the right hand is advanced, resting on a long shaft, apparently a spear; the left arm is dropped at the side, supporting an object which has been incompletely impressed, but which is probably a shield. This is a representation of Athena Promachos rather similar to that which appears on coins of certain Seleucid kings (Babelon, Pl. V, 3; Gardner, *Syria*, Pl. XVIII, 9; R. H. McDowell, "Coins," *Preliminary Report upon the Excavations at Tel Umar, Iraq* [Ann Arbor, 1931], p. 54, No. 19). On an impression found at Orchoi this same figure occurs as the type of an official seal (Rostovtzeff, "Seleucid Babylonia," p. 41, No. 57). The impression from Seleucia appears to furnish an exception to the general rule concerning distinctions between the types of official and private seals (see p. 29). The wide popularity of this particular motif throughout the Greek world may serve to explain the exception.

Sealing No. AIc(16), as under No. (5), above.

(7) Oval; the lower half not impressed; very worn; w. 12.5 mm.; execution obscure.

Type: Figure, apparently female, fully draped, standing right. The head is obscure but is probably helmeted. The left hand clasps a long shaft, which I take to be a spear. The right hand is dropped at the side, but from the wrist down the arm has not been impressed. Though the whole impression is very obscure, it appears to be another representation of Athena Promachos, in this instance facing right instead of left.

Sealing No. AIc(16), as under No. (5).

(8) Circular; diam. 11 mm.; execution mediocre. Pl. III, Fig. 37.

Type: Figure, female, fully draped, standing right. The head is covered by a crested helmet. The left arm supports a shield; the right hand holds a spear held diagonally from behind the shoulder to the ground in front of the feet. The sweep of the drapery from the knees to the ground suggests that we may have here a representation of Athena-Nike. But what is apparently a chlamys attached at the waist, as on No. (4) above, is not typical of such an assimilation. Apart from the chlamys the impression is closely similar to an early Roman seal shown by Furtwängler (Pl. LXIII, 29).

Sealing No. AIIa(31), appended; convex; clay. Archive B.

(9) Oval; incompletely impressed at the bottom; counter-impressed with thumb nail (cf. p. 10 above); $13^+ \times 13$ mm.; execution fair. Pl. III, Fig. 38.

Type: Figure, female, fully draped, standing right. The head is covered by a high-crested helmet; a spear rests against the left shoulder, a shield against the knees. The outstretched hand (right) holds a Nike who faces left and extends a wreath toward the goddess. Representations of Athena Nikephore occur on coins of Alexander Bala, Demetrius II, and other later Seleucid kings (Babelon, Pl. XVII, 18; Gardner, *Syria*, Pl. XVII, 10). On the coins, however, Athena stands left, and there are other variations in detail. An official seal from Orchoi had as type Athena Nikephore, but the Victory is turned away from the goddess (Rostovtzeff, "Seleucid Babylonia," p. 39, No. 51). On gems of the Roman period Athena Nikephore is shown facing and turned left (Furtwängler, Pls. XLIV, 66; LXII, 19).

Sealing No. AIc(24), a bulla, whole; multiple; clay. Great House, Level III, Room 141 sub (equivalent to Level IV).

(10) Oval; slightly incomplete at top and bottom, marred by flaw in seal; $12^+ \times 11$ mm.; execution fair.

Type: Head right, in crested helmet. The features are idealized, and there can be no doubt that the representation is of Athena. The head of Athena Promachos, as well as the full figure, formed a very popular motif throughout the Hellenic and Hellenized world. As coin type it appears in the reigns of Seleucus I, Antiochus I, Seleucus II, and Antiochus IV (Babelon, Pls. I, 11, 12; IV, 1; VII, 11; XV, 5). The impressions of five different seals from Seleucia, Nos. (10)–(14), bear this motif. None of them may be associated in a particular way with the similar coin types.

Sealing No. AIIa(27), appended; convex; clay. Archive B.

(11) Oval; badly worn; 8 × 6.5 mm.; execution obscure.

Type: Head right, in crested helmet, as above. Another impression of the same seal is No. (12), below.

Sealing No. AId(58), a bulla fragment; indeterminate; clay. Archive A.

(12) A duplicate impression of No. (11).

Sealing No. AId(59), a bulla fragment; indeterminate; clay (?). Archive A.

(13) Oval; badly worn; 10 × 9 mm.; execution obscure.

Type: Head right, in crested helmet, as on No. (10).

Sealing No. AIc(2), a bulla complete in two pieces; multiple; clay. Archive B.

(14) Incompletely impressed, no dimensions obtainable; execution fair.

Type: Head right, in crested helmet, as on No. (10).

Sealing No. AIc(9), a bulla complete in two pieces; multiple; bitumen. Archive B.

(15) Oval; 11 × 7.5 mm.; execution crude.

Type: Herm with head of Athena Promachos right.

Sealing No. AIIa(26), appended; convex; clay. Archive B.

d. Artemis

(1) Oval; badly abraded and cracked; 15.5 × 9.5 mm.; execution fair.

Type: Figure, female, standing right, clad in short tunic and ankle boots. The headdress is obscure. The left arm is extended and holds a bow; the right is raised behind the shoulder, apparently in the act of drawing an arrow from a quiver which has become obscured. This is without doubt a representation of Artemis. It occurs on the impressions of four different seals from Seleucia, Nos. (1)–(5). Impression No. (1) almost exactly reproduces the type found on a coin of Timarchus minted in Babylonia, presumably at Seleucia (Gardner, *Syria*, Pl. XXVIII, 6). The popularity of the motif locally suggests that it was derived from a statue of the goddess erected in Seleucia. The general motif of Artemis the Huntress was of course common to the Greek world, although based on Anatolian mythology. An intaglio in the Southesk Collection reproduces the same type with some variations in detail (Carnegie, Vol. I, Pl. IV, C25).

Sealing No. AId(60), a bulla fragment; indeterminate; clay. Archive A.

(2) Oval; slightly broken and cracked; $13^+ \times 8.5$ mm.; execution fair. Pl. III, Fig. 39.

Type: Artemis standing right, as above, but the impression of another seal. On this impression the hair can be distinguished. It is drawn into a knot behind and is bound with a fillet. The pose of the body is slightly different and shows greater movement and perhaps grace. The seals were the work of two different engravers. A duplicate of this impression is No. (3), below.

Sealing No. AId(61), a bulla fragment; indeterminate; bitumen. Archive A.

(3) A duplicate impression of No. (2).

Sealing No. AId(62), a bulla fragment; indeterminate; bitumen. Archive A. It is probable that the two fragments, AId(61) and (62), are parts of a single bulla.

(4) Oval; incompletely impressed; badly worn; $14^+ \times 10.5$ mm.; execution obscure but apparently fair.

Type: Artemis standing right, as above. The impression is very obscure, and the bow cannot be distinguished. But in respect to the position of the arms and to the pose of the whole body there is a very close similarity to impression No. (1). It is quite possible that both are the work of one artist.

Sealing No. AId(63), a bulla fragment; indeterminate; clay. Archive A.

(5) Oval; the edges broken, badly abraded; $8^+ \times 7^+$ mm.; execution apparently good.

Type: Artemis standing right, as above. Although obscured by abrasion the impression appears to represent a higher degree of workmanship than do the others of the group.

Sealing No. AId(53), a bulla fragment; indeterminate; clay. Surface.

(6) Oval; incompletely impressed, abraded; 11+ × 7 mm.; execution mediocre.

Type: Bust, female, turned left. The hair is drawn into a knot behind and bound with a fillet. Above the head is a crescent. There is no evidence of portraiture. The presence of the crescent suggests an identification as either Artemis or Aphrodite. The latter is usually represented with some form of rather elaborate headdress, whereas Artemis is frequently shown with simple fillet or with a diadem. On our impression the object described as a fillet may be a diadem, but this is doubtful. With little hesitation I assign the type to Artemis. An impression of an official seal from Seleucia has as type an Artemis head crowned with a diadem (see p. 48, impression No. IA3v(1)). The head or the bust of Artemis is found as type on the coins of Seleucus II, Seleucus III, Antiochus III, Seleucus IV, and the two Demetrii (Babelon, p. 38, No. 283; p. 42, No. 314; Pls. X, 14; XI, 18; XVI, 5, 6; XXII, 11). On the coins the goddess wears at times the fillet, at times the diadem. The crescent, however, does not appear.

Sealing No. AIc(14), a bulla fragment; multiple; bitumen. Archive A.

e. Nike

(1) Oval; the lower half broken off, badly worn; w. 10 mm.; execution fair.

Type: Winged figure, female, draped, standing right. The hair is somewhat obscured, but is apparently drawn into a knot behind. Owing to a break the lines of the lower drapery cannot be distinguished. A wreath is held in front close to the body. The representation is clearly of Nike. The goddess of victory carrying either a wreath or a palm enjoyed a popularity both as an official and as a private emblem that extended to the very limits of the influence of Hellenization. Besides its common use on the Seleucid coinage this type is found on Armenian and Parthian

issues (Babelon, p. 212, No. 6; p. 215, No. 25; p. 216, No. 27; Wroth, p. 8, No. 17; p. 116, No. 20; p. 169, No. 72; etc.). However, with the sense in which we use the term the motif is Greek rather than Oriental. The five impressions in this group that have Nike as type appear to represent as many engravers.
Sealing No. AId(64), a bulla fragment; indeterminate; clay. Archive A.

(2) Oval; incompletely impressed; worn; 13+ × 11 mm.; execution crude.
Type: Winged figure, female, draped, standing left. The details of the headdress are obscure. There is no flare to the lower folds of the drapery. The outstretched right hand holds a wreath from which hang fillets. The impression occurs in duplicate on a single bulla.
Sealing No. AIa(3), a whole bulla; single; clay. Archive A.

(3) Circular; badly worn; diam. 10 mm.; execution obscure.
Type: Winged figure, female, draped, standing left. Nearly all details, including that of the drapery, are obscure. In one outstretched hand is held an object, probably a wreath with fillets.
Sealing No. AId(4), a bulla fragment; indeterminate; bitumen. Archive A.

(4) Oval; worn and obscure; 9 × 7 mm.; execution obscure.
Type: Winged figure, female, draped, standing right. Details of headdress and drapery have been obscured. One arm is advanced holding an object that is probably a wreath. Two other impressions of the same seal occur on the fragment.
Sealing No. AId(111), a bulla fragment; indeterminate; clay. Great House, Level III, Room 160.

(5) Oval; worn; 16 × 11 mm.; execution good. Pl. III, Fig. 40.
Type: Winged figure, female, draped, standing facing with head turned right. The wings rise well above the head, a feature not found on the preceding impressions. The drapery from the knees down flares as though driven by the wind. The right arm is dropped at the side, and the left arm has been obscured. On an intaglio of the Southesk Collection there is a very similar

type with the right arm dropped at the side and holding a wreath (Carnegie, Vol. I, Pl. IV, D6). The details of figure, wings, and especially drapery establish a close relationship between the two seals. Somewhat similar is a Graeco-Roman gem shown by Furtwängler (Pl. XLII, 3).

Sealing No. AIIb(4); appended; plane. Great House, Level I, Room 38.

(6) Oval; broken at the bottom, abraded; $11^+ \times 19$ mm.; execution crude.

Type: Winged figure, female, draped, standing left. The hair is dressed high on the head in a manner really exaggerated. The details of the lower part of the robe have been lost. In the outstretched left hand is held a palm branch disproportionately large in comparison with the figure.

Sealing No. AId(65), a bulla fragment; indeterminate; clay. Archive A.

f. Tyche

(1) Oval with short sides straight; 12×8 mm.; counter-impressed with thumb nail (cf. p. 10); execution fair. Pl. III, Fig. 41.

Type: Figure, female, draped, standing right. The hair is drawn into a knot at the back of the head. Behind the left shoulder appears a cornucopiae. The outstretched right hand holds a short scepter in a diagonal position. Immediately behind the cornucopiae may be observed an object that resembles a cluster of fruit or flowers. This appears to be suspended from the lip of the horn. Three other impressions of the same seal are Nos. (2)–(4). These are undoubtedly representations of Tyche. On coins of the two Demetrii this goddess is shown holding a short scepter (Babelon, Pls. XVI, 3, 9, and 14; XVII, 1; XIX, 3). The object described as a cluster is peculiar. A similar object is found associated with Tyche on a coin of Antiochus IX. Babelon describes this as a rose and takes it to be a symbol, not necessarily an attribute of the goddess (*ibid.*, p. clxiii). Certainly on the impression and probably on the coin the cluster cannot be dissociated from the horn of plenty. I suggest that it may represent an idea of overflowing abundance. The motif of the goddess of Fortune was particularly popular in the late Hellenistic and the Partho-Roman periods; it was common to the religious concept of a great part of the Orient that was in any way influenced by the process of Hellenization. In the general sense, therefore, the motif is Greek.

Sealing No. AId(66), a bulla fragment; indeterminate; bitumen (?). Archive B.

(2) A duplicate of No. (1); counter-impressed with thumb nail.

Sealing No. AId(67), a bulla fragment; indeterminate; bitumen (?). Archive B.

(3) A duplicate of No. (1); counter-impressed with thumb nail.

Sealing No. AId(68), a bulla fragment; indeterminate; bitumen (?). Archive B.

(4) A duplicate of No. (1); counter-impressed with thumb nail.

Sealing No. AId(69), a bulla fragment; indeterminate; bitumen (?). Archive B. The four fragments, sealings AId(66)–(69), are perhaps parts of two bullae, each of which bore two impressions of a single seal.

(5) Nearly circular; 11+ × 11 mm.; execution fair.

Type: Figure, female, draped, standing left. The headdress is obscure. In the left arm is a cornucopiae; the outstretched right arm holds a long scepter.

Sealing No. AId(70), a bulla fragment; indeterminate; clay. Archive A.

(6) Oval; incompletely impressed, worn; 14.5 × 12.5 mm.; execution mediocre. Pl. III, Fig. 42.

Type: Figure, female, draped, standing left. The hair is dressed in a large knot at the back of the head. The left arm holds a cornucopiae and rests on a short column; the right arm advances a short flaming torch. The identification of this figure presents difficulties. The horn of plenty is an attribute of Demeter as well as of Tyche. Even Isis is so represented, although in such instances her peculiar attributes make identification simple (Furtwängler, Pl. XXXIV, 13). Babelon (Pl. XIX, 12) identifies as Demeter a female figure which holds a torch but lacks the cornucopiae. Furtwängler (Pl. XXXIX, 10) shows a gem bearing a figure with both horn of plenty and torch, but he does not attempt to identify the goddess represented. It is possible that Demeter furnishes the type of our impression, but I have tentatively assigned it to Tyche, a more popular concept in the period with which we are concerned. This impression occurs on the fragment in duplicate.

Sealing No. AId(71), a bulla fragment; indeterminate; clay. Surface.

(7) Probably oval; incompletely impressed and broken; execution perhaps fair.

Type: Figure, female, draped, standing either facing or turned one quarter left. The head is partly broken off, but there are traces that indicate either a turreted crown or a kalathos. In the outstretched right hand is an object that appears to be a torch. The left elbow rests on a short column. The left shoulder is broken off, and hence there is no direct evidence as to the presence of a cornucopiae. The position of the elbow, however, suggests that an object was held in the left arm, and I have tentatively assumed the occurrence of a horn of plenty on this type. Though the turreted headdress is more common in the later period, on autonomous coins of Seleucia belonging to the first and second centuries B.C. we find instead Tyche wearing the kalathos (Hill, p. 141, No. 4). The date of the impression is fixed by the association with it on the same bulla of another impression concerned with the salt tax that belongs to the year 187/86 B.C. Owing to the rather close relationship in style between impressions (6) and (7) it is possible that both were made by the same engraver.

Sealing No. AId(12), a bulla fragment; indeterminate; clay. Archive B.

(8) Oval; incompletely impressed at the right and bottom, worn; $15^+ \times 14^+$ mm.; execution obscure, probably fair; counter-impressed with thumb nail.

Type: Figure, female, draped, standing left. The head is somewhat obscured, but it appears to be surmounted by a turreted crown. In the outstretched right hand is held an object that has a short shaft. This may be either a scepter or a torch; I am inclined to think it is the latter. Held in the left arm is an object that has been only partly impressed and is further obscured by wear. At first glance this object may be taken for a scepter, but the position of the arm in relation to the object suggests that we have here again a cornucopiae, only one edge of which was impressed. Any identification of the figure is necessarily tentative. If the headdress is a turreted crown, the representation is of Tyche. The probable occurrence of the horn of plenty strengthens this assumption. The impression is found in duplicate, on two parts of a single bulla.

Sealing No. AIb(3), a bulla complete in two pieces; dual; clay. Archive A.

(9) Oval; the lower half broken off; w. 9 mm.; execution crude. Pl. III, Fig. 43.

Type: Figure, female, draped, standing right. The head is surmounted with a crude representation of a turreted crown. In the left arm is a cornucopiae; the right hand rests on an object having a long shaft which may represent either a torch or a scepter, probably the latter. On the basis of the horn and the turreted crown I identify the figure as Tyche, the "city goddess." The turreted crown as an attribute of Tyche appears very rarely on Seleucid coins, as, for example, on a tetradrachm of Alexander Bala (Babelon, Pl. XVII, 8). On the autonomous civic coins of Seleucia and on the Parthian issues this form of headdress is perhaps the most characteristic symbol of the goddess. That is, this representation of Tyche became a prevalent coin type only after 143 B.C. Since it is found crudely executed on a seal impression of the Seleucid period, it is probable that the crowned city goddess constituted a popular motif before its adoption as an official type.

Sealing No. AId(72), a bulla fragment; indeterminate; clay. Archive A.

(10) Oval; the lower half broken off, worn; w. 9 mm.; execution mediocre.

Type: Figure, female, draped, probably standing facing with head turned left. The body from the waist down has been destroyed by a break. The head is bare, with the hair drawn into a knot behind. In the left arm is a cornucopiae; there are traces at the edge of the break which suggest that the elbow of this arm rested on a short column. In the outstretched right hand is an object held perpendicularly that appears to be either a torch or a short scepter. This impression has some elements in common with No. (6) above, but the torch is quite different.

Sealing No. AIc(7), a bulla practically complete in two pieces; multiple; bitumen (?). Archive B.

(11) Oval; very worn; 13 × 11 mm.; execution obscure, probably mediocre.

Type: Figure, female, draped standing left. The head is bare, with the hair drawn into a knot behind. The left arm holds a cornucopiae; the hand of the right outstretched holds an object entirely obscure. I presume that this was either a torch or a scepter, as on the impressions listed above.

Sealing No. AId(46), a bulla fragment; indeterminate; clay. Archive A.

(12) Oval; badly worn; 12.5 × 7.5 mm.; execution obscure.

Type: Figure, female, draped, standing left. The head is bare, and the hair is drawn into a knot behind. In the left arm is held a cornucopiae; in the outstretched right hand, a scepter or torch. There is a definite relationship between this impression and No. (11), but they were not made by a single seal.

Sealing No. AId(73), a bulla fragment; indeterminate; clay. Archive A.

(13) Oval; 12 × 8 mm.; counter-impressed with thumb nail; execution fair.

Type: Figure, female, draped, standing facing. The hair is rolled over the forehead and is surmounted with what is probably a kalathos. In the left arm is a cornucopiae; the right arm has been obscured by the nail impression. Note the reference to the kalathos under No. (7), above.

Sealing No. AIIa(8), appended; convex; clay. Archive B.

(14) Oval; incompletely impressed; 11+ × 10.5 mm.; execution crude. Pl. III, Fig. 44.

Type: Figure, female, draped, standing facing. The upper part of the head has not been impressed. The figure holds under each arm a large cornucopiae. Owing to this unusual feature as well as to the absence of the headdress the identification of the type as a representation of Tyche is purely tentative.

Sealing No. AIc(24), a whole bulla; multiple; clay. Great House, Level III, Room 141 sub (equivalent to Level IV).

x. Deity types not identified

(1) Oval; badly gouged and abraded; 12 × 10 mm.; execution at least fair. Pl. III, Fig. 45.

Type: The face of the impression is occupied by two figures. The one on the right half of the impression is seated right on an object of trapezoidal section that approximates some representations of the omphalos. The trunk and head of this figure have been entirely destroyed. The figure appears to be male. The legs are nude, and the pose is that of Apollo seated on the omphalos with the left leg retracted. Behind, and executed on a smaller scale, a second figure stands. It is female and is clothed in a long robe of Greek style. Whether it is facing or is turned right is difficult to determine. The head is very peculiar; it does not, in fact, resemble a head. The closest analogy which I have been able to find is that of the Ephesian Artemis on an intaglio in the Southesk Collection. Here, however, the body of the goddess is triformed (Carnegie, Vol. I, Pl. IV, C26). On our impression the figure holds what may be a wreath over the head of the seated personage. The details of the robe suggest a representation of Nike, but there are no indications of wings. Above both figures is a large crescent. I am unable to offer an explanation of the type. The seated figure suggests Apollo or an athlete. The smaller size of the standing figure implies its subordination in the motif. On the other hand, it scarcely can be taken as a representation of a mortal. Again, the crescent does not harmonize with the male figure seated apparently on an omphalos. The peculiar formation of the head on the standing figure and the crescent show Oriental influence, but the style of the dress on the female personage and the nudity of the male figure on the omphalos are characteristics natural only in a Greek motif.

Sealing No. AIIa(9), appended; convex; bitumen. Archive A.

(2) Oval; short sides straight; worn; 11 × 8 mm.; execution obscure. Pl. III, Fig. 46.

Type: Figure, female, fully draped, seated left on throne. The head is surmounted with an elaborate headdress, all details of which have been obscured. The left arm of the figure rests on an arm of the throne. Held in the right hand, close to the body, there is an obscure object that suggests an elaborate scepter. The absence of any of the distinctive attributes of deity and the poor condition of the impression render identification doubtful. Possibly it was intended to represent Tyche. In any case the motif is Greek rather than Oriental.

Sealing No. AIb(4), a whole bulla; dual; clay. Archive A.

(3) Oval; incompletely impressed, worn; 17+ × 12 mm.; execution crude. Pl. III, Fig. 47.

Type: Figure, female, draped, standing with the body turned one quarter right and the head facing. The head is encircled with a wreath; the features have been entirely obscured. The left hand rests on a long shaft, neither extremity of which has been impressed. The position of the hand and arm suggests that this object is a spear or staff rather than a scepter. The right elbow appears to be resting on a short column. Beside rather than within the right arm is an object that must be either a cornucopiae or a quiver. It has perhaps more of the characteristics of a quiver than of a horn, but its position favors the latter supposition. The representation of a quiver unaccompanied by a bow is difficult to explain. The wreath on a female head is likewise confusing. The form of the garment worn has been obscured by incomplete impression. Though identification of the figure is not practicable, there can be no doubt that the motif is Greek. The impression occurs in duplicate on a single fragment.

Sealing No. AIc(11), a bulla fragment; multiple; bitumen. Archive A.

(4) Oval; very narrow, deeply inset; 9.5 × 4 mm.; execution obscure.

Type: Herm with facing head, on which there appears to be a kalathos. Beneath the herm is a wreath. All details of the head have been obscured. The motif is Greek.

Sealing No. AId(112), a bulla fragment; indeterminate; bitumen. Great House, Level III, Room 306.

2. *Representations of minor deities*

a. Hermes

(1) Circular; diam. 13 mm.; worn; execution mediocre. Pl. III, Fig. 48.

Type: Bust right, male, youthful. The head is covered by a petasos. Behind the bust are traces that may represent the kerykeion. A rather similar treatment of Hermes is found on a seal in the Metropolitan Museum of Art (Richter, p. 106, No. 159). Our impression is of inferior workmanship. The motif is, of course, Greek.

Sealing No. AIc(26), a bulla fragment; multiple; clay. Surface.

(2) Oval; incompletely impressed; 13 × 8+ mm.; execution fair.

Type: Bust right, male, the head covered by a petasos. Since the impression is incomplete, it is not possible to determine whether any of the usual attributes of Hermes formed a part of the original seal. The impression does not represent portraiture; that is, it does not form one of the group of private royal portraits (see p. 65). On the other hand, it does show a relationship to the type of No. (1). The identification adopted appears, therefore, to be required.

Sealing No. AIb(2), a whole bulla; dual; clay. Archive A.

b. Eros

(1) Oval; 13 × 10 mm.; counter-impressed with thumb nail; execution good. Pl. III, Fig. 49.

Type: Winged figure, male, nude, standing facing. The head is bare, with the hair cut close. In the right hand is held a short scepter. The position of the left arm has been largely obscured by the nail impression, but it appears to be holding a wreath. There is no doubt of the identification, and the motif is Greek.

Sealing No. AIIa(10), appended; convex; clay. Archive B.

(2) Oval; 11 × 5.5 mm.; execution good.

Type: Winged figure, male, nude, advancing right. In the outstretched left hand is a wreath with long fillets; the right arm is dropped at the side. This characteristic portrayal of Eros is reproduced below on Nos. (3)–(5), but with differences in detail and in execution.

Sealing No. AIc(18), a whole bulla; multiple; clay. Archive B.

(3) Oval; the lower half broken off; w. 7.5 mm.; execution fair.

Type: Winged figure, male, nude, advancing or standing right. Held immediately in front of the body is a wreath of somewhat exaggerated size.

Sealing No. AId(74), a bulla fragment; indeterminate; bitumen. Archive B.

(4) Oval; broken at bottom, worn; w. 8 mm.; execution crude.

Type: Winged figure, male, nude, standing or advancing right. A wreath is held in the left hand close to the body; the right arm is dropped at the side. In details this impression is akin to No. (2), but the execution differs widely.

Sealing No. AId(75), a bulla fragment; indeterminate; clay. Archive B.

(5) Oval; incompletely impressed, worn; 12 × 6+ mm.; execution mediocre.

Type: Winged figure, male, nude, standing right and holding a wreath in front of the body. All details are obscured. Another impression of the same seal is No. (6), below.

Sealing No. AIIa(25), appended; convex; bitumen. Archive B.

(6) A duplicate impression of No. (5).

Sealing No. AIIa(21), appended; convex; bitumen. Archive B.

(7) Oval; abraded; 12 × 8.5 mm.; execution crude.

Type: Winged figure, male, nude, standing one quarter left. The legs appear to be crossed; this is possibly a crude attempt to denote movement. The figure holds in both hands a wreath with long fillets.

Sealing No. AId(76), a bulla fragment; indeterminate; bitumen. Archive A.

(8) Oval; the seal has been partly applied twice, and neither impression is complete; w. 9 mm.; execution fair.

Type: Winged figure, male, nude, seated right on a dolphin, right. The arms are outstretched, holding an object that has not been impressed. Eros on a dolphin, playing the lute, is shown on an intaglio in the Metropolitan Museum of Art (Richter, Pl. 39, No. 150).
Sealing No. AId(77), a bulla fragment; indeterminate; clay. Archive A.

(9) Circular; badly worn; diam. 8 mm.; execution mediocre.
Type: Winged figure seated left on a dolphin, left. All details have been obscured, but the figure apparently represents Eros. The motif is that of No. (8), but the execution is very different.
Sealing No. AId(72), a bulla fragment; indeterminate; clay. Archive A.

(10) Oval; 15 × 8 mm.; execution obscure, but apparently good. Pl. III, Fig. 50.
Type: Winged figure, presumably Eros, seated right on a sea horse, right. The figure has the arms outstretched toward the head of the sea horse, apparently in the act of driving. Furtwängler (Pl. XLI, 40) shows a seal of the Hellenistic period, to which our impression is very similar.
Sealing No. AIc(18), a whole bulla; multiple; clay. Archive B.

(11) Oval; incompletely impressed; 9+ × 8+ mm.; execution mediocre.
Type: Winged figure, male, nude, flying right. The arms have been obscured by incomplete impression. An intaglio reproduced by Furtwängler (Pl. X, 10) shows Eros flying right and holding a wreath. Our impression appears to be of similar character.
Sealing No. AId(78), a bulla fragment; indeterminate; bitumen. Archive A.

(12) Nearly circular; 12 × 11 mm.; execution very crude. Pl. III, Fig. 51.
Type: Winged figure, male, nude, advancing right, apparently pursuing a large bird. Eros is frequently represented as playing with a bird (cf. Furtwängler, Pl. LXIV, 15). Another impression

of the same seal is No. (13), below. These impressions represent the poorest execution in our collection.

Sealing No. AIIb(7), appended; unfinished; clay. Archive B.

(13) A duplicate of No. (12).

Sealing No. AIIb(8), appended; unfinished; clay. Archive B.

c. Psyche

(1) Oval; 11 × 10 mm.; execution mediocre. Pl. III, Fig. 52.
Type: Winged figure, female, apparently nude, seated left on the ground. The hair is drawn into a flat knot behind. The right knee is raised and is clasped by the right arm. The left arm is dropped at the side, and the hand rests on the ground, partly supporting the body. In spite of the lack of quality in the execution the pose is full of grace. With slight variation in detail the same pose is reproduced in Nos. (2) and (3), below. The original work from which the motif of the seals was drawn would appear to have been of considerable merit. The assignment to Psyche appears necessary. The informality of the motif is, of course, typically Greek of the Hellenistic period.

Sealing No. AId(79), a bulla fragment; indeterminate; clay. Archive A.

(2) Oval; the lower edge slightly broken; 13+ × 10 mm.; execution mediocre.
Type: Winged figure as above, No. (1). Both pose and execution of the two impressions are similar, but I do not consider that the two seals by which the impressions were made represent the work of a single engraver.

Sealing No. AIc(17), a bulla fragment; multiple; clay. Archive A.

(3) Oval; broken at the top, incompletely impressed; 9+ × 6+ mm.; execution apparently fair.
Type: Winged figure as above, but seated right. The pose is exactly that of Nos. (1) and (2), but reversed. The execution, however, is superior and shows the hand of still a third engraver. Another impression of the same seal is No. (4), below.

Sealing No. AIc(19), a bulla fragment; multiple; clay. Archive B.

(4) A duplicate of No. (3).

Sealing No. AIc(20), a bulla fragment; multiple; clay. Archive B. The impressions on this fragment appear to be duplicates of those on the preceding piece. Both fragments may be parts of a single bulla.

(5) Oval; worn; 12 × 9 mm.; execution obscure, but probably fair.

Type: Winged figure, female, clad apparently in a short tunic, seated right on a stool. The hair is drawn into a large knot behind. The figure is bent forward, with the left knee raised as though in the act of attaching a sandal. This representation of Psyche has the same informality noticed on the preceding impressions. The execution, however, is superior, and must be taken as the work of another engraver. There is a certain similarity in both the pose and the execution of this type and of those of No. IC2c(1), below, the representation of a woman seated on a similar stool.

Sealing No. AIc(3), a whole bulla; multiple; clay. Archive B.

(6) Oval; no dimensions obtainable, owing to breakage and incomplete impression; execution obscure.

Type: Winged figure, female, apparently nude, seated right. The hair appears to be drawn into a bunch at the top of the head. The right arm is dropped at the side. Further details have been obscured. The traces suggest that the pose may be that of No. (3), above, but the details of the head and the wings are quite different.

Sealing No. AIc(8), a bulla practically complete in two pieces; multiple; bitumen. Archive B.

(7) Oval; 14 × 11 mm.; execution crude. Pl. III, Fig. 53.

Type: Female figure seated left, draped. The hair is done in a "Psyche knot" of exaggerated proportions. Along the back is what I take to be a crude representation of wings. The right arm is advanced, holding an obscure object. Another obscure object appears in the field to the left. The identification of the figure as Psyche is entirely tentative.

Sealing No. AId(109), a bulla fragment; indeterminate; clay. Surface.

d. Silenus

(1) Oval; 13 × 10 mm.; execution fair.

Type: Head right, male, crowned with a heavy wreath and bearded. The features are gross. The peculiar ears, characteristic of representations of Silenus, cannot be distinguished on the impression. All the other details, however, appear to require this identification. The motif is Greek.

Sealing No. AIc(9), a bulla complete in two pieces; multiple; bitumen. Archive B.

(2) Oval; incompletely impressed, chipped; 16+ × 13 mm.; execution mediocre. Pl. III, Fig. 54.

Type: Mask, facing, gross features, heavy beard. The hair is arranged over the forehead in a manner suggestive of horns. I have not been able to find close parallels to this type in the catalogs of antique gems. The identification as Silenus, however, appears to be required.

Sealing No. AId(110), a bulla fragment; indeterminate; bitumen. Surface.

(3) Oval; badly worn; 11.5 × 5.5 mm.; execution obscure.

Type: Figure seated or crouched left, with back to a herm. The figure is very obscure, but appears to have a bushy beard. The herm bears an object which I take to be the head of Dionysus, with beard and garland. With some reservation I identify the figure as Silenus.

Sealing No. AIc(18), a whole bulla; multiple; clay. Archive B.

e. River god

(1) Circular; diam. 14 mm.; execution mediocre.

Type: Head, facing, male, with horns and ears of bovine type. This is a characteristic portrayal of a river god. A rather similar type is found on a gem of the late Hellenistic period (Furtwängler, Pl. XXVI, 10). On the intaglio, however, stars occur in the field beside the head. It should be noted that on some autonomous coins of Seleucia a river god is found associated with Tyche (Hill, p. 141, No. 6).

Sealing No. AIc(23), a whole bulla; multiple; clay. Surface.

3. *Representations of acts of religious observance*

a. Priests or worshipers

(1) Oval; incompletely impressed, worn; 14⁺ × 17 mm.; execution obscure. Pl. III, Fig. 55.

Type: Figure standing right, male, bearded, clothed in long robe and conical hat. Further details of the clothing have been obscured. In front of the figure may be seen the upper part of an object, the rest of which has not been impressed. This appears to be a tripod with cover. The right hand of the figure rests on this cover. The left hand is held above the right and bears an obscure object, possibly a small vessel. The poor condition of the piece makes identification difficult. There can be little doubt that the type represents a scene of sacrifice in an Oriental [5] cult. One may go farther and state that the motif represents Semitic rather than Iranian elements. The image of the worshiper who wears a conical hat is reminiscent of the mural paintings from Doura-Europos (Breasted, Pls. VIII–IX; Cumont, p. 286).

Sealing No. AIc(17), a bulla fragment; multiple; clay. Archive A.

(2) Oval; incompletely impressed, worn; 14 × 8⁺ mm.; execution mediocre. Pl. III, Fig. 56.

Type: Figure, male, standing right. The features have been obscured, and it is not possible to determine whether the face is bearded. The figure wears an ankle-length garment, with a cloak rolled back over the shoulders. On the head is a high conical hat. Both arms are outstretched in front and hold an object that is obscure. The feet are executed in one plane, one in front of the other. This feature and the ankle-length garment suggest an older Babylonian influence. The cloak is peculiar and unlike anything I have been able to find on Oriental seals. The motif is certainly Oriental and probably represents Semitic influence. The impression occurs in duplicate on a single bulla.

Sealing No. AIa(4), a whole bulla; single; clay. Archive A.

---

[5] This term is defined on page 224.

(3) Oval; very narrow; abraded and worn; 11 × 4 mm.; execution obscure.

Type: Figure, probably male, standing apparently facing, clothed in a long, tight-fitting robe. The head is obscure, but appears to be covered by a large wig that descends on both sides of the face. The shoulders are markedly broad. Held diagonally across the breast from the right shoulder down is a macelike object. The shape of the body and the wig produce an effect that recall Egyptian art. The shape and the position of the mace suggest Phoenician influence. The poor condition of the impression makes any effort at further identification impracticable. The motif is distinctly not Greek.

Sealing No. AId(46), a bulla fragment; indeterminate; clay. Archive A.

B. REPRESENTATIONS OF HEROES, MYTHOLOGICAL PERSONAGES, AND FANCIFUL FIGURES

1. *Heroes*

a. Hercules

(1) Oval; incompletely impressed; 12+ × 8 mm.; execution mediocre. Pl. III, Fig. 57.

Type: Figure, male, nude save possibly for a cloak, standing left. The head is bare and heavily bearded. Resting on the ground in front and held by the right hand is a heavy, knobbed club. Over the left arm is an object that is either a part of the cloak or the skin of an animal. This is a characteristic representation of Hercules, a motif that is Greek. Another impression of the same seal is No. (2), below. It is interesting to note that these two impressions of one seal occur on different bullae that are separated by an interval of several years. The bulla on which occurs impression No. (1) is stamped with the date equivalent to 175/74 B.C.; that bearing impression No. (2), with the date 184/83 B.C.

Sealing No. AIc(5), a bulla complete in two pieces; multiple; clay. Archive B.

(2) A duplicate of No. (1).

Sealing No. AId(14), a bulla fragment; indeterminate; clay. Archive B.

(3) Oval; 11 × 10 mm.; execution mediocre.

Type: Figure, male, nude, standing facing with head turned right. The details of the head are obscure. The body is of heavy build. The left hand rests on a large club; the right holds a skin. This impression and Nos. (1) and (2) represent seals made by different engravers.

Sealing No. AId(112), a bulla fragment; indeterminate; bitumen. Great House, Level III, Room 306.

(4) Crescent-shaped, that is, with the long sides forming concentric arcs; 9.5 × 5 mm.; execution fair. Pl. IV, Fig. 58.

Type: Head right, male, massive, heavily bearded. The impression is closely related to a representation of Hercules on a seal described by Furtwängler (Pl. XXVI, 31).

Sealing No. AId(87), a bulla fragment; indeterminate; clay. Archive B.

(5) Circular; diam. 15.5 mm.; execution at least fair.

Type: Head right, male, massive but with a low forehead, heavily bearded. Although similar in concept the seals represented by this impression and No. (4) were not, I think, executed by the same engraver. The impression occurs in triplicate on the one bulla.

Sealing No. AIc(23), a whole bulla; multiple; clay. Surface.

b. Odysseus

(1) Oval; 15 × 10.5 mm.; execution fair. Pl. IV, Fig 59.

Type: Figure, male, standing right, nude save for a long cloak slung over the back. The head is bare, but there are traces suggesting a hat hanging at the back of the neck. The figure leans on a long staff and has the left leg crossed in front of the right. The scabbard of a sword protrudes behind the waist from the left side. The body is rather heavy in proportion to height. Nos. (2) and (4), below, show the same figure in a similar pose. On some the pylos-shaped hat is distinctly visible. Nos. (5) and (6) have the same general motif, but with variations. The identification of the figure as Odysseus is supported by Furtwängler, who so names a similar figure that occurs as the type of a large number of Greek seals. The build of the figure, the cloak, the hat, the sword, and the staff are all elements common to the seals as well as to the impressions. One seal of the late Hellenistic period is especially close to the style of our impression even in respect to the position of the legs (Furtwängler, Pl. XXVII, 45; cf. Pls. XXIII, 61; XXXIV, 26). The motif of the type is distinctly Greek.

Sealing No. AIc(17), a bulla fragment; multiple; clay. Archive A.

(2) Oval; worn; 13 × 10 mm.; execution obscure, but apparently mediocre.

Type: Figure standing right, as on No. (1). The pose is the same on the two impressions, but there are slight differences in execution and in quality. On this impression the hat hanging at the back of the neck is more distinct and suggests a pylos.

Sealing No. AId(80), a bulla fragment; indeterminate; clay. Archive A.

(3) Rectangular; worn; 14 × 6.5 mm.; execution mediocre.

Type: Figure standing right, as on No. (1). On this impression the hat may be easily distinguished. In details of execution Nos. (2) and (3) are closely related, and the seals with which they were impressed may well have been the work of a single artist.

Sealing No. AId(81), a bulla fragment; indeterminate; clay. Archive A.

(4) Oval; incompletely impressed, worn; 12+ × 7 mm.; execution mediocre.

Type: Figure standing right, apparently as on No. (1). The impression is very obscure, and the hat may not be distinguished. The pose, however, appears to be the same. The staff is somewhat thicker.

Sealing No. AId(82), a bulla fragment; indeterminate; clay. Archive A.

(5) Oval; the lower third broken off; w. 7 mm.; execution probably fair. Pl. IV, Fig. 60.

Type: Figure standing left, male, perhaps nude. The head is covered by a pylos. Owing to a break the figure is incomplete below a point above the knees. The sword and the staff occur as on the preceding impressions. On the present specimen, however, the left hand grasps an object which appears to be a rope that extended down beyond the break. The head is bent forward, as though looking down. In spite of these differences there seems to be no reason to doubt the similarity of the motif to that of the foregoing types.

Sealing No. AId(83), a bulla fragment; indeterminate; clay. Archive A.

(6) Oval; partly broken; 12+ × 7 mm.; execution fair. Pl. IV, Fig. 61.

Type: Figure, male, apparently nude, seated right on an object that appears to be a rock. The head is covered with a pylos. The scabbard of a sword protrudes from behind the left side. The left knee is raised and clasped by the two hands. The characteristics in common between this type and the preceding five are the style of the hat, the sword, the general build of the body, and a certain pensiveness of attitude. A late Hellenistic gem shows Odysseus seated on a rock. The hat and sword are similar, but he is clad and holds a spear or staff. On this gem the pensive air is marked (Furtwängler, Pl. XXVII, 49). The quality of execution represented by impression No. (6) is, perhaps, the best within the group.

Sealing No. AId(84), a bulla fragment; indeterminate; bitumen. Archive A.

c. Penelope

(1) Oval; badly chipped; 12 × 8 mm.; execution obscure, but at least fair.

Type: Figure, female, fully draped, seated right, probably on a chair. The hair is arranged in a knot on top of the head. The figure is bent forward with the chin cupped in the right hand, the elbow resting on the knees. Furtwängler (Pls. IX, 35; X, 20) shows two seals to which the type of our impression appears to be closely related and which he describes as having a "Penelope" motif. They are of the classical period in Greece. This impression should be considered one of the group of Odysseus types. The motif is, of course, Greek.

Sealing No. AIIa(11), appended; convex; bitumen. Archive A.

2. *Mythological personages*

a. Medusa

(1) Oval; worn; 8 × 5 mm.; execution mediocre.

Type: Head facing, very obscure. Beneath the chin is a knotted bowlike arrangement similar to one on a seal shown by Furtwängler (Pl. L, 47) and described by him as a snake knot associated with Medusa. The character of this snake knot is sufficient to identify the type of our impression as a representation of Medusa. The Medusa motif in its successive forms was one common to the Greek world from the archaic period to the Roman. Variant treatments of the same motif are found on Nos. (2)–(5), below.

Sealing No. AId(85), a bulla fragment; indeterminate; clay. Archive B.

(2) Oval; incompletely impressed; 13+ × 11+ mm.; execution fair. Pl. IV, Fig. 62.

Type: Head facing, with the hair waving around it and the cheeks. This appears to portray the "dead Medusa," characteristic of the art of the Hellenistic period (cf. Richter, p. 126, No. 212).

Sealing No. AIc(24), a whole bulla; multiple; clay. Great House, Level III, Room 141 sub (equivalent to Level IV).

(3) Oval; worn and chipped; 13+ × 10 mm.; execution obscure.

Type: Head facing with waving locks. At the side of the throat may be seen a snake knot. The style is intermediate between those of Nos. (1) and (2).

Sealing No. AIIa(23), appended; convex; bitumen. Archive B.

(4) Oval; incompletely impressed; 15+ × 10 mm.; execution obscure but fair.

Type: Face viewed from the front. The dressing of the hair has been obscured. The impression does not appear to represent a mask. It is not portraiture. I tentatively identify the type as a Medusa motif on the general grounds that it more nearly approximates conventional representations of the Medusa features than those of any deity or other mythological personage.

Sealing No. AId(86), a bulla fragment; indeterminate; clay. Archive A.

(5) Oval; incompletely impressed; 11+ × 7+ mm.; execution mediocre.

Type: Head right, entwined by a snake. The features have been very much obscured by the incomplete impression.

Sealing No. AIc(6), a bulla fragment; multiple; bitumen. Archive B.

b. Opheltes and the dragon

(1) Oval; incompletely impressed, worn; 13+ × 10 mm.; execution fair.

Type: Serpent partly coiled, grasping a small human figure. This figure has been impressed only in part, but it appears to represent a child. The type is somewhat similar to that of an intaglio in the Metropolitan Museum of Art, described by Dr. Richter (Pl. 51, 200) as "Opheltes and the dragon." My identification is based on this similarity. The motif is Greek.

Sealing No. AId(88), a bulla fragment; indeterminate; clay. Archive A.

3. *Fanciful figures*

a. Winged demon

(1) Oval; cracked and worn; 15 × 9 mm.; execution mediocre. Pl. IV, Fig. 63.

Type: Winged figure advancing right. The figure has a human trunk and arms, "cupid" wings, the legs and feet of a goat, long tail, a human head with long straight horns, a bushy beard, and a nose characteristic of Silenus types. It holds a lyre. The commingling of different attributes exemplified by the type is rather characteristic of seal motifs of the Hellenistic period. I have found, however, no reference to gems that fits the description of our impression. It should be noted that this demon obviously was not intended to be an object of fear; rather it was of a jovial character. The motif is definitely Greek.

Sealing No. AId(89), a bulla fragment; indeterminate; clay. Archive A.

(2) Oval; incompletely impressed, worn; dimensions very incomplete; execution obscure.

Type: Winged figure standing right. It has a human trunk, with the legs of a goat. The head is very obscure, but appears to be human save for horns. There are traces which suggest that the artist started to engrave wings of the long Nike type, but, changing his mind, cut over the original lines to form wings of the cupid type. The creature holds a large lyre. The motif of this impression is that of No. (1), but the execution was by a different hand.

Sealing No. AId(90), a bulla fragment; indeterminate; clay. Archive A.

b. Griffin

(1) Oval; cracked and abraded; 14 × 10 mm.; execution mediocre. Pl. IV, Fig. 64.

Type: A griffin springing right. The style is about that of a so-called Graeco-Persian seal described by Furtwängler (Pl. XI, 41), but the execution of the impression is inferior. The griffin motif was one common to both Greek and Oriental concepts. The style of execution of our impression was the product of the Western culture.

Sealing No. AId(70), a bulla fragment; indeterminate; clay. Archive A.

(2) Oval; 17 × 9.5 mm.; execution mediocre.

Type: A griffin running or springing left. The motif is that of No. (1), but there is considerable difference in the details of execution.

Sealing No. AId(54), a bulla fragment; indeterminate; clay. Surface.

(3) Probably circular, diam. 13 mm.; incompletely impressed; execution obscure.

Type: Griffin crouching left. All details have been obscured. The general motif is that of No. (1).

Sealing No. AId(113), a bulla fragment; indeterminate; clay. Surface.

(4) Oval; 12 × 8 mm.; execution mediocre.
Type: The fore part of a griffin right, showing head, neck, fore legs, and wings. The style and execution of this impression differ in details from those of the preceding impressions.
Sealing No. AIc(18), a whole bulla; multiple; clay. Archive B.

C. REPRESENTATIONS OF MORTALS

1. *Draped women in formal pose (religious connotation?)*

a. Holding palms

(1) Oval; worn and cracked; 16.5 × 9 mm.; execution fair. Pl. IV, Fig. 65.
Type: Figure, female, fully draped, standing left. The head is bare, and the hair is drawn into a large knot behind. The left elbow rests on a short column; the right hand outstretched holds a palm branch. This motif, with variations in details, is repeated on Nos. (2)–(5), below. No definite attributes of deity or of mythological characters can be distinguished. The representation is, therefore, of mortal women. On the other hand, the formal pose and the stereotyped repetition of the theme suggest a possibility that a religious significance should be attached to the type. The presence of the column and the style of the hair and the robe indicate that the motif is Greek.
Sealing No. AId(93), a bulla fragment; indeterminate; clay. Archive A.

(2) Oval; incompletely impressed, worn; 13+ × 11 mm.; execution obscure.
Type: Figure standing left, as above. The hair is bunched rather than drawn into a knot, and the palm is of different shape. The impression is repeated four times on one bulla.
Sealing No. AIc(16), a whole bulla; multiple; clay. Archive A.

(3) Shape and dimensions obscured by overimpression; execution mediocre.
Type: Figure as above, but standing either facing or turned one quarter left. The head has been obscured. The execution differs in details.
Sealing No. AId(13), a bulla fragment; indeterminate; clay. Archive B.

(4) Oval; incompletely impressed; 11+ × 8 mm.; execution crude.

Type: Figure as above, standing facing. The hair is bunched. The object held in the hand has not been completely impressed, but apparently is a palm. The artist has distorted the normal position of the body in an effort to indicate its dependence on the support of the column. The impression occurs in duplicate on two parts of a single bulla.

Sealing No. AIa(5), a bulla complete in two pieces; single; clay. Archive A.

(5) Rectangular; broken at the bottom; 12+ × 7 mm.; execution mediocre.

Type: Figure as above, standing right. The hair is drawn into a knot. The execution is perhaps superior to that of the preceding impressions.

Sealing No. AId(94), a bulla fragment; indeterminate; clay. Archive A.

b. Holding lyres

(1) Oval; 12 × 6.5 mm.; execution very crude. Pl. IV, Fig. 66.

Type: Figure, female, fully draped, standing left. The hair is drawn into a knot at the upper back of the head; there is possibly a flower-like ornament over the forehead. The right arm holds a large lyre; the left arm is dropped at the side. Over the left shoulder appear three large dots, rather obscure, but possibly intended to represent flowers. A similar concept is represented by No. (2), below. The question must be raised whether the type can best be identified as a muse or as a mortal woman. The details of the impressions do not provide direct proof, and I have tentatively assumed that the types represent ordinary mortals. These women, however, must be distinguished from that class of musicians portrayed by impressions Nos. IIIC2a(1)–(3) below, who were associated with the lighter festivities of the city. For the two impressions with which we are now concerned a religious connotation is very possible. Whatever the identification the motif is definitely Greek.

Sealing No. AIIa(12), appended; convex; clay. Archive B.

(2) Oval; abraded and worn; 14 × 9 mm.; execution mediocre.

Type: Figure, female, draped, standing facing. The head is somewhat obscured, but there are traces that suggest a wreath of flowers. A large lyre is held in the left arm; the right arm is dropped at the side. The concept is that of No. (1), but the execution differs widely.

Sealing No. AId(91), a bulla fragment; indeterminate; clay. Archive A.

2. *Nude women*

a. Musician

(1) Oval; incompletely impressed; 12+ × 9+ mm.; execution mediocre. Pl. IV, Fig. 67.

Type: Figure, female, nude, standing turned three quarters away. The legs are crossed, and the head is thrown back. Held in front of the figure is a large lyre, from which hang long streamers. The hair appears to be done up on top of the head and bound around with a fillet which hangs down over the shoulders. Furtwängler (Pl. XLI, 24) shows a seal of the Hellenistic period that has a similar motif, a nude woman viewed from the back, with legs crossed. She is playing a wind instrument. The motif is Greek. This impression as well as the others in the group, nude dancers and musicians, probably represents the class of entertainers to which some reference is made in certain of the classical authors. The impression left by their remarks, that the Seleucians were, to say the least, light-minded, is not borne out by the proportional relation of this group to the total number of seal types in our collection (see p. 225, below). A second impression of the same seal is No. (2), below, found on another bulla with a different provenance.

Sealing No. AId(17), a bulla fragment in two pieces; indeterminate; clay. Archive B.

(2) A duplicate of No. (1), very incompletely impressed.

Sealing No. AIc(25), a bulla fragment; multiple; clay. Surface.

(3) Oval; broken and chipped; 11+ × 7 mm.; execution fair.

Type: Figure, female, nude, standing or advancing right. The legs from the thighs down have been destroyed. The head is obscure, but there are traces that suggest some sort of elaborate headdress. The figure is represented playing on a wind instrument. The general motif is that of No. (1).

Sealing No. AIIa(13), appended; convex; clay. Archive B.

b. Dancer

(1) Oval; incompletely impressed; 10 × 8.5 mm.; execution crude. Pl. IV, Fig. 68.

Type: Figure, female, nude, turned left, apparently in the act of dancing. The head is obscure, but the hair is drawn into a large knot behind. The figure rests on the left foot, and the left knee is slightly bent. The right leg is raised, with the knee bent at right angles. Behind the figure is a column or possibly a thymiaterion. For the general concept see the remarks under No. a(1), above. The motif is Greek. Another impression of the same seal is No. (2).

Sealing No. AId(92), a bulla fragment; indeterminate; clay. Archive B.

(2) A duplicate of No. (1).

Sealing No. AIc(18), a whole bulla; multiple; clay. Archive B.

(3) Oval; badly worn; 10 × 5.5 mm.; execution obscure.

Type: Figure, female, apparently nude, standing right. The headdress is obscure. The figure appears to be poised on the toes of the left foot, with the right knee raised to the chest; the arms are thrown out in front. Furtwängler (Pl. XLIII, 42) shows a seal described as Aphrodite in the act of putting on her sandals. This nude figure stands flat on one foot, with the other leg raised. The type of our impression, however, is distinctly different and must be taken to represent a dancer. It contains an element of the Bacchanalian. The general motif is Greek.

Sealing No. AIc(18), a whole bulla; multiple; clay. Archive B.

c. Posed informally

(1) Oval; abraded; 10.5 × 6 mm.; execution good. Pl. IV, Fig. 69.

Type: Figure, female, nude, seated right on a slender stand. The head has been partly destroyed by abrasion, but the hair appears to be bound with fillets. The legs are crossed, with the feet resting on a cubical hassock. The elbows rest on the knees; the lower arms are not shown. The pose is graceful. The motif is Greek.

Sealing No. AIIa(14), appended; convex; clay. Archive B.

(2) Oval; worn; 10 × 5 mm.; execution obscure, but apparently good.

Type: Figure, female, draped from the waist down, seated right on a low chair. The trunk and head are bent to the left, with the right arm raised over the head and the left brought back toward the shoulder. The type appears to represent a woman handling her hair, which, however, cannot be distinguished. The knees are crossed. The motif is Greek and characteristic of the informality found on seals of the Hellenistic period.

Sealing No. AIIa(15), appended; convex; clay. Archive B.

3. *Various representations of men*

a. Warrior

(1) Oval; badly worn; 15 × 9 mm.; execution crude.

Type: Figure, male, clad in short tunic, standing left. The head is covered by a high conical helmet. In the right hand is a heavy spear, and the left rests on a grounded shield. No sword may be distinguished, but this may be due to the poor condition of the piece. The shape of the helmet resembles rather closely that found on a Hellenistic seal (Furtwängler, Pl. XXVIII, 73). It is interesting to note that on Seleucid coins the characteristic emblem of Tryphon (142–139 B.C.) was a helmet of similar form, but decorated with a long horn. Babelon (Pl. XXI, 1; p. cxxxix) quotes Eckhel's suggestion that the form represents the national Macedonian helmet. The figure certainly does not represent the traditional Greek warrior; the details are obviously not Oriental. Whether the stock represented was Macedonian, Thracian, or "barbarian" from farther north cannot, I think, be determined. The motif is definitely not Oriental; in the general sense it may be classed as Greek.

Sealing No. AId(95), a bulla fragment; indeterminate; clay. Archive A.

(2) Circular; the right half broken off; diam. 12 mm.; execution in high relief and very good. Pl. IV, Fig. 70.

Type: Warrior kneeling left on right knee. On the head is a high-crested helmet. The right hand holds a spear advanced; a large shield rests on the ground in front supported by the left arm. On the shield seen in profile is an episema which I take to represent a Medusa head. Furtwängler (Pl. LXI, 55) shows an intaglio of a craftsman at work on a similar shield that is ornamented with the Gorgon head. The motif is distinctly Greek. The execution is very good, but there appears to be a certain lack of finish.

Sealing No. AId(87), a bulla fragment; indeterminate; clay. Archive B.

(3) Oval; broken; 11+ × 7+ mm.; execution fair.

Type: Figure, male, nude, crouching or kneeling left. On the head is a crested helmet. The left arm supports a shield in front of the body; the right hand, slightly retracted, grasps a weapon. Whether this is sword or spear cannot be determined, owing to the condition of the impression. For the same reason the presence or absence of ornamentation on the shield must remain doubtful. There is an obvious resemblance between this type and that of the preceding impression. The quality of the design is distinct as, possibly, were the sources from which the concept was drawn. The motif of the impression is, of course, Greek. Another impression of the same seal is No. (4).

Sealing No. AIIa(35), appended; convex; clay. Archive B.

(4) A duplicate of No. (3).

Sealing No. AIIa(34), appended; convex; clay. Archive B.

(5) Probably circular; incompletely impressed; diam. approx. 8 mm.; execution crude.

Type: Figure, male, nude, kneeling or crouching right. The head has not been impressed. On the right arm is an undecorated shield; the left hand holds a spear advanced. The motif is that of No. (3), but the execution is inferior.

Sealing No. AIIa(33), appended; convex; clay. Archive B.

b. Pastoral

(1) Oval; broken at the bottom; w. 12 mm.; execution fair. Pl. IV, Fig. 71.

Type: Figure, male, apparently nude, standing left, leaning on a staff. The head is bare. The figure has been destroyed below the middle of the trunk. In the absence of any attributes to suggest a particular significance I have assumed that the representation is general in the manner of Hellenistic gem engraving. The motif suggests nothing more than a pastoral scene and is, of course, Greek. Furtwängler (Pl. LXI, 61) describes as a herdsman a somewhat similar figure on a Hellenistic seal.

Sealing No. AIb(1), a bulla nearly complete; dual; clay. Archive A.

c. Convivial

(1) Nearly circular; cracked; 11.5 × 10 mm.; execution very crude. Pl. IV, Fig. 72.

Type: Figure, male, clad in short tunic, seated left on a stool. The head is covered by a flat hat. The left hand rests on the hip. In the outstretched right hand is a vessel tilted as though the figure were about to drink. The vessel is of exaggerated size, approximately that of the trunk of the figure. Though somewhat obscure it appears to have a single handle, a long slightly curved spout, and a broad base. The whole effect is one of rustic conviviality. The motif is obviously Greek.

Sealing No. AId(96), a bulla fragment; indeterminate; clay. Archive A.

D. REPRESENTATIONS OF SYMBOLS AND OBJECTS

1. *Of religious significance*

a. Tripod

(1) Circular; edges broken; diam. 11 mm.; execution fair.

Type: Tripod-lebes of light design, rather squat. The form differs considerably from that found as the type of the seal of the bybliophylax (see p. 39, No. IA1a(1)).

Sealing No. AIc(12), a bulla complete in two pieces; multiple; bitumen. Archive A.

b. Crescent and star as parts of design

(1) Oval; chipped; 15+ × 12+ mm.; execution fair. Pl. IV, Fig. 73.

Type: The partial destruction of the design by chipping renders identification difficult. The central part of the design is occupied by a mummy-shaped figure or pillar. It suggests the form given at times to the Ephesian Artemis (Furtwängler, Pl. XLIV, 2, 6). In details, however, it fails to show the characteristics usually attributed to this idol. No head or other parts of the body may be distinguished; one cannot be certain that they were intended to be shown. In the upper left-hand corner of the field is a crescent and, to the right, a star of eight rays. Below each of these symbols and about midway in the field appear two similar stars. Whether a third pair occupied the lower corners cannot be determined. These symbols are, of course, known attributes of Artemis, but as evidence for identification they are inconclusive. The motif is probably Anatolian, possibly Syrian.

Sealing No. AIIa(32), appended; convex; clay. Archive B.

c. Star or sun as design

(1) Probably circular; abraded; diam. 12 mm.; execution good. Pl. IV, Fig. 74.

Type: A star or possibly the sun. It is formed of eight broad rays around a central point. The object closely resembles the ornament shown on the cuirass of the Parthian king Orodes I (57–37 B.C.), as portrayed on his coins (Wroth, Pl. XIV, 11). It appears also as the reverse type on a coin of the same king (*ibid.*, Pl. XVIII, 7). A star occurs as a symbol on the coins of a number of the Seleucid kings, but the shape is different, and I have found none with eight rays. With some reserve I have classed the motif as Oriental.

Sealing No. AId(101), a bulla fragment; indeterminate; bitumen (?). Archive A.

d. Caduceus as part of design

(1) Circular; badly worn; diam. 12 mm.; execution obscure. Pl. IV, Fig. 75.

Type: Column on top of which is an obscure object the nature of which cannot be determined. To the right is a caduceus;

over this is an object that appears to be a short torch. Between the column and the caduceus is a wreath. The values of these symbols I do not understand. The motif is Greek.

Sealing No. AId(115), a bulla fragment; indeterminate; bitumen. Surface.

e. Ceremonial lamp (?)

(1) Oval; incompletely impressed, worn; 15 × 10+ mm.; execution fair. Pl. IV, Fig. 76.

Type: A shallow covered vessel apparently circular, mounted on the end of a shaft. From the center of the top of the vessel rises an object that appears to be a perpendicular spout with a rim around its extremity. From the rim issues a flame. At each side of the base of the spout stands an obscure object that resembles a tuft of feathers. I have been unable to determine either the motif or the significance of this type.

Sealing No. AId(97), a bulla fragment; indeterminate; bitumen (?). Archive A.

f. Ceremonial standard (?)

(1) Circular; partly overimpressed by another seal; execution obscure; diam. 12 mm.; Pl. IV, Fig. 77.

Type: Standard head mounted on the end of a shaft. The head is formed by a perpendicular cone which rests on a short cross bar. Surmounting the cone is an arrangement that can best be described as a spearhead between two curved blades. The general effect is that of a halberd with two blades. Notwithstanding the superficial resemblance I do not think that the representation is of a weapon. The blades are entirely ornamental. I do not understand the significance of the type. The motif is likewise obscure. This impression and the one just preceding occur on one bulla and may perhaps be related.

Sealing No. AId(97), a bulla fragment; indeterminate; bitumen (?). Archive A.

g. Thunderbolt

(1) Oval; broken; 14 × 9.5 mm.; execution good. Pl. IV, Fig. 78.

Type: Winged thunderbolt accompanied by a single stalk of grain. The motif is Greek.[6]

Sealing No. AIIb(17), appended; plane; bitumen. Surface.

2. *Herms*

a. With crescent

(1) Circular; worn; diam. 9 mm.; execution mediocre.

Type: Herm facing; to the left a crescent. Owing to the poor condition of the piece the identity of the herm cannot be established. The presence of the crescent is insufficient to determine the significance of the type. In a general sense the motif is Greek.

Sealing No. AIc(2), a bulla complete in two pieces; multiple; clay. Archive B.

b. Alone

(1) Oval (?); broken; no dimensions obtainable; execution obscure.

Type: Herm facing. All details have been obscured, and no identification is possible. The motif is Greek.

Sealing No. AIc(8), a bulla practically complete in two pieces; multiple; bitumen. Archive B.

3. *Masks*

a. Comic

(1) Oval; worn; 12 × 8 mm.; execution fair. Pl. IV, Fig. 79.

Type: Comic mask turned one quarter right. The type of our impression approximates that of a Hellenistic-Early Roman seal shown by Furtwängler (Pl. XXVI, 65). The motif is, of course, Greek. Impressions (2) and (3), below, have been made by the same seal as was No. (1). Nos. (4) and (5) probably are

---

[6] I owe to Dr. Eugene S. McCartney of the University of Michigan the realization of the significance of this association of symbols. In Greek lore thunder in certain instances was supposed to have a direct relation to plant fertility, and in this sense Zeus might be looked to as a source of fertility. Dr. McCartney has discussed this relationship in an article, "Phenology and Lore of Good and Bad Crops in Greek and Latin." He expects to publish this in *The Classical Weekly*, probably some time after October 1, 1935. See also *ibid.*, 25 (1932), 201.

impressions of this seal. If not, I think there can be no doubt that the various seals with which the five impressions were made represented the work of a single engraver. The five impressions occur on different bullae, each of which bears in addition a dated impression. There is an interval of one year between Nos. (1) and (2); of three years between (2) and (3); of ten years between (3) and (4); of nine years between (4) and (5). Impressions (6) and (7) represent different seals, but these again, I believe, were the work of the artist responsible for the others.

Sealing No. AIc(2), a bulla complete in two pieces; multiple; clay. Archive B.

(2) A duplicate of No. (1).

Sealing No. AIc(1), a bulla practically complete in two pieces; multiple; clay. Archive B.

(3) A duplicate of No. (1).

Sealing No. AIc(3), a whole bulla; multiple; clay. Archive B.

(4) Owing to incomplete impression the original form and dimensions cannot be stated; execution fair.

Type: Comic mask, as on No. (1). There appear slight differences in execution that may be due only to the manner of impression. See the discussion under No. (1).

Sealing No. AIc(9), a bulla complete in two pieces; multiple; bitumen. Archive B.

(5) Owing to incomplete impression the original form and dimensions cannot be stated; execution fair.

Type: Comic mask, apparently as on No. (1). See the discussion under No. (1).

Sealing No. AId(28), a bulla fragment in two pieces; indeterminate; bitumen. Archive B.

(6) Oval; broken; 12+ × 10 mm.; execution fair.

Type: Comic mask. The style closely approximates that of the related impressions above, but is executed rather more in profile. Note the discussion under No. (1).

Sealing No. AIIa(16), appended; convex; clay. Archive A.

(7) Oval; 12 × 11 mm.; execution fair.

Type: Comic mask. The style is similar to that of the other impressions in the group. It is somewhat larger. See the discussion under No. (1). On the same bulla occurs the impression of an official seal, incomplete, but without doubt a royal portrait (see p. 45, No. IA3m(1)). The impression under discussion is of value for the identification of this portrait. The evidence of style and execution afford a reasonable basis for the assumption that impression No. (7) was made by a seal which was the work of the same hand responsible for those represented by impressions (1)–(5). By the dates associated with these impressions we know that this engraver worked during the reigns of Seleucus IV, Antiochus IV, and Demetrius I. This in turn establishes a presumption that the royal portrait associated with impression No. (7) is of one of these kings. Since the features approximate those on coins of Antiochus IV, the identification of the portrait is confirmed.

Sealing No. AIc(26), a bulla fragment; multiple; clay. Surface near trial trench 4.

(8) A duplicate of No. (7).

Sealing No. AIc(23), a whole bulla; multiple; clay. Surface near trial trench 4.

b. Tragic

(1) Oval; incompletely impressed; 11+ × 8+ mm.; execution good. Pl. IV, Fig. 80.

Type: Tragic mask viewed in profile, elderly, bearded. The type suggests that of a seal shown by Furtwängler (Pl. XXVI, 53).

Sealing No. AIIa(17), appended; convex; bitumen. Archive A.

c. Multiple

(1) Oval; broken and badly abraded; 10+ × 9 mm.; execution perhaps fair.

Type: Apparently a double mask, in profile back to back. Owing to the abrasion details cannot be distinguished.

Sealing No. AIc(13), a bulla fragment; multiple; bitumen. Archive A.

4. *Vessels*

a. Amphora

(1) Oval; cracked; 12 × 8 mm.; execution fair.

Type: Amphora of normal shape. Another impression of the same seal is No. (2), below. Vessels of different forms are represented by Nos. (3)–(10). It would be difficult to determine the symbolic value of each form. Indeed there is no ground for an assumption that symbolism always played a part in the selection of a seal type. The motifs of vessels are Greek. They were particularly popular in the Graeco-Roman period (cf. Furtwängler, Pls. XIII, 41; XXXI, 14; XLVI, 56–59, 61–69).
Sealing No. AIc(19), a bulla fragment; multiple; clay. Archive B.

(2) A duplicate of No. (1).
Sealing No. AIc(20), a bulla fragment; multiple; clay. Archive B. It is probable that sealings Nos. AIc(19) and (20) are parts of a single bulla. The shape and color are the same, and the impressions on one appear to be duplicated on the other.

b. Jar or urn

(1) Oval; badly abraded; 11+ × 8 mm.; execution probably fair.

Type: A jar or urn apparently supported within a stand. It is not possible to determine the character of the vessel. It has a short neck with a wide rim. The greatest diameter is found midway of the length. The proportions are very slender just above the base, which has been obscured. The jar stand is obscure, but appears to have been elaborate; its upper extremities rise higher than the rim of the vessel.
Sealing No. AId(98), a bulla fragment; indeterminate; clay. Archive A.

(2) Oval; incompletely impressed; 11+ × 9.5 mm.; execution mediocre. Pl. IV, Fig. 81.

Type: Two vessels of a single form and size. They have large flat bases, slender short necks, and wide lips. They are provided with stoppers that have knoblike tops. The bodies taper but slightly from top to bottom. The greatest width occurs at about two thirds of the distance from bottom to top. The general effect of the form is crude, but this is perhaps due to the execution rather than to the concept in the engraver's mind. Another impression of the same seal is No. (3).

Sealing No. AId(99), a bulla fragment; indeterminate; clay. Archive A.

(3) A duplicate of No. (2).

Sealing No. AId(100), a bulla fragment; indeterminate; clay. Archive A.

c. Twin jars inverted

(1) Practically rectangular, the short sides slightly curved; worn; 11 × 8 mm.; execution mediocre. Pl. IV, Fig. 82.

Type: Two vessels of the same form and size, inverted. The diameter of the rim is only slightly less than the greatest diameter of the body. At the bottom the body tapers abruptly to a point. Another possible identification must be considered: May these objects represent the pilei or hats of the Dioscuri? The pilei appear on Seleucid coins both as types and as symbols. At times they are shown surmounted by stars and provided with straps for attaching (Gardner, *Syria*, Pl. XIV, 10). Occasionally they are portrayed without accessories and resemble rather closely the type of our impression (Babelon, Pl. XV, 5). A careful examination reveals, however, an essential difference in the two forms. The greatest diameter of the hats occurs at the bases corresponding to the rims of the vessels, which, however, are actually contracted at the rim. We have the evidence afforded by the preceding impressions in this group that vessels did form the types of seals at Seleucia. I raise the question whether on coins the twin objects without accessories may not be vessels rather than pilei. A symbolic value for such a coin type would not be difficult to find. We have the example afforded by one of our impressions of official seals that has a vase associated with the emblem of a department of state (see p. 41, No. IA1c(1) and pp. 138–141). Whatever the identification the motif is Greek. Nos (2)–(5), below, are of similar form.

Sealing No. AIc(21), a bulla fragment; multiple; clay. Archive A.

(2) Oval; 10 × 6 mm.; execution crude.

Type: Twin vessels as on No. (1), but smaller.

Sealing No. AIc(3), a whole bulla; multiple; clay. Archive B.

(3) Circular; incompletely impressed; diam. approx. 12 mm.; execution mediocre.

Type: Similar to that of No. (1).

Sealing No. AIc(24), a whole bulla; multiple; clay. Great House, Level III, Room 141 sub (equivalent to Level IV).

(4) Oval; broken; obscure; 13$^+$ × 10 mm.; execution obscure.

Type: Similar to that of No. (1).

Sealing No. AIIa(36), appended; convex; bitumen. Great House, Level III, Room 14.

(5) Owing to incomplete impression the form and dimensions cannot be recorded; execution obscure.

Type: Similar to that of No. (1).

Sealing No. AIc(12), a bulla complete in two pieces; multiple; clay. Archive A.

5. *Miscellaneous*

a. Column

(1) Owing to incomplete impression the form and dimensions cannot be recorded; execution crude.

Type: A short column with simple base and capital. The column is not fluted. It should be noted that all remains of columns found in the excavations at Seleucia were made of burnt brick without fluting. The execution of the impression may, therefore, have been influenced by local forms. The motif is, of course, Greek.

Sealing No. AId(14), a bulla fragment; indeterminate; clay. Archive B.

(2) Oval; broken; 11$^+$ × 9 mm.; execution mediocre. Pl. V, Fig. 83.

Type: A short column with simple base and capital. On each side of the column is a wreath with streamers. The column is not fluted. The concept and motif are again Greek.

Sealing No. AIc(17), bulla fragment; multiple; clay. Archive A.

b. Hand clasping an object

(1) Probably oval; incompletely impressed; $11^+ \times 8^+$ mm.; execution obscure.

Type: Forearm and hand clasping an object that has been obscured. The value of the symbolism is dependent upon the nature of this object. The type appears to represent a motif more Greek than Oriental.

Sealing No. AId(87), a bulla fragment; indeterminate; clay. Archive B.

6. *Plant life*

a. Palm tree

(1) Oval; incompletely impressed; $15^+ \times 12$ mm.; execution mediocre.

Type: Palm tree showing the branches and the upper part of the trunk. An attempt has been made to portray a cluster of the fruit as well as the characteristic roughness of the bark. The palm occurs as seal type on the gems of many periods in Greek art, including the archaic (Furtwängler, Pl. LXI, 1, 7). Associated with other objects it is found on the seals of the various non-Greek civilizations (Carnegie, Pls. Qd9, Qd15). The two concepts are quite distinct, and the motif of our impression is Greek. The impression occurs in duplicate on two parts of a single bulla.

Sealing No. AId(91), a bulla fragment; indeterminate; clay. Archive A.

(2) Oval; slightly broken; $12 \times 7^+$ mm.; execution mediocre. Pl. V, Fig. 84.

Type: Palm tree. It appears to be standing on a base, but I take this to be simply a representation of the ground. Above the tree and at right angles to its length is an object which appears to be a ladder having three rungs. Ladders occur as a part of the design on Greek seals of the classical period (Furtwängler, Pl. XXXVI, 19). There is usually no symbolical significance attached; the design shows, perhaps, an attack on fortifications or a group of cupids picking fruit. In the present instance there appears to be symbolism. I suggest that the ladder associated with the palm represents some concept connected with the cultivation of palms. The impression occurs on a bulla concerned with a wholesale transaction in salt. The seal by which the impression was made belonged to one of the witnesses. A simple cultivator of palms would not have served in this capacity. It is doubtful whether a large landowner would have chosen as his emblem a motif that so directly connected him with the cultivation of his lands. In the East today a class of entrepreneurs exists who contract for the harvesting of fruit crops. It is very possible that the owner of the seal was a member of such a group, a man of some standing in the commercial world and at the same time intimately associated with the harvesting of dates. If this theory is warranted, the impression affords, I believe, the sole example in our collection of a seal type that refers directly to the occupation of the seal owner. The association of the ladder and the palm is interesting because today in the area around Seleucia ladders are never used in climbing these trees. To the left of the palm on the impression and parallel to it are a series of markings that have some resemblance to characters. I have become convinced that they are not characters, but I am unable to explain their significance. Possibly they are a crude representation of falling fruit. The design as a whole is one that would be more apt to occur, I think, to a person of Greek rather than of Oriental culture, and I designate the motif as Greek. Another impression of the same seal is No. (3).

Sealing No. AIc(4), a bulla nearly complete in two pieces; multiple; clay. Archive B.

(3) A duplicate of No. (2).

Sealing No. AIc(5), a bulla complete in two pieces; multiple; clay. Archive B.

b. Fruit on a branch

(1) Ovoid; 14 × 8 mm.; execution mediocre. Pl. V, Fig. 85. Type: An upright branch having three pairs of stems at right angles to the branch; on each stem hangs a globular object. These objects are probably pomegranates, possibly citrous fruit. The execution is highly conventionalized. The motif is Greek rather than Oriental.

Sealing No. AId(114), a bulla fragment; indeterminate; clay. Débris.

c. Grain

(1) Oval; 12 × 6 mm.; execution fair. Pl. V, Fig. 86.

Type: Head of wheat on a short stalk. That the grain is wheat rather than barley is suggested by the character of the "beard." Similar types are found on Graeco-Roman gems (see Furtwängler, Pl. XXX, 49–51). The motif is Greek.

Sealing No. AIIa(24), appended; convex; clay. Archive B.

E. REPRESENTATIONS OF ANIMAL LIFE

1. *Quadrupeds*

a. Lion

(1) Oval; worn; 16.5 × 9 mm.; execution mediocre. Pl. V, Fig. 87.

Type: Lion advancing right toward an obscure object that probably represents a bullock's head. Animal portrayals form the type of seals common to a number of cultures. The concept was one very popular with Iranian peoples. The execution of such seals, however, is generally in Western style. The motif is commonly designated "Graeco-Persian." In terms of the general culture which such seals represent I am forced to classify this impression and some others in the group as "general" (see discussion of terms on page 224). Another impression of the same seal is No. (2), below.

Sealing No. AId(58), a bulla fragment; indeterminate; clay. Archive A.

(2) A duplicate of No. (1).

Sealing No. AId(59), a bulla fragment; indeterminate; bitumen. Archive A. The impressions on this fragment duplicate those on fragment AId(58), but they are parts of different bullae.

(3) Oval; abraded; worn; 13.5 × 8 mm.; execution crude.

Type: Animal crouched right. The head has been obscured, but the body appears to be that of a lion. There are traces that suggest a mane. For the motif see under No. (1).

Sealing No. AIc(17), a bulla fragment; multiple; clay. Archive A.

b. Bullock's head

(1) Almost circular; incompletely impressed; 10⁺ × 10 mm.; execution crude. Pl. V, Fig. 88.

Type: Bullock's head facing. This motif is found on Greek seals of the classical period as well as later (Furtwängler, Pls. XXXI, 1; XXVII, 70). A somewhat similar impression occurs on sealings of the Parthian levels of the excavations (see p. 239, No. B3d(1)). The motif is "general." The impression occurs in duplicate on a single bulla.

Sealing No. AIb(4), a whole bulla; dual; clay. Archive A.

c. Camel

(1) Oval; incompletely impressed; 14⁺ × 11 mm.; execution crude. Pl. V, Fig. 89.

Type: Camel standing right, single hump, tail erected. A variant form of this type is No. (2), below. The camel is portrayed on seals of several periods of Greek culture, the classical period in Asia Minor, the Italic, and the Graeco-Roman periods (Furtwängler, Pls. XII, 49; XXV, 55; XLII, 49). The type does not appear to have been used on Oriental seals of earlier periods, and was not at all common as late as the Sassanian period. In the Parthian levels of the excavations at Seleucia animal figurines occur frequently; the camel, however, appears only in levels that belong to the first century A.D. The lack of popularity of this type on Oriental seals in comparison with other animal types such as the lion or the bullock may be explained by the lack of a symbolic value which might be attached to it. The types of the lion and the bullock both had such values as, for instance, power. Only in areas of Greek culture does there appear to have been developed a feeling for motifs without symbolism. The motif, therefore, is classed as Greek.

Sealing No. AIIa(18), appended; convex; bitumen. Archive A.

(2) Oval; broken; 9⁺ × 7⁺ mm.; execution crude.

Type: Camel standing right. Most details have been obscured by reason of a break. It is probable that the camel had a single hump. This impression and that above are very closely related, but they are of different seals. They may represent the work of one engraver.

Sealing No. AIc(22), a bulla fragment; multiple; bitumen. Archive A.

2. *Birds*

a. Peacock

(1) Oval; 9 × 5 mm.; execution crude. Pl. V, Fig. 90.

Type: Bird standing right, with long heavy tail and large crest, apparently intended to represent a peacock. This bird is frequently portrayed on gems of the later Hellenistic and the Roman periods (Furtwängler, Pl. XXIX, 55, 60, and others). I think the motif may reasonably be classed as Greek. Another impression of the same seal is No. (2).

Sealing No. AId(103), a bulla fragment; indeterminate; clay. Archive B.

(2) A duplicate of No. (1).

Sealing No. AId(104), a bulla fragment; indeterminate; clay. Archive B.

b. Dove

(1) Oval; 12 × 7 mm.; counter-impressed with thumb nail; execution fair. Pl. V, Fig. 91.

Type: A bird about to alight on a tree or shrub, apparently a dove. The informal treatment of the motif suggests that no formal symbolism was intended. The motif, therefore, is Greek.

Sealing No. AIIa(19), appended; convex; clay. Archive B.

c. Pheasant

(1) Oval; incompletely impressed, worn; 12+ × 10 mm.; execution fair. Pl. V, Fig. 92.

Type: Bird standing right. An upright crest as well as the general form make reasonable an assumption that the representation is of a pheasant. The motif again is Greek.

Sealing No. AId(105), a bulla fragment; indeterminate; clay. Archive A.

d. Eagle

(1) Oval; damaged by salt incrustation; 13 × 7 mm.; execution mediocre. Pl. V, Fig. 93.

Type: Eagle standing with outstretched wings. The eagle is of common occurrence on Greek seals of many periods, partly no doubt as a result of its associations in mythology. It is almost as common in Oriental art, especially of the Sassanian period (Carnegie, Pl. I, P13). It occurs also on sealings from the Parthian levels at Seleucia (see p. 240, Nos. B3e(1)–(4)). The motif must be classed as "general."

Sealing No. AIIb(5), appended; plane; clay. Surface.

3. *Miscellaneous*

a. Insect

(1) Oval; 11 × 6 mm.; execution fair. Pl. V, Fig. 94.

Type: An insect, possibly a fly, viewed from above. Flies and other insects formed fairly common subjects for seal types in the Graeco-Roman period and sometimes in earlier periods (Furtwängler, Pls. XLV, 58, 68, etc.; X, 53). The motif is Greek.

Sealing No. AIc(21), a bulla fragment; multiple; clay. Archive A.

b. Crab or frog

(1) Oval; worn; 13 × 10.5 mm.; execution obscure.

Type: Very obscure, but apparently a frog or crab viewed from above. Both these forms occur as types of seals in the late Hellenistic and Graeco-Roman periods (Furtwängler, Pls. XLV, 52, 60; XXVIII, 77; and others). If the representation is of a crab, it may be considered that the concept is astrological and hence possibly Babylonian. If so, it is the only impression from Seleucia that has astrological connotations. Owing to the obscure condition of the piece I have classed the motif as "general." Another impression of the same seal is No. (2).

Sealing No. AId(58), a bulla fragment; indeterminate; clay. Archive A.

(2) A duplicate of No. (1), equally obscure.

Sealing No. AId(59), a bulla fragment; indeterminate; bitumen (?). Archive A.

CHAPTER IV

IMPRESSIONS OF SEALS OF DEPARTMENTS OF STATE AND THEIR SUBDIVISIONS

In the catalog the impressions of official seals are divided into three classes: A, those of departments of state and their subdivisions; B, those that identify individual officials; and C, those of collectors of taxes and other dues. Impressions of Class A, with which this section is concerned, is subdivided into three groups: 1, with a principal type and a secondary legend; 2, with a principal type and a secondary symbol; and 3, with no visible legend or symbol. The last group have been incompletely impressed and may, therefore, belong to either Group 1 or Group 2. Class A is thus composed of two kinds of impressions, both of which have principal types, with which in one case are associated symbols and in the other, legends.

AN OFFICE OF THE TREASURY CONCERNED WITH THE ISSUE OF CURRENCY

Group 2 of our category is at present represented by a single type of impression, comprising Nos. IA2a(1)–(4), having as design the associated Seleucid dynastic emblems, the anchor and the horse's head. It has been pointed out that the circumstances of the use of the anchor appear to require an assumption that it became the particular emblem of the royal treasury. It is suggested that, as used on the impressions of Group 2, with which we are now concerned, the anchor, accompanied by the horse's head, represents the office of the treasury which was responsible for the placing of newly coined money in circulation. The sealings on which these impressions occur are of one form, rather large, flat, and roughly finished. It is clear that they were intended not for the sealing of documents, but, rather, of containers. Their roughness and the fact that as many as four sealings of this one form have been found on the surface, indicating their relative abundance, suggest their use in some frequently recurring routine situation. That the same type of impression, again only on the one form of sealing, has been found at Orchoi [1] proves that the operation was common to various parts of the empire. Since the anchor was the particular emblem of the dynasty, it must be presumed that it would have been used as the seal design of only a very important department of state, such as the royal treasury. The use of the anchor as the general type on stamps of tax collectors demonstrates that the department which it represented was concerned with fiscal matters, whereas its appearance on the other impressions not concerned with the collection of taxes indicates that it represented more than a subdepartment having to do with revenues. These conditions again point to the treasury. In modern Persia, before the use of paper currency was accepted by the general public, it was customary to make large payments by means of sacks of silver coins that had been sealed officially as a guarantee of the contents. This practice was made necessary by the lack of a gold currency. In the Seleucid Empire silver tetradrachms rather than gold coins were the medium of exchange in large transactions that required the payment of currency. It is not suggested that any relation exists between the practice in modern Persia and that of the Seleucid Empire, but the similarity of conditions and the circumstances under which the anchor occurs as seal type on our impressions makes reasonable the explanation that these impressions represent the seal of an office in the treasury responsible for the issue of currency.

THE BYBLIOPHYLAX

Group 1 of the class of seals of departments of state and their subdivisions, consisting of nine impressions, represents either four or five offices or functions. Two impressions, Nos. IA1a(1) and (2), have as type the tripod-lebes and the legend βυβλιοφυλακικός. This term is a variant form of βιβλιοφύλαξ, "keeper of archives," [2] which is known from an inscription found at Didyma and dated in the reign of Antiochus II.[3] An impres-

---

[1] M. I. Rostovtzeff, "Seleucid Babylonia: Bullae and Seals of Clay with Greek Inscriptions," *Yale Classical Studies*, 3(1932), 47, No. 80.

[2] Liddell and Scott, *A Greek-English Lexicon*, ed. H. Stuart Jones.

[3] Theodor Wiegand, ed., *Milet, Ergebnisse der Ausgrabungen und Untersuchungen seit dem Jahre 1899* (Königliche Museen zu Berlin), VI, 36.

sion similar to those from Seleucia was found at Orchoi; it has been discussed by Rostovtzeff.[4] He suggests that the duties of the *bybliophylax* may have been, not those of an official charged with the registration of general documents, but the "keeping in evidence the royal estates in Babylonia." That is to say that he was in charge of "a special cadaster, a 'grundbuch,' of royal lands." He is somewhat hesitant in his definition of the term because of a possible alternative interpretation. On the sealings from both Orchoi and Seleucia there occurs the title of another official in charge of some form of registration, the *chreophylax*.[5] On the basis of the evidence from Orchoi Rostovtzeff is led to believe that the functions of this official were probably developed later than were those of the bybliophylax. He is faced, therefore, with the possibility that the two officials had similar functions. The evidence from Seleucia establishes the fact that the chreophylax was in existence at Seleucia as early as the period immediately after the death of Seleucus I. In Seleucia, at least, the two offices were contemporary, and their functions were distinct. So far as the new evidence throws further light on the problem, it supports the hypothesis of Rostovtzeff that the bybliophylax was in some way responsible for the recording of certain transactions involving the royal estates.

I would not limit the functions of this official to the recording of transfers of title in estates — the one function suggested by the document from Didyma. The two impressions from Seleucia form a part of Archive A. The transactions recorded in this archive appear to be limited to those concerning slaves or salt, principally salt. The sealings on which the impressions occur are rather large and flat and clearly were not used to seal single documents. They are of the type which apparently was used to seal containers. So far as it is possible to determine from the illustration of the corresponding sealing from Orchoi,[6] it is of a similar form. These sealings have all been found in archives of documents. In Archive A there occurs also a class of impressions which have been termed "private seals of royalty."[7] They appear to represent seals used by personal agents of members of the dynasty who were concerned with transactions in salt,

---

[4] *Op. cit.*, pp. 70–71.
[5] The significance of this title will be discussed on pages 131–138.
[6] Rostovtzeff, *op. cit.*, Pl. IX, No. 1. [7] They are discussed in Chapter VI.

and it is suggested that they were stewards of royal estates in the vicinity of Seleucia. There is no evidence that the transactions of Archive A involved transfers of land. Though the impressions of private royal seals found in the archives are numerous, only two impressions of the seal of the bybliophylax have been preserved. While some impressions of the seal of this official which were originally a part of the archives may have been lost, yet the disproportion in the numbers of the two kinds of impressions is so great that it must be presumed that a sealing impressed by the bybliophylax did not accompany each document recording a transaction in which a royal estate was involved. It follows that this official was not concerned with individual transactions in the produce of the royal estates. Rather he reviewed such transactions. On the basis of this hypothesis the sealings with the stamp of the bybliophylax may be considered to have been used on packages containing documents that had been registered by this official in connection with transactions of purchase or sale by stewards of the estates. In short, he may be termed a controller.

If we leave aside all direct evidence, but take into consideration the purpose served by the royal estates as probably the principal source of private income for the royal family, and the fact that a satisfactory income from this source was dependent upon the honest and efficient administration of the estates by the royal stewards, especially in the disposal of their produce, it would be necessary to assume, in the complete absence of evidence, that some form of control was provided over the activities of the stewards. The registration of purchases, sales, or grants of royal lands is insufficient to account for the maintenance in each great center of the empire of a special royal official. The existence of a system of control of the administration of these estates as suggested by the evidence from Seleucia, added to the recording of changes in title, does furnish a satisfactory explanation for the presence of the bybliophylakes at Seleucia, Sardis, and other centers. The close similarity of the impressions of the seal of this official found on the two sites in Babylonia and the fact that the title is unaccompanied by a qualifying term suggest that one office, placed probably in Seleucia and directly under the governor-general, controlled all the estates in Babylonia.

Too little is yet known with regard to the bybliophylax or to the functions of officials such as the oikonomoi and the dioiketai to permit of a schematic arrangement of the various offices which appear to have had some part in the administration of the royal lands. Neither is it possible to assume that the administrative hierarchy was uniform throughout the empire. It is very probable, however, that the official who controlled the royal estates of the province in which lay one of the three capital cities, Antioch, Seleucia, and Sardis, at the same time supervised the activities of his colleagues in the provinces surrounding and politically dependent upon that center. The title of this official may have differed even though within his province he performed precisely the same duties as did those in charge of outlying provinces.

THE CHREOPHYLAX

Four impressions of Group 1 of the class of seals of departments of state and their subdivisions, Nos. IA1b(1)–(4), have as type the portrait head of Antiochus I. On No. (1) may be seen a single line of legend reading χρεοφυλάκων. On the other three no legend is visible. Since they are incompletely impressed, and since the type figures on all four appear to be identical, it is assumed that the same legend is to be understood on each impression. The form χρεοφυλάκων is the genitive plural of χρεοφύλαξ. A rather full bibliography covering the various occurrences of this term is given by Weiss,[8] and the material has been covered again by Rostovtzeff.[9] The word, which was in use as early as the fourth century B.C., was frequently employed in the records of Roman Asia. Both Weiss and Rostovtzeff suggest that the chreophylakia may have been originally offices for the registration of loans. In time their functions included the registration of general private contracts. In the earlier period they were, of course, a part of the administration of the various city-states. As Rostovtzeff notes, in the Roman period they were municipal. The position occupied in Seleucid Babylonia by the chreophylakes and the nature of their functions involve various problems. Besides the impressions just listed, the direct evidence embraces a number from Orchoi.

---

[8] *Griechisches Privatrecht*, I, 408.
[9] *Op. cit.*, pp. 57–60.

Some of these have been published.[10] Rostovtzeff has gathered together all examples of this class of impressions from Orchoi in the study to which reference has already been made. The material is extensive and presents variations. Some of the impressions occur on bullae, others on appended sealings. As types there are found portrait heads of reigning kings and representations of deity. Two forms of legend appear: χρεοφυλακικός Ὄρχων and χρεοφυλακικός ἐν Ὄρχοις. All these impressions that may be definitely dated are of the reigns of Antiochus III and his successors down to and including Demetrius II. The legend form with the city name in the dative case occurs on impressions that have a royal portrait as type. This portrait has been variously taken to represent Seleucus II, Seleucus III, or Antiochus III. Whichever may be the correct identification, this group is the earliest from Orchoi.

The provenances of these impressions from Orchoi are of importance for an appreciation of their significance. As Rostovtzeff [11] has pointed out, the exact provenance of the greater part of the sealings listed by him is not known. They had been picked up by Arabs and sold to dealers. Those found in the course of scientific excavation lay in the ruins of a temple.[12] They constituted, therefore, a part of the archives of the temple. It is very probable that the sealings removed by the Arabs came from the same building, but this cannot be demonstrated. Rostovtzeff thinks of this archive as the depository of the records of the chreophylakion of Orchoi.[13] Apparently he is led to this conclusion by the facts that there have been found in the archive so many impressions of seals of these officials and that, apart from the bybliophylax with his specialized duties, no other official in charge of records is mentioned on the legend-bearing impressions. The nature of the archives in which were housed the sealings from both Orchoi and Seleucia has an important bearing on any

---

[10] A. T. Clay, *Babylonian Records in the Library of J. Pierpont Morgan*, Part IV (Yale University Press, 1923), pp. 52–54; J. Jordan, *Uruk-Warka, Wissenschaftliche Veröffentlichungen der deutschen Orient-Gesellschaft*, p. 65; L. Speleers, *Catalogue des intailles et empreintes orientales des Musées royaux du Cinquantenaire*, p. 234; G. R. Driver, "A New Seal in the Ashmolean Museum," *The Journal of Hellenic Studies*, 43 (1923), 55; K. Friis Johansen, "Tonbullen der Seleukidenzeit aus Warka," *Acta Archaeologica*, 1 (1930), 45.   [11] *Op. cit.*, p. 6.

[12] J. Jordan, *Uruk-Warka, Nach den Ausgrabungen der deutschen Orient-Gesellschaft*, p. 63.   [13] *Op. cit.*, pp. 49, 72.

complete interpretation of the various forms of administrative organization revealed by the impressions. The argument concerning the nature of the archives from which came the sealings from Seleucia is given elsewhere.[14] The evidence clearly demonstrates, I believe, that these archives belonged to a family firm of salt merchants. As to the archive in the temple at Orchoi, there appears to be some evidence that suggests a conclusion other than that given above.

In the first place, it should be noted that the impression of the seal of the chreophylax does not appear on every sealing from Orchoi. If the temple archive represents the depository of this official at Orchoi, his seal would have been impressed either on all or on none of the sealings. Actually I can find no adequate grounds for an assumption that the chreophylax would seal documents intended to be kept within his archives. The purpose of the seal of this or any other official was to afford evidence that a particular function had been accomplished. The presence in the files of an office of registration of a document representing a contract is evidence that the contract had been registered.[15]

In the second place, there appears to be no evidence that the act of registration by a chreophylax involved the filing of the documents themselves in official archives. Such may have been true in an earlier period when the control of commerce by governments was less complicated. In the period with which we are concerned the evidence is opposed to such an assumption. It will develop in the course of the discussion that commercial contracts were liable to several forms of registration. To have required the filing in each governmental office involved of actual copies of all contracts registered would have resulted in a slowing down of the business life — a result hostile to the principles upon which the Hellenistic governments were conducted. Though they subjected business to strict control for the purpose of increasing revenue, for the same purpose they encouraged the development and expansion of the commercial activities within their borders. The filing of copies of documents in the various offices could have served no purpose useful to the government.

[14] Pp. 179-198.

[15] In this connection reference should be made to the discussion of the use of bullae and other forms of sealings on page 7. It is there argued that the impression of the seal of the person in whose archives a document was filed never occurs on the bulla which encased the document.

To the business man concerned such a practice could have afforded but one advantage, that of security against fraud by the other party to a contract. But since it must be presumed that each party to any commercial contract would desire to retain a copy of the document in his own files, the affixing of the seals of the various officials concerned to both copies of every contract registered would serve the same purpose, provided at least one of the offices of registration maintained a register in which were entered the essential details of each transaction.

That the chreophylax did maintain such a register appears to have been demonstrated by the results of the excavations at Doura-Europos. Doura Documents I–IV have been described by Cumont as fragments of a register kept by the chreophylax of Doura in the χρηματιστήριον. This term he defines as the office "où l'on conservait une transcription ou du moins un résumé des contrats passés entre particuliers."[16] The evidence from Doura-Europos belongs to the opening years of Parthian control of that city, but it reflects the administrative system of their predecessors, the Seleucid kings.[17] On the basis of the extant evidence it appears reasonable to assume in regard to the act of registration performed before a chreophylax and probably to other acts of registration that the officials concerned entered in a journal the essential points of each document presented, and affixed their seals to one or more copies of the contract which were retained by each principal in the transaction. In particular, I would assume that the archive uncovered at Orchoi represents transactions in which the temple as a business unit was interested.

The nature of the ownership of the archives from Seleucia and Orchoi is of importance for a determination of the classes of transactions that were customarily entered for registration with the chreophylax. Under the assumption that the archives represent the files of such officials, it is difficult to explain the lack of variety in the kinds of transactions recorded in the archives. Once they are recognized as private files whether of a temple or of a business firm, it becomes evident that only limited deductions as to the classes of transactions that were customarily

---

[16] F. Cumont, *Fouilles de Doura-Europos*, pp. 281, 288, 294, 297.

[17] M. I. Rostovtzeff, "Syria and the East," *The Cambridge Ancient History*, VII, 5, 167.

registered may be safely made from the nature of the contents of the archives.

The question whether registration with the chreophylax was or was not compulsory must be raised in this connection. The answer to this question involves in turn the problem of the determination of the essential purpose served by this form of registration. Rostovtzeff states: "The organization of these chreophylakia was no doubt dictated by the necessity for efficient collection of new taxes introduced by the Seleucids.[18] That is to say, the essential purpose of this form of registration is considered fiscal. Now the original purpose of the offices of registration found in the earlier city-states was juridical, the protection of individuals against fraud or misunderstanding in connection with loans and other forms of private transactions. Rostovtzeff has pointed out that in this earlier period the primary purpose of registration was supplemented in the course of time by an attempt on the part of the city governments to control the collection of taxes through this same form of registration.[19] As has been pointed out above, the material from Orchoi contains references to only two forms of registration, that with the bybliophylax and that with the chreophylax, with the latter strongly emphasized. In many instances the seal of this official has been impressed on bullae that bear also impressions of stamps of tax collectors. Such coincidences make natural an assumption that registration of contracts with the chreophylax was directly connected with the collection of taxes. The sealings from Seleucia, however, throw a somewhat different light on the situation. Of the four impressions of seals of the chreophylax two are found on bullae and two on appended sealings of the container type. The bullae bear no stamps of tax collectors. One shows in addition to impressions of private signets three impressions of different official seals representing officials of registration other than the chreophylax or bybliophylax.[20] In other words, the transaction which this bulla represents was subjected to four acts of registration. The second bulla, besides impressions of private seals, bears the impression of an official seal that attested the accomplishment of the act of *katagraphe*, a form of registration required

---

[18] M. I. Rostovtzeff, "Seleucid Babylonia: Bullae and Seals of Clay with Greek Inscriptions," *Yale Classical Studies*, 3 (1932), 73.

[19] *Op. cit.*, p. 58.   [20] For a discussion of these impressions see page 149.

in connection with the sale of certain commodities.[21] Still another act of registration concerned with slaves is represented by impression No. IA1c(1), to be discussed just below. The material from Seleucia clearly points to the existence in Seleucid Babylonia of numerous forms of registration in addition to that with the chreophylax. Now it is evident that one form of registration would suffice to serve the original purpose for which the chreophylakia were organized — the protection of contracts. The other forms must be presumed, therefore, to have been concerned with the protection of certain governmental policies. The act of katagraphe served to secure the collection of a sales tax. The full significance of the other forms cannot be determined on the basis of the material in hand, but it is probable that all were organized by the Seleucid dynasty to further their fiscal policy. In the light of the evidence from Seleucia the following generalization is suggested in regard to the purpose served by the chreophylakia in Seleucid Babylonia. Those responsible for the organization of an administrative system for the new empire found already in existence in the various Greek cities offices of registration that served a multiple purpose, including both juridical and fiscal elements. Either because it was found impracticable to make over existing "city" institutions, or because the single office in each community was inadequate to take care of the increased volume and variety in trade that was characteristic of the period, or, probably as a result of both conditions, a number of new offices were created, each with its particular function, but all serving a fiscal purpose. It is to be expected that the new organization was flexible, that the number of new forms created would depend on local conditions in each community. In the smaller centers dual or even multiple functions were perhaps retained by single offices. It is to be presumed that, in proportion to the number of new offices established in each community, the local chreophylakion would be stripped of its fiscal functions. In view of the variety of different seals of officials of registration found at Seleucia, it is reasonable to suggest that in this important center the chreophylakes were simply notaries with a function purely juridical. In a city such as Orchoi, of less importance as a center of commerce, it is very possible that the chreophylax exercised dual functions.

[21] This form is discussed on pages 141–148.

On the basis of this interpretation of the functions of the chreophylakes in Seleucid Babylonia the question whether this form of registration was compulsory must necessarily depend on the complexity of the administrative organization of each community. That the registration of private contracts for the purpose of avoiding misunderstanding or fraud was made obligatory is possible but doubtful. When the purpose of registration was fiscal, to aid in the efficient collection of taxes, it is obvious that all contracts involving commodities liable to tax must have been subjected to compulsory registration. Since registration for fiscal purposes would actually tend to establish the basic terms of a contract against misinterpretation, it is reasonable to assume that in centers such as Seleucia, where the fiscal and juridical purposes of registration were separated, recourse to registration with the chreophylakes was limited to contracts involving other than routine transactions.

As has been stated above, the chreophylakes originally were a part of the organization of the various city-states, and in the Roman period they were municipal. What, then, was their status in Seleucid Babylonia? Rostovtzeff finds that these officials were part of the royal administration. This conclusion is based principally on the character of the seal types with which the title is associated.[22] With this question is involved the status of other officials and of official functions represented by the impressions. Still another problem has a bearing on this question: In Seleucid Babylonia were the administrative forms imposed by the royal government uniform in all centers, or were local conditions permitted to affect the organization? It has just been suggested that the number of offices of registration in a community depended upon its size and importance. It is to be noted also that the chreophylax seals from Orchoi have the city name as a part of the legend, whereas the corresponding seals from Seleucia show only the title. Various other distinctions in form between the official seals and stamps from the two sites will appear.[23]

The portrait of Antiochus I on the impressions of the seals of the chreophylakes at Seleucia determines their date. Whether the office of chreophylax was established by Antiochus or by his father cannot be definitely settled on the basis of the evidence

[22] *Op. cit.*, p. 63.   [23] See pp. 165–173.

available. This evidence points, however, to Antiochus I as the great organizer of the Seleucid administrative system.

REGISTRATION FOR APPRAISAL

The seals of the bybliophylax and of the chreophylakes of Seleucia identify the titles of officials. Associated with them in the class of seals of departments of state and their subdivisions are impressions of seals that identify a function, but that do not name the official or the office concerned with the accomplishment of the function. One of these, No. IA1c(1), has as type the Seleucid anchor accompanied by a vessel and a legend of two lines, the first of which is ἀνδραποδικῆς.[24] The anchor appears to have been the particular emblem of the royal treasury. The symbol associated with the anchor on this impression is more difficult to explain. To judge by the form of the vessel, it was a small vase rather than a jar. A vessel of rather similar form was used by the Romans as a unit of measure, the congius.[25] Its appearance on a seal alongside the emblem of a general department of state suggests that it represented a subdivision of the department. Of interest in this connection is a seal in the Southesk Collection.[26] The design is composed of several elements. At about the center of the field is a monogram; to its left are a star and a crescent; to the right there is a vase very similar in form to the vessel on our impression; above appear a lizard and the legend παραλίου. The star-and-crescent motif was used as an official emblem by the Parthian and Sassanian empires and by kingdoms dependent on them. In the East it became as characteristic a symbol as was the anchor in the Seleucid Empire and in dependent principalities. To what particular country this seal in the Southesk Collection is to be attributed need not be determined. Of immediate interest is the association of the vase with a national emblem in a manner similar to its use with the anchor on our impression. In both cases the vessel may be taken to be symbolical of some function within a principal department of state. We possess a number

---

[24] See p. 41.
[25] W. Smith, *A Dictionary of Greek and Roman Antiquities* (London, 1901), I, 529.
[26] Lady Helena Carnegie, ed., *Catalogue of the Southesk Collection of Antique Gems*, I, 110.

of impressions of what seem to be official seals that bear monograms. This form appears to have been used to designate a special class of inspectors in the public service who were responsible, apparently, for standards of various sorts. Each monogram represented a particular individual, not an office.[27] The association on the Southesk seal of a national emblem, of a vessel similar in form to a standard unit of measure, and of a monogram, suggest that the vessel was the symbol of a subdepartment responsible for the maintenance of standards. I assume tentatively that the vessel associated with the anchor on the impression with which we are now concerned was the emblem of such an office. The presence of the anchor indicates that the office was attached to the treasury.

The term ἀνδραποδική does not seem to occur elsewhere than on the sealings from Seleucia and from Orchoi, where it is always incomplete. It is clearly a derivative of ἀνδράποδον, "slave." [28] Since it is formed by adding -ικο- to a stem, the literal meaning is "concerning slaves." It has been established that in Ptolemaic Egypt ἀνδράποδον was used in a general sense much as was δοῦλος.[29] At Orchoi the term *andrapodike* occurs only on stamps attesting the satisfaction of a tax. On one impression from Seleucia, No. IB1c(1), it is used in connection with a tax on imported slaves. The impression with which we are concerned at present, however, was not made by the stamp of a tax collector. It lacks a date and the half-anchor, both characteristic of all tax stamps. The type occupied the center of the field, with the legend secondary to the type. The form, therefore, is that of seals of registration. On the basis of the character of the type figures and of the first line of the legend it is reasonable to assume that the impression represents the seal of an office attached to the treasury that, among other functions, undertook some form of registration of slaves.

The second line of legend is, unfortunately, very obscure. In part the traces suggest [ἐ]πιιη[or [ἐ]πιφη[. We may have here a derivative of ἐπίφημι, "to agree," or of ἐπιφημίζω, "to pledge," "to declare." [30] Whatever the word may be, it is not

---

[27] See pp. 151–155.
[28] Liddell and Scott, *op. cit.*
[29] W. L. Westermann, *Upon Slavery in Ptolemaic Egypt*, p. 8.
[30] Liddell and Scott, *op. cit.*

found on other seal impressions from Orchoi or from Seleucia. The meanings "to appeal" and "to declare" could be satisfied by an assumption that the act of registration served to appraise the value of certain commodities prior to the payment of a tax. In the present instance the assessment was concerned with slaves. In Ptolemaic Egypt the tax on the sale of slaves was based on the value of the slave as stated in the contract of sale.[31] That a sales tax was levied in Seleucid Babylonia is demonstrated by the sealings from both Orchoi and Seleucia.[32] Though the basis for the assessment is not known, it is reasonable to suppose that it was the same as in contemporary Egypt. The collection of a sales tax affects the interest of both buyer and seller, whichever party actually pays the tax. In the present-day Orient, in areas where a sales tax is enforced, collusion between buyer and seller to avoid payment of the full tax is common practice. This is effected by a false evaluation of the commodity in the formal contract, and is so successful that a serious problem has been created for the authorities concerned. The regulation of commerce by the Seleucid kings was very strict and appears to have resulted in complex forms of administration. It is not unreasonable, therefore, to assume that there was established at Seleucia an office charged with the duty of appraising the value of commodities subject to the sales tax. Not all contracts necessarily passed through such an office; it is rather to be expected that recourse to it would follow only in the case of a dispute between the tax authority and the parties to the contract. Such a function would logically fall to the treasury, the department interested in the efficient collection of revenues, and within the treasury to the particular office charged with the maintenance of standards. This interpretation of our impression is offered tentatively, but it appears to satisfy the requirements of the elements composing the seal design. The impression, therefore, is considered to represent a particular function — the appraisal of the value of a commodity subject to tax — performed by an office of the treasury charged with the maintenance of standards. As has been pointed out at the beginning of the discussion, this form of seal emphasized a function without naming the office charged with the function. An examination of the fragment of bulla on which the impression occurs

---

[31] Westermann, *op. cit.*, p. 14.   [32] See p. 195.

demonstrates that the enclosed document was small. The fragment constitutes approximately half of the original bulla, and this half is entirely taken up by the one impression. It is evident that the document was not a contract. On the basis of the interpretation of the impression it may rather be taken as a unilateral document, a statement of appraisal, containing such necessary details identifying the commodity as would establish its relationship to the contract of sale with which it was concerned. No exact date may be assigned to the impression. As a part of Archive A it belongs to the general period of Seleucid control of Babylonia.

THE ACT OF KATAGRAPHE

We have next to consider two other impressions that identify functions performed by an unnamed office of some department of state. These impressions, Nos. IA1d(1) and IA1e(1), are very fragmentary. On each a single line of legend has been preserved, with only traces of the seal types. These traces are sufficient, however, to demonstrate that the type occupied the principal part of the field, with the legend secondary to the type. Whether the complete legend on each was composed of one or of two lines cannot be determined by an examination of the sealings. The characteristics of the design, so far as it has been preserved on each impression, do preclude the possibility that the impressions represent stamps of tax collectors, and establish at least presumptive evidence that they identify an official act performed in the name of some department of state.

On one impression the legend reads ἀνδραποδικῆς; on the other, καταγραφῆς. With the first term we have become familiar as a result of its occurrence on an impression already discussed.[33] The literal meaning should be retained, "concerning slaves." The term καταγραφή is, of course, well known through its occurrence on documents of Ptolemaic Egypt, but our impression supplies, I believe, the sole instance of its use in the Seleucid Empire. According to Professor Westermann, its more general meaning, "list" or "register,"[34] was developed in the Ptolemaic administrative usage to refer to "the official recording of a sale" by the agoranomus. In connection with this registration a

---

[33] See p. 139.   [34] See Liddell and Scott, op. cit.

sales tax was collected by the appropriate tax farmer.[35] It is reasonable to assume that in Seleucid Babylonia the term was used to denote a somewhat similar form of registration. References to a sales tax, the ἐπώνιον, occur frequently on the sealings from Orchoi.[36] Though not yet found in the excavations at Seleucia, and though minor differences in administrative forms existed between the two cities, there can be no doubt that a general sales tax such as the *eponion* was enforced throughout Seleucid Babylonia. On the sealings from Orchoi occur references to a sales tax on slaves, which, in the view of Rostovtzeff, was distinct from the eponion.[37] Finally, at Seleucia we have the salt tax which, I believe, was clearly a sales tax.[38] Whether the act of katagraphe was required in connection with all sales taxes in Babylonia cannot be definitely determined on the basis of the extant evidence. However, the absence of the impression of a particular seal from a bulla does not constitute evidence that the seal had not been affixed to the document originally associated with the bulla.[39] Specifically, the fact that the impression of the katagraphe stamp does not occur on the bullae from Orchoi which bear the stamp impression attesting the satisfaction of the eponion can be taken only as indicating that the party who had paid the sales tax had not been responsible for the act of registration.

Let us take, for instance, a transaction involving the sale of a slave. Let us assume that the contract was registered by the act of katagraphe, and that a sales tax was collected in connection with the registration. In Ptolemaic Egypt the responsibility for the execution of the katagraphe rested on the seller, though in general practice the purchaser paid the sales tax.[40] Whether the same usage prevailed in Seleucid Babylonia does not immedi-

---

[35] *Op. cit.*, pp. 9–11. I recognize the fact that the alternative meaning referring to the drawing up of a deed by the principals concerned is more generally applied to the word katagraphe as found in the papyri. The fact, however, that the form occurs at Seleucia on an official seal appears to me to require, so far as Seleucid administrative practice is concerned, a translation in the sense of "registration." As I have already explained under the discussion of the chreophylakia at Seleucia (p. 131), I use "registration" in a general sense as having a significance at times juridical, at times fiscal, and, again, the two values may be combined. As applied to the act of katagraphe the registration implied was, of course, not juridical but fiscal only.

[36] Rostovtzeff, *op. cit.*, p. 65. [37] *Ibid.*
[38] See p. 195. [39] See pp. 7–9.
[40] Westermann, pp. 9 and 42.

ately interest us. It is evident that one principal was especially concerned with the accomplishment of the act of registration, and one, perhaps the same but probably the other, with the payment of the tax. Each principal would wish to have on the bulla to be kept by him the impression of the seal of the opposite party and probably those of the witnesses. The principal who paid the tax would require the impression of the tax collector's stamp; the one responsible for the drawing up of the deed, which probably involved the payment of a fee, would have affixed on his bulla the seal that attested the act of katagraphe. Since the act of registration was always accompanied by the levying of a tax, and the tax was collected only in connection with the registration, and since the impressions of seals on bullae were for purposes of a file record, an impression that identified either the act of registration or the satisfaction of the tax would serve as a record of both. One would expect to find on a single bulla impressions both of the stamp of a tax collector and of the seal attesting the act of katagraphe only in case one principal had initiated the registration and had also paid the tax. Similarly, no deduction may be drawn from the fact that on the bullae from Seleucia stamped by the collector of the salt tax no impression attests an act of registration.[41]

Some value attaches to the provenance of our impression bearing the legend "katagraphe." Archive A, of which it formed a part, appears to have been concerned with two commodities, principally with salt, but to a degree with slaves. Since references on the bullae to the former commodity are numerous, whereas the latter is mentioned but three times, it is probable that the particular act of katagraphe of which we have record took place in connection with a sale of slaves. The bulla fragment on which the impression occurs has also a value in an effort to understand the act of katagraphe as used in Seleucid Babylonia. This fragment shows in addition impressions of the seal of the chreophylax and of three private seals. These four impressions occupy one side of the bulla. The seal attesting the act of katagraphe was stamped on the top of the bulla. By analogy with other bullae it is almost certain that the side now missing bore the impression of a large, that is, official seal and of at least one private seal. If the original bulla had been impressed with

[41] Cf. p. 197.

but two official seals, they would have occupied the two sides, with the private seals impressed on the top.

This presumptive evidence for the existence of a third official impression on this bulla raises another question. Did the word καταγραφή represent the entire legend on the incomplete impression under discussion, or was the name of the act of registration accompanied by the name of the commodity registered? There can be no doubt that the name of the commodity appeared on each bulla that recorded the registration of a transaction. If the stamp of a tax collector appeared on a bulla in addition to the impression attesting the act of registration, the former would identify the commodity. But since, as has been shown above, there are no grounds for belief that both kinds of impressions necessarily appeared on one bulla, it must be assumed that the official charged with the registration possessed seals that would identify each particular commodity concerned as well as the general act. This could have been accomplished in two ways. He may have had both a general seal bearing the name of the act of registration and a series of stamps each of which bore the name of a particular commodity. On the other hand, there may have been a series of seals each with a two-line legend comprising the name of the act and the name of a commodity. Analogous with the latter supposition is the form of our impression, discussed above, that identified an act of registration concerning slaves, probably an appraisal. The office responsible for this act must have been concerned with commodities other than slaves. It is to be presumed, therefore, that this office possessed a series of seals, each dealing with a particular function in respect to a particular commodity. The waste of space consequent upon the necessity of impressing two seals on a bulla in order to identify a single act must have militated against the adoption of the first supposition. In the absence of more definite evidence it is tentatively assumed, therefore, that on our impression the word καταγραφή was accompanied by the name of the particular commodity registered. As has been pointed out, the nature of the provenance of this impression suggests that this commodity was a slave or slaves.

The third official seal which must be presumed to have been impressed alongside the seal of the chreophylax and that attesting the act of katagraphe represents, therefore, an act or function distinct from both of these. If in the transaction represented by this particular bulla the owner of Archive A had both initiated the act of katagraphe and paid the tax on the sale, the third official impression may have been that of the stamp of the tax collector. That another possibility exists is demonstrated by a bulla to be discussed below.[42] On this sealing there occur the impressions of four different official seals, none of which is the stamp of a tax collector. One impression represents the office of the chreophylax; the others cannot be identified, but their form classifies them as of seals of departments or their subdivisions. These impressions afford evidence that a single transaction might involve at least four different offices or officials of the government aside from tax collectors. On the bulla fragment with which we are now concerned, therefore, the third official impression may have attested another act of registration or of appraisal.

The impression of the seal of the chreophylax alongside that representing the act of katagraphe is worthy of note. In commenting on the impressions from Seleucia Rostovtzeff states that this act was performed by the chreophylax.[43] The only evidence for this conclusion is the association of the two impressions on one bulla. In the discussion of the probable functions of the chreophylakes of Seleucia it has been argued that the existence of impressions representing several other offices of government, whose functions must be presumed to have been fiscal, makes it likely that the duties of the chreophylakes were juridical only. On the basis of the evidence there presented I can find no grounds that necessitate an assumption that the act of katagraphe was performed by the chreophylax. On the other hand, the very fact that the two impressions are found on the one fragment appears to demonstrate that each represents a different function. If the act of katagraphe was regularly performed by the chreophylax, this fact must have been known to the business public. There would have been no necessity for the impression of the seal bearing the title of the official; the impression that attested the act of registration would have identified the official responsible. It is assumed, therefore, that in the transaction represented by our fragment the interest of the chreophylax was purely notarial. The impression of his seal

[42] P. 149.   [43] *Op. cit.*, p. 63, note 7a.

indicates simply that the document was of such importance that the principals desired its registration for their own protection.

As has been stated above (p. 141), in Ptolemaic Egypt the agoranomus may have been responsible for the act of katagraphe. No reference to this official has been found at Seleucia. That the title was known in Parthian Babylonia appears certain as the result of the finding of an inscribed bronze weight at Hillah near the site of Babylon. The legend reads: Θεοδοσίου τοῦ 'Ανδρομάχου ἀγορανομοῦντος χρυσόι δύο ἔτους ϛΝΣ.[44] The date is equivalent to either 56/55 or 55/54 B.C. The existence under Parthian rule of an official having a Greek title in an area formerly a part of the Seleucid Empire affords reasonable evidence that the office had been a part of the earlier administration. Though it is not certain that Seleucia and Babylon would have had common administrative organizations, the office of agoranomus was so characteristic of the Hellenistic period that its existence in Babylon affords presumptive evidence of a similar establishment in Seleucia. There is a possibility, therefore, that in Seleucid Babylonia, as in Ptolemaic Egypt, the act of katagraphe was performed in the presence of the agoranomus.

The impression with the legend καταγραφῆs has associated with it on the one bulla an impression of the seal of the chreophylax. This seal dates from the reign of Antiochus I, shortly after the death of his father, Seleucus.[45] The act of registration known as "katagraphe" was, therefore, in existence in Seleucid Babylonia as early as about 280 B.C. Westermann has noted that the earliest uncontested use of the term in Egypt is dated in the third century, and the next to the earliest occurrence is in 198/97 B.C.[46] The impression from Seleucia is of significance, therefore, for any estimate of the relative rapidity of development of administrative forms in the two states.

We have now to consider the second fragmentary impression identifying an act or function of government. This impression, No. IA1d(1), shows the legend ἀνδραποδικῆs, "concerning slaves." The legend is clearly not complete, and the name of the act to which the commodity was subjected has been lost. It is natural to see in this impression another example of the

---

[44] A. Dumont, "Poids grec trouvé à Babylone," *Revue archéologique*, N. Sér., 20 (1869), 191–192.   [45] See pp. 210–211.   [46] *Op. cit.*, p. 9.

act of katagraphe applied to slaves. There is no serious objection to the assumption. Traces of a type figure may be distinguished directly below the legend. Though the form of the type cannot be determined, it is clear that it occupied a principal position on the field. In respect to the form of the design, therefore, the two fragmentary impressions are similar. It would not be necessary to assume that the type figures are the same in order to establish the identity of the function represented by the two impressions. The sealings from Orchoi afford evidence that the seal type used by the chreophylax of that city varied in different periods. In contradistinction to the emblems of principal departments these types were general in character, and in successive periods different designs may well have served to represent the same office, the definite identification of which would be established by the accompanying legends. Though the impression with the legend καταγραφῆς can be dated to about 280 B.C., the other fragmentary impression concerning slaves may be assigned to the period from 150 to 145 B.C., as a result of the association with it of an impression bearing the portraits of Alexander Bala and Cleopatra Thea.[47] Under these conditions the incomplete legend ἀνδραποδικῆς may be restored as καταγραφῆς | ἀνδραποδικῆς, and the two impressions, Nos. IA1d(1) and IA1e(1), may be taken to represent the one act.

Other possibilities, however, exist. In the first place there must be noted the impression referring to slaves that has been classified as an appraisal of value.[48] May the fragmentary impression with which we are now concerned represent a similar act? The objection to such an interpretation lies in the nature of its type. The traces that may be discerned suggest a bar; it is impossible that the type comprised an anchor.[49] The impression attesting an act of assessment has as type the Seleucid anchor accompanied by a vessel. The interpretation would require, therefore, an assumption that the seal type representative of this act was changed in successive periods, as was the seal of the chreophylax at Orchoi. Now it has been shown that the anchor became the special emblem of the royal treasury, and there is considerable evidence to support a conclusion that this emblem was retained by this department over a long period.

[47] P. 68, No. IIA1q(1).   [48] Cf. pp. 138–141.
[49] It has not been practicable to reproduce these traces photographically.

While the evidence is insufficient to require the rejection of this interpretation, it must be classed as doubtful. There remains, of course, the possibility that the fragmentary impression represents some act or function concerning slaves, of which we have no knowledge. In spite of these other possible interpretations, it has seemed best, on the basis of the evidence available, to classify this impression, No. IA1d(1), as one attesting an act of katagraphe concerning slaves.

VARIOUS UNIDENTIFIED ACTS OF REGISTRATION

In the opening paragraph of this chapter dealing with seals of departments of state and their subdivisions, attention was called to a group of impressions that have been incompletely made. They have as types portrait heads and representations of deity. Each type occupies a principal position in the center of the field. No legend appears, but on each one those parts of the original seal on which a legend would have been engraved have been partly or entirely obscured by incomplete impression or by the overimpression of another seal. In no case is it possible to determine that a legend did not form a part of the seal design. In the discussion of the characteristics of official seals it was argued that the portrait of the reigning monarch in any period would not have been used to identify the seal of a particular office. Rather as seal type it served to identify the general authority of the government and must be presumed to have been accompanied in each case by a legend giving the title of a particular official or the name of a function. On the basis of this reasoning those impressions with which we are now concerned that have as types the portraits of rulers represent seals which bore legends identifying various offices or functions. Such impressions are Nos. IA3a(1), IA3c(1), IA3f(1), IA3m(1), and IA3o(1)–(2).

Three impressions, Nos. IA3u(1)–(3), have as type representations of Apollo, and one, No. IA3v(1), has a likeness of Artemis. In general, it may be assumed that representations of deities would not have a significance as seal types corresponding to that of a royal portrait. However, owing to the peculiar relationship between the dynasty and the Apollo cult, it is very possible that certain representations of the god were reserved as the emblem of some important department of state. If they were so reserved, the likeness may have appeared on the general seal of the department, unaccompanied by a legend. On the other hand, at Orchoi a portrayal of Apollo leaning on the tripod occurs as the seal type of the chreophylax and is accompanied by a legend. Under the circumstances it does not appear possible to determine whether or not legends formed a part of the seals represented by the three impressions showing likenesses of Apollo. Although the goddess Artemis appears as the type of some Seleucid coins, and although her cult was popular in both Antioch and Seleucia,[50] no particular dynastic significance may be attached to it. It is probable that the Artemis head was adopted in some particular reign as a general type for certain official seals to be accompanied in each case by an appropriate legend.

The offices or functions represented by these eleven impressions cannot be accurately determined. As has been stated, one or more of the portrayals of Apollo may have identified some principal department; the royal portraits almost certainly represent particular offices or acts, such as the chreophylakia and the act of katagraphe. Three of the impressions — No. IA3a(1), bearing the portrait of the deified Seleucus; No. IA3c(1), having the portrait of Seleucus, son of Antiochus I; and No. IA3u(2), showing an Apollo head — occur on a single bulla alongside an impression of the seal of the chreophylax. The last has as type the portrait of Antiochus I. In the discussion above repeated reference has been made to this bulla because of the evidence it affords of the complicated system of control over commerce instituted by the Seleucid kings. The bulla had encased a document kept in Archive A of the Great House. To judge by the number of private as well as official impressions on the bulla, this document was the record of some sort of contract. The principal commodity in which the owners of the archive dealt appears to have been salt. That this contract was not a routine transaction in salt is demonstrated by the unique character of the bulla in respect to the number and nature of the impressions it bears. In these details it differs radically from the two series of bullae that bear the impression of the stamp of the collector

[50] Compare the description of representations of this deity on private seals, pp. 81–83.

of the salt tax.[51] A few bullae in the archive refer to transactions in slaves. It is possible, therefore, that the document recorded a purchase, a sale, or other disposal of slaves. One may not exclude the possibility, however, that the bulla represents a different sort of transaction, not a part of the regular business of the firm — a purchase or sale of land, the settlement of an estate, or some other act.

That this bulla bears no impression of the stamp of a tax collector is of significance. The impression representing the chreophylakes has a juridical value; the impressions of three other official seals must have been required as a part of the fiscal policy of the state. Only the exigencies of a stern revenue service offer a satisfactory explanation of such a complicated system of registration. That is, the three impressions represent acts required of one of the principals to the contract in connection with the collection of one or more taxes. That no stamp of a tax collector appears on the bulla demonstrates the necessity for the assumption, already advanced, that all the seals represented on a document did not necessarily appear on the bulla which encased the document. The absence of the impression of the stamp of a tax collector from our bulla indicates that the owner of Archive A did not pay the tax or taxes involved. The presence of the four impressions of seals of registration implies that, if fees were exacted for these functions, they were paid by the owner of the archive, and that in any case he initiated the acts of registration.

For our immediate purpose the bulla is of importance as indicative of the necessity for caution in attempting to identify the functions represented by the eleven incomplete impressions with which we are now concerned. From the various sealings we have learned of the existence in Seleucid Babylonia of the chreophylax, of the bybliophylax, of the act called katagraphe, and of still another act involving a registration of slaves. As is inevitable in the partial excavation of a major site such as Seleucia, what is known of these offices and functions has been due in large measure to chance. In spite of the fact that our direct knowledge of the administrative system in Seleucid Babylonia is based largely on the recovery of only three archives, one in Orchoi and two in Seleucia, it would not be unnatural to interpret our incomplete impressions as representing these same

[51] Cf. pp. 186–187.

offices and functions. This Rostovtzeff has done in respect to similar impressions from Orchoi that lack an identifying legend.[52] The occurrence on one bulla of three impressions of seals of registration other than that of the chreophylakes forces the conclusion that there were practiced in Seleucia administrative functions which with our present knowledge can be neither named nor explained. That only one bulla of this sort has been recovered, instead of indicating merely the rarity of these new forms, should serve to emphasize the possibility that still other functions and offices existed of which we have no direct knowledge. Only further excavation at Seleucia and at other comparable sites may serve to supply the identification of the functions represented by these eleven incomplete impressions. At present they may be classed simply as illustrative of acts of registration required in the case of certain contracts by various departments or offices. The portraits of Seleucus I and of Antiochus I on the bulla establish the early date at which we find the Seleucid administrative system in Babylonia fully organized.

CONTROLLERS

In the preceding paragraphs there have been discussed seals of departments of state and their subdivisions. Their design was such as to emphasize what may be called the bureaucratic point of view. On certain of these seals the title of the official concerned was omitted; when it was inscribed the individuality of the particular officeholder was obviously of no importance. We have now to consider a small group of seal impressions that have characteristics essentially the opposite.

There are four such impressions. Their common characteristic consists of monograms as a part of the design. In Chapter II an effort has been made to show that the use of a monogram as a part of a seal design, so far, at least, as the impressions from Seleucia are concerned, must be taken as demonstrating the official nature of the seal.[53]

An attempt should now be made to identify the functions represented by this class of seals. The evidence is largely indi-

---

[52] *Op. cit.*, p. 53.
[53] Cf. pp. 26–28. In the catalog these impressions are numbered B1a(1) to B3a(2), pp. 49–50.

rect, and consists partly of the peculiar characteristics that distinguish the impressions from other classes of seals. Of great importance, however, is a consideration of the occurrence of monograms on other classes of objects. It is now generally accepted that most if not all monograms on coins of the Hellenistic period refer to the names of a certain class of officials connected with the issue of money.[54] Mr. Newell describes these officials as "controllers." A bronze weight from Seleucia bears a monogram incised on one of the principal faces. On other faces have been inscribed the unit of weight, the date, and a personal name. The name can refer only to the owner of the weight, and the monogram can be adequately explained only on the supposition that it stands for the name of an official.[55] Its purpose was certainly to inspire confidence in the accuracy of the weights on the part of buyers of merchandise. Yet the monogram refers not to an impersonal office but to an individual known by his personal name although having an official character. Such an individual may properly be called a controller of standards. Monograms occur on still another class of objects from Seleucia — on the handles or bases of pots which appear to have been employed to measure liquids.[56] Here again each monogram refers to the name of a particular individual, not to an office. These individuals may likewise be denominated controllers of standards.

It now becomes necessary to inquire why these controllers, whether in the mint or concerned with weights or measures, were identified by their names rather than by a reference to their official titles. At once a distinction must be made between actual circumstances and inherited tradition. The original motives that led to the adoption of monograms based on personal names to identify certain classes of officials may have been forgotten, though the usage still persisted. In view of this distinction, there appears to be but one answer to the question: In theory at least such controllers were men of standing in their communities, and their names were widely known and carried with them the confidence of the public. It follows, again in

---

[54] P. Gardner, *The Parthian Coinage* (London, 1887), p. 23; W. Wroth, *Catalogue of the Coins of Parthia*, p. lxxiii; E. T. Newell, *The Seleucid Mint of Antioch* (New York, 1918), pp. 134–135.

[55] For further discussion of this weight, see pp. 256–258. [56] See pp. 250–252.

theory, that these controllers were not officials of career, were not a part of the bureaucracy of government, but rather were elected or appointed for a limited term. That such was the origin of the use of personal monograms on official monuments is entirely consistent with what is known regarding the organization of government in the older Greek centers, especially the duty of the citizen of rank in a city-state to serve in some official capacity. The perpetuation of this idea in the administrative forms of the Seleucid Empire becomes a reasonable assumption. The carry-over of some older practices into the new administration was, of course, inevitable. But beyond this influence of tradition practical necessity must have been a compelling factor. Upon its organization the empire was made up of very heterogeneous elements that had behind them deep-rooted traditions. The problem of the early kings was that of enforcing upon each center administrative forms that to a degree, at least, would be uniform for the whole empire. If one bears in mind the compelling economic motives that determined the political policies of the great Hellenistic kingdoms, especially in relation to trade, it becomes evident that each government would seek to enforce a uniform currency and a system of weights and measures that, if not uniform, would at least meet certain required standards. In many communities such a program must have necessitated the acceptance of new forms and especially new units of currency and of weights and measures. That bitter opposition ensued is inevitable. In each local center the official emblems adopted by the newly organized government can have inspired little confidence. The retention of Alexander types on the early coinages of the successful *Diadochi* is evidence of an effort to dispel such fear. It is entirely reasonable to suppose that in each center of the empire the new administration appointed as controllers of the currency and of weights and measures men whose names in monogram on the new pieces would inspire that confidence which was necessary for the survival of trade, but which the strange emblems of the royal government could not secure. In time, the necessity for a consideration of local prejudices must have passed. Under the changed circumstances the class of officials that had been represented on official monuments by their personal monograms may have become absorbed into the general bureaucracy, and the essential purpose of the use of monograms may have been disregarded. That this purpose was not entirely forgotten is suggested by certain occurrences of monograms as types on the autonomous coinage of Seleucia during periods of civil commotion.[57]

To summarize the conclusions drawn from the evidence, it is suggested that the class of officials whose personal monograms appeared on the coinage was originally chosen from among citizens of high standing in each mint center; that this practice either was continued to, or was revived at, a later date; and that the primary duty of this class of officials was to provide a check on the standard of the currency on behalf of the public. I suggest, further, that a similar class of officials, chosen originally in the same manner, was responsible for the maintenance of the standards of weights and measures; that there were probably still other classes of officials with similar duties; and that the use of personal monograms as official symbols was limited, in the Seleucid Empire at least, to these classes of controllers. In the light of the evidence cited I assume that the impressions with which we are now concerned were made by the seals of such controllers. The peculiar characteristics of three of these impressions, especially the commingling of private and official elements, are well explained on the basis of the conclusions that have been drawn. They indicate that the owners of the seals possessed official attributes, yet did not form a part of the bureaucracy. As their personality formed the basis of their value as officials, so their seals expressed their individuality. It was noted of impression No. IB1b(1) that the monogram appears foreign to the unity of the seal design. It is not unreasonable to see in this the formation of an official seal by the addition of the monogram to the personal seal of the individual before his selection as controller. On Nos. IB2a(1) and (2) the names of the individuals in monogram form the types of the official seals. The size of the fourth impression, No. IB1a(1), and the use of the royal portrait as type render it characteristically official. Here again, however, the emphasis is on the individual represented by the personal monogram. The seal was not that of an impersonal office or department; it could have been used only by the particular controller whose name it bore. The exact

[57] These will be discussed in my forthcoming volume No. XXXVII in this series, *Coins from Seleucia on the Tigris*.

functions of the controllers represented by these four impressions cannot be determined. No. IB2a(1) occurs on a bulla concerned with a transaction in salt, but apparently represents a witness to a contract; that is, the seal was used in a nonofficial capacity. The provenances of the other three impressions have no significance for the determination of their use.

CHAPTER V

STAMPS OF COLLECTORS OF TAXES AND OTHER DUES

THE groups and individual impressions that represent the class of stamps of collectors of taxes and other dues have certain characteristics in common that serve to establish their relationship with one another and at the same time to distinguish them from other classes of official seals. These common elements are: a typical shape; extensive legends that invariably include a date; and the relegation of the type representing the general authority of government to a minor position in the field or its complete disappearance.

The careless application of the stamps has rendered impossible an accurate determination of the shape of all the impressions. The form of the greater number is essentially the same. They are ovoid, with the short sides straight. Though the size differs, the proportion between height and length varies little. This uniformity of shape common to the class maintains itself between impressions having differing legends and dates that are widely separated in time. It applies also to the impressions of a similar class found at Orchoi.

The legends that distinguish the class occupy either three or four lines, one of which comprises the date. The type, when it occurs, is placed after the date in a very secondary position. The relative importance accorded legend and type is the reverse of that characteristic of seals of departments and offices of state in which the type occupies the center of the field. The presence of a date on each individual of the class, whatever the subject-matter, is evidence that the impressions attest the payment of something due or its satisfaction in another form. That is, the impressions constitute receipts or acknowledgments from the person or office that had affixed the stamp to the holders of the bullae on which the impressions occur. It must be kept in mind that a date never forms part of the legend on a seal that attests simply an act of registration.

It will be remarked that the date on the impression identifies the year only, not a month within the year. If the value of the date applied to the document that was contained within the bulla, one must assume that the transaction represented by the document occurred but once each year. If, on the other hand, the date had reference to the official seal or stamp itself and not to the document, one must conclude that the person who had the right to employ the stamp held an annual appointment. Whichever the conclusion may be, it must be recognized that the year was inscribed on the stamps for a definite purpose. Among the dated impressions from Seleucia there occurs a long series dealing with transactions in salt, all found together in one archive. It will develop in the course of the discussion that this series in its original state was composed of one document for each successive year over a period of thirty odd years.[1] This fact, taken with the recording of the year date only on the stamps, suggests that the act represented by the impression of the official stamp in respect to transactions by any one individual was performed but once each year. In his catalog of impressions of official seals from Orchoi Rostovtzeff has listed impressions from different bullae that bear the same date.[2] The provenance of these impressions within the ruins cannot be determined accurately. None, apparently, were found in the course of excavation. They do not constitute proof, therefore, that a single individual performed more than once each year the act which the impression of the stamp represents. The evidence, however, is insufficient to demonstrate that the dates on the stamps refer to the acts which the stamps attest rather than to the terms of appointment of the officials who employed the stamps. If, as will be shown below, these officials were tax contractors and thus clothed for a limited period only with a certain degree of authority, it would not be unreasonable to suppose that the stamps which identified their authority limited by a date the period of its application.

THE COMMERCIAL CALENDAR USED IN SELEUCIA

The system of dating employed on the stamps was, of course, that commonly referred to as the Seleucid Era. In the transposition of the dates to our present era it has been assumed that

[1] See p. 183.
[2] M. I. Rostovtzeff, "Seleucid Babylonia: Bullae and Seals of Clay with Greek Inscriptions," *Yale Classical Studies*, 3 (1932), 30 ff., Nos. 16, 17, 20, 21, and 22.

the Babylonian rather than the Macedonian calendar was employed in their calculation; that is, that the Seleucid Era opened with the spring (Nisan) of 311 B.C. rather than with the fall of 312 B.C. The problem of the calendar employed in Seleucid Babylonia by the royal administration remains unsettled.[3] In any consideration of the two calendars it must be borne in mind that there is an essential distinction between the value of the dating employed on coins and that found on official stamps such as those with which we are now concerned. A date on a coin has a value which concerns the administration, but which is of little import to the general public. The stamps, however, were impressed on business documents and their envelopes; it was certainly of importance that the date on these stamps should be in such a form as to be readily understood by the business public. One might assume, of course, that a desire for administrative uniformity led to the employment of the Macedonian calendar by all the royal mints. Official stamps and seals intended for use in one particular community, on the other hand, must be supposed to have complied with local usage in form although not in content. The problem resolves itself into the question of whether the Macedonian or the Babylonian calendar was the one commonly used by the business community in Seleucia during the period with which we are concerned.

It should be remarked in passing that the form of the type found on the stamps, the half-anchor, appears to reflect a similar distinction between official documents intended for local use and those that had a wide distribution. There was discussed above (pp. 127–128) a class of sealings that shows the full anchor as type. It has been presumed that these sealings were employed to close bags of coin issued by the mints, and that the full anchor, the emblem of the treasury, impressed on each sealing guaranteed the contents. It follows that the sealings might be transferred

---

[3] Cf. W. Kubitschek, "Grundriss der antiken Zeitrechnung," in I. Müller und W. Otto, *Handbuch der klassischen Altertumswissenschaft*, I (1928), 227 ff.; F. X. Kugler, *Sternkunde und Sterndienst in Babel*, I (1907), 214; A. Bouché-Leclercq, *Histoire des Séleucides*, II, 516; J. K. Beloch, *Griechische Geschichte*[2], IV, 2, 50; E. Cavaignac, "La Chronologie des Séleucides," *Revue d'Assyriologie*, 28 (1931), 73; J. Johnson, "The Dura Horoscope and the Seleucid Calendar," *Dura Studies*, 1–15. Evidence pointing to the use of the Babylonian calendar by the mint at Seleucia during the Parthian period will appear in my forthcoming volume on coins (see page 154, note 57).

with shipments of currency to various parts of the empire. Examples of such sealings have been uncovered at both Orchoi and Seleucia. They have a uniform shape, and impressed on each is an anchor of one common form. This anchor is closely related in style to that so frequently found as the type or symbol on Seleucid coins. Now the shape of the half-anchor employed as the type on the dated impressions which were intended for use in Seleucia only is that to be seen on Parthian coins presumably minted at Seleucia.[4] The style of the emblem on the impressions and later on the Parthian coins is clearly a local concept of an anchor. The distinction between the two representations of anchors exemplifies the lack of a required uniformity throughout the empire in respect to the forms of such official documents as had a localized use.

There is no direct evidence available for determining the particular calendar employed by the business community of Seleucia in the third century. The impressions of private seals which have been found would appear to support an assumption that Hellenic rather than local culture prevailed. In the discussion it will be seen that the motifs representing the seals of business men are overwhelmingly Hellenic in character, with but little indication of a superficial Hellenization of native ethnic elements.[5] On the basis of this material it appears that the individuals represented by our impressions, probably comprising the upper strata of the business community, were Greek by descent. In the absence of other evidence it would be reasonable to assume that they introduced and retained the Macedonian calendar. Upon analysis, however, the problem becomes more complex. Seleucia as developed by Seleucus I and his successors was the principal center for commerce in Mesopotamia and Babylonia. The business community in the city was, therefore, a highly organized unit or series of units. If this organization was due primarily to the Hellenic and Hellenized elements brought into Seleucia by the efforts of the dynasty, it must be presumed that the Macedonian calendar was the one commonly used by the business community. If, however, the Western elements, which we find dominating the commercial life of the city in the third century, were not the creators of this

[4] See W. Wroth, *Catalogue of the Coins of Parthia*, Pl. XVII, 7–14.
[5] See Chapter VIII.

organization, but had gradually taken over and developed units of commerce and finance that formed a part of the pre-Seleucid community, Opis, the chances are at least equal that the native calendar was retained.

Historical evidence suggests that the formal foundation of Seleucia was inaugurated while Seleucus was yet satrap, perhaps as early as 318 B.C., and that it consisted of little more than the fortification of Opis and possibly the organization of a *polis*. At this time Opis was a recognized center of trade and shipping. It had, therefore, well-developed institutions of commerce and finance. Not only is there no evidence of the importation of masses of colonists at an early date, but the political and military conditions of the empire would not have favored extensive efforts toward colonization for a period of perhaps twenty-five years after the formal foundation of Seleucia. During this time there was without doubt a constant stream of settlement on the part of Hellenic elements, traders as well as veterans, who became absorbed in part by the commercial life of the reorganized Opis. The large influx of colonists from the West took place perhaps during the period in which the inhabitants of Babylon were transferred to Seleucia by Antiochus I. As a result of this transfer the long record of economic supremacy held by Babylon must have had its effect upon the development of the commercial life of the new center. The Greek bankers and merchants who settled in Seleucia were intelligent men; we cannot presume that they would have countenanced the destruction of the older channels of trade. They were necessarily dependent upon the great number of native traders throughout the East, who possessed the confidence of the various peoples. Nor may it be overlooked that Greek traders had settled in the East in earlier periods. These foreigners must have adapted themselves to the usages of the country, and their influence would in turn have its effect upon the new organizations. In short, though the evidence is inconclusive, it points definitely toward an acceptance by the incoming westerners of the already existing organizations for commerce and banking, and the application of their own superior technique to the further development of these institutions, rather than to the creation of new forms. I believe in particular that the imposition of a strange calendar upon the business world of the East by the newcomers would have been foreign to the general trend of the development of Greek commercial supremacy as revealed by the evidence. It is assumed, therefore, that the Babylonian calendar was in common use by the business community of Seleucia, and that this calendar was recognized by the government to the extent at least that official stamps intended for use on commercial documents were dated by it. In this connection it should be noted that some years ago Bouché-Leclercq argued that the Seleucid Era itself was a concept of Babylonian minds, and that from Babylonia the idea was carried to the West after the death of the first Seleucus. The era was first calculated on the basis of the Babylonian calendar and was subsequently adapted to the Macedonian reckoning.[6]

THE ANCHOR AS THE EMBLEM OF THE ROYAL TREASURY

A uniform shape and a design that comprises a long legend with a date are characteristics common to all the individuals of the class of impressions with which this chapter is concerned, but on the basis of the presence or absence of a type and of the city name the class must be separated into two groups. This division is at present unequal: we have but one impression which conforms to the class characteristics in regard to shape, length of legend, and the presence of a date, but on which neither type nor city name appears.[7] The impressions from Orchoi that constitute a similar class in respect to common characteristics may be divided into two groups on the basis of the same distinction. Rostovtzeff has listed two impressions that exemplify the common elements of shape, legend, and date without the addition of type or of city name.[8] On the specimens from both sites the type representing the general authority of government and the name of the particular city are invariably associated.

It becomes necessary to examine the values of these two elements in the design in order to establish the significance of their association and of their presence or omission. The impressions from Seleucia comprising the class number forty-nine. As has been stated above, in one of these, No. IC2a(1), the type emblem and the city name have been omitted from

---

[6] *Op. cit.*, II, 517–518.
[7] No. IC2a(1) in the catalog; it is discussed below on pages 173–175.
[8] *Op. cit.*, pp. 43–44, Nos. 65, 66.

the design. Of the forty-eight impressions which constitute the other group within the class, one, No. IC1c(1), refers to the importation of slaves and forty-seven, Nos. IC1a(1)–(12) and IC1b(1)–(35), refer to transactions in salt. The city name, Σελευκείας, forms a part of the legend on the forty-eight examples. Twelve of the forty-seven impressions concerned with salt show no type emblem, but they are incompletely impressed. Since in all other respects they conform to the characteristics of the group, there can be no doubt that a type formed a part of the design of the seals with which they were impressed. Aside from these twelve, incompletely impressed, and from one other that has a distinct form of type and will be discussed below, on all the impressions of the class with which we are dealing, whether from Seleucia or from Orchoi, with whatever commodity they may be concerned, the common type emblem is the half-anchor. In the course of the discussion of the Greek words that occur on the class of impressions with which we are engaged it will be shown that they all refer to the satisfaction of taxes. This holds true also for the impressions of this class from Orchoi.[9] The half-anchor, therefore, is the normal type of all impressions that concern the satisfaction of taxes and is found on no other class of impressions. This emblem must, then, be presumed to represent that branch of the government that was responsible for the administration of taxes. That this emblem has the form of a half-anchor suggests that the full anchor represented a great department of which a subdivision was identified by the half-anchor. The collection of taxes was a normal function of the treasury. I assume, therefore, that the half-anchor identified a subdivision of the treasury, which was itself represented by the full anchor, and that this subdivision was responsible for the administration of the various general taxes.

Although as type it represents not only a particular branch but the general authority of the government, the half-anchor occupies a position in the design very secondary to that of the legend. This arrangement of the design sets apart as fundamentally distinct the impressions that are concerned with taxes from those that represent departments, offices, or officials of the administration. The distinction finds a reasonable explanation in an assumption that the stamps which attest the satis-

[9] See Rostovtzeff, *op. cit.*, pp. 30–43, Nos. 16–26, 42, 48, 51, 59–64.

faction of taxes were used by tax contractors, who, while clothed for a term with a degree of official power, were essentially private individuals.

On three of the impressions concerned with salt the half-anchor is accompanied by a subsidiary symbol: No. IC1b(19), dated in 169/68 B.C., shows a caduceus; No. IC1b(20), 168/67 B.C., a star; and No. IC1b(26), 162/61 B.C., another star of similar form. A satisfactory explanation for these occurrences is not apparent. It should be noted that similar secondary symbols may have formed part of the original stamps with which a number of the impressions were made. Their absence is due to the incomplete impression of many examples and to the fact that any symbol following the anchor would necessarily occupy the extreme right edge of the seal design. Yet there are numbers of impressions in our series that are complete; no subsidiary symbols could have formed part of the stamps by which these impressions were made. An examination of the political events of the years in which these symbols occur throws little light on the problem. The year 162/61 B.C. marks the assumption of royal power in Babylonia by Timarchus. For this year we find a star added to the normal type. But the same form of star appears in the year 168/67 B.C. in the reign of Antiochus IV. To the same reign belongs the caduceus in the year 169/68 B.C. To neither of these dates may a definite significance be attached. It is probable that the symbols have reference to some administrative change within the department concerned with the tax contractors.

Though the half-anchor forms the normal type on the impressions of the class with which we are now concerned, one exception has been noted. No. IC1a(2) has as type a representation of Nike in the act of crowning a head that appears to be that of Helios. The impression is dated in 229/28 B.C., and is the second earliest in our series. The earliest, 286/85 B.C., has the normal type emblem. Since impressions for the years immediately preceding and succeeding 229/28 B.C. have not been recovered, it is not possible to determine accurately whether the emblem is symbolic of an event peculiar to the one year, or whether it replaced the anchor as type over a longer period. I am inclined to accept the former supposition. The anchor, originally the particular emblem of Seleucus I, became a symbol characteristic of the dynasty as a whole. So far as numismatic evidence affords light, Nike was not associated in any peculiar way with the reign of Seleucus II. In spite of the surname popularly attached to him, Callinicus, there are no grounds for believing that this monarch would have substituted a representation of this goddess for the dynastic emblem as seal type. The motif of Nike crowning Helios, or Apollo, the deity most closely associated with the royal family, suggests the commemoration of some victory.

In 229–28 B.C. Antiochus Hierax, who had dispossessed Seleucus of all his domain north of the Taurus, was himself decisively defeated by Attalus of Pergamon. To associate the new seal type with this victory would require the assumption that Attalus and Seleucus were allies. Of this there is no evidence. An explanation may be found in another quarter. The Parthians under Tiridates had thrown off Seleucid rule in eastern Persia some time during the previous war between Seleucus and Antiochus, apparently as a result of the loss of prestige incurred by the former through his defeat. Tarn says of these circumstances: "The establishment of the new kingdom [Parthia] had been favored by the troubles of Seleucus II; but once his hands were free Seleucus made an expedition eastward and Tiridates fled.[10] Peace in the west had been arranged by 236 B.C., according to Tarn;[11] by 234 B.C., according to Beloch.[12] Just when the campaign against Tiridates was opened is not known. Tarn assumes that by 228 Seleucus was in the east, and it is established that in 227 he was recalled by a renewed offensive on the part of Antiochus.[13] The details of the campaign in Persia given by the literary sources are obscure. Upon the advance of Seleucus, Tiridates took to flight; how far Seleucus pursued him is not known. According to Justin, the Parthian king later met and defeated Seleucus.[14] Both Tarn[15] and Beloch[16] treat this reference as of little significance. Seleucus broke off the campaign only because of the threat in the west. There is no evidence of a sweeping victory by either side. Since, however, the

[10] "Parthia," *The Cambridge Ancient History*, IX, 576.
[11] "Egypt against Syria and Macedonia," *The Cambridge Ancient History*, VII, 720.
[12] *Griechische Geschichte* ², IV, 1, 680.   [13] *Ibid.*
[14] *Historicae Philippicae*, lxi. 4. 9.
[15] "Parthia," *The Cambridge Ancient History*, IX, 576.
[16] *Griechische Geschichte* ², IV, 1, 684, note 1.

Seleucid army was forced to withdraw from enemy country only because of an entirely distinct threat elsewhere, it must be granted that such victory as resulted could well be claimed by Seleucus. This would be the more reasonable in 229/28, while the campaign was yet in progress. In the absence of definite evidence the circumstances favor an assumption that the unusual seal type was introduced during this year to commemorate a victory over the Parthians.

THE STATUS OF THE *POLIS* WITHIN THE ROYAL ADMINISTRATION

We must now consider the significance of the use of the city name and of its association with the half-anchor, representative of the royal treasury. In the discussion of the seals of chreophylakes it was pointed out that at Seleucia the legend comprised the title alone, whereas at Orchoi the title of the official was accompanied by the name of the city in the form of the ethnikon, Ὄρχων or ἐν Ὄρχοις. The stamps of tax contractors from Orchoi bore the ethnikon as the normal form, but an exception must be noted at two periods. Two bullae dated in the year 220/19 B.C. bear impressions both of the seal of the chreophylax and of stamps of tax collectors. On the former occurs the normal form, Ὄρχων; on the latter, Ὀρχηνοῦ. Another bulla of the year 146/45 B.C. reveals in the form of the city name the same distinction between the two classes of impressions. In this instance, however, we find the phrase Ὀρχηνοῦ λιμένος.[17] As Rostovtzeff has pointed out, λιμήν has here the value "fiscal area."[18] On the impressions of tax stamps from Seleucia we find the one form Σελευκείας. In referring to Seleucia the ancient writers employed the same term, with the addition of a phrase descriptive of its position on the Tigris River.[19] On the autonomous coins of the city, issued during the period from about 140 B.C. to 43 A.D., the regular formula is Σελευκέων τῶν πρὸς τῶι Τίγρει.[20] Imhoof-Blumer has noted a single variant reading

---

[17] Rostovtzeff, *op. cit.*, p. 30, Nos. 16, 17; p. 39, No. 51.

[18] *Ibid.*, pp. 78–80.

[19] Appian, *Syriaca*, lvii; Plutarch, *Lucullus*, xxii; Strabo, xvi. 2. 5; Pliny, vi. 26. 122, and others.

[20] G. F. Hill, *Catalogue of the Greek Coins of Arabia, Mesopotamia, and Persia*, p. cxiv.

Σελευκία τῆς πρὸς τῶι [Τίγρει].[21] From the excavations we have a coin with Σελευκίας followed by the same phrase. Our piece is dated in 41/40 B.C.; that of Imhoof-Blumer, in 38/37 B.C. The well-known letter from Antioch in Persia to the city of Magnesia, belonging to the period around 200 B.C., is subscribed to by the city of Seleucia with the formula Σελε[υ]κεῦσιν τοῖς πρὸς [τ]ῶι Τίγρει, the ethnikon found on the autonomous coinage.[22]

We have now to consider what conclusions may be drawn from this body of material. Do the variant forms of the city name have each a particular significance? On the autonomous coinage the city name clearly refers to a political entity, a governing body that exercised a certain independence. In the inscription from Magnesia, likewise, Seleucia appears as a body politic. In the literary sources, on the other hand, the city is referred to as primarily a geographical unit. In the first case we have as the normal form the ethnikon; in the latter, the place-name proper. With the exception of the two coins cited and of our sealings every known reference to the city of Seleucia on a document of an official character employs the ethnikon. The ethnikon is regularly found on the official monuments of contemporary cities. In the correspondence to which reference has been made between the cities of the east and Magnesia the several parties were exercising that degree of independence which was permitted them under the suzerainty of the Seleucid kings. By the issue of a coinage on which the royal types do not appear Seleucia is shown to have enjoyed a very real degree of autonomy under the Parthians. The political status of the city during this period has been well described by one of the Latin writers: "Rerum publicarum tria genera sunt, regium, optimatum, populare. Aut enim sub regum sunt potestate, ut Seleucia Parthorum."[23] The question now arises, Does the use of the ethnikon imply a certain degree of independence on the part of a city, and, conversely, when on official monuments such as coins or seals the ethnikon is replaced by a simple place-name, does it follow that a city possessed at that time a more restricted degree of self-government?

The occurrence of the place-name rather than of the ethnikon

---

[21] *Monnaies grecques*, p. 452, No. 67.
[22] Dittenberger, *Orientis Graecae Inscriptiones Selectae*, I, 233, ll. 101–102.
[23] Lucius Ampelius, l.

on the autonomous coins of Seleucia in the years between 41 and 37 B.C. must be examined to determine whether the political events during that general period may offer a reasonable explanation for the change. About 56/55 B.C. two brothers of the Arsacid line were engaged in a struggle for the throne. One, Mithradates III, had been a protégé of Rome.[24] Seleucia adhered to Mithradates and the other brother, Orodes, was able to capture it only by assault.[25] This is the first instance, but not the last, during the long period of Parthian intradynastic strife in which Seleucia sided with the pro-Roman candidate for the throne. Orodes, who reigned until 37 B.C., was engaged in an almost constant struggle with Rome. In 54 B.C. there took place the ill-fated expedition of Crassus into Parthian territory. Plutarch in his account of the campaign is very emphatic in his belief that Seleucia favored the western power.[26] The story, related by the same author, of the actions of the Parthian commander-in-chief in Seleucia after the defeat of Crassus demonstrates that the Parthians were of the same opinion.[27] Between 52 and 38 B.C. the Parthians were the aggressors in battles fought largely in Roman territory. To this period belong the two coins that have the place-name rather than the ethnikon. No coins of the city can be assigned to the period from 37 B.C. until the reign of Artabanus III (10–40 A.D.). As early as 15 A.D. we begin to find coins with civic types, but with no legend descriptive of the city name in any form. Such issues continued until 43 A.D., when the right of coinage was taken away from the city. During the interval from 37 B.C. to the reign of Artabanus no mention of Seleucia is made by the ancient writers. What the status of the city was during this period cannot be determined. A passage in Tacitus, however, states that Artabanus arrived at some sort of convention with the *primores* of Seleucia, by which all power in the city was placed in their hands.[28] From the context it is clear that the reference is to the traditional governing class, the "Hellenic" elements that must have constituted the original polis. The sequence of political events may be summarized as follows. After the first occupation of Seleucia by the Parthians the city enjoyed full autonomy, and the civic

---

[24] Appian, *Syriaca*, viii. 51.
[25] Plutarch, *Crassus*, xxi–xxvii. See also Alfred von Gutschmid, *Geschichte Irans*, p. 87. [26] *Crassus*, xvii. [27] *Ibid.*, xxxii. [28] *Annals*, vi. 41–42.

coinage bore the city name as an ethnikon. An interval of unrest followed when the city was to a degree disloyal to her overlords. Within this period fall the coins on which the place-name has been substituted for the ethnikon. It should be noted that the contemporary Parthian royal issues bear for the first time the type representing a city goddess, sometimes kneeling, offering a palm or diadem to the king.[29] There follows a half-century during which there appears to have been no new issue of civic coinage. Only with the accession of a monarch who is known to have come to some agreement favorable to the old ruling class in Seleucia do we find a revival of civic issues, and on these pieces the city name is entirely omitted. After another interval of less than thirty years the city is deprived of the right of issue. Viewed in the light of these circumstances, the change from ethnikon to place-name in the legend on the civic coins stands out as one element in a process resulting in the loss of the autonomous rights of the city within the Parthian Empire.

It has been stated in regard to the sealings from Orchoi that the place-name Ὀρχηνοῦ was substituted for the ethnikon Ὄρχων at two periods, in 220/19 B.C. and in 146/45 B.C. An examination of the historical source material demonstrates that these two years were characterized by major political disturbances in Babylonia. The revolt of Molon has been described in detail by Polybius,[30] and it has been possible to establish definitely the date limits. The successful advance of Antiochus III took place in the spring of 220 B.C., and after crushing the revolt he returned to Syria, by the end of the year.[31] Orchoi is not mentioned by Polybius, but as a part of Babylonia it lay within the area of revolt. The rapid success of Molon's effort may be well explained only on the supposition that he was supported by the mass of the "natives," the Babylonians and Iranians. It is noteworthy that Babylon, not Seleucia, became his headquarters. It has been argued that even in Seleucia the native elements favored the rebel.[32] Orchoi, a predominantly Babylonian center, may be presumed, therefore, to have been concerned in the effort to throw off the Seleucid yoke. Now Polybius relates that for

[29] Wroth, *op. cit.*, Pls. XIV, 10–12; XVIII, 15–16; XIX, 1–2.
[30] v. 41–54.
[31] See E. R. Bevan, *The House of Seleucus*, I, 303–304; E. Babelon, *Les Rois de Syrie, d'Arménie et de Commagène*, p. lxxxvi.
[32] E. E. Fabian, *De Seleucia Babylonia* (Leipzig, 1869), p. 29.

her part in the revolt Seleucia was subjected by Hermias, the first minister of Antiochus, to a severe persecution. In view of the circumstances a curtailment in 220/19 B.C. of the political rights possessed by the polis of Orchoi under the Seleucid kings would not be unnatural.

The second seal impression from Orchoi, upon which we find the place-name rather than the ethnikon and which is dated in 146/45 B.C., has been described by Rostovtzeff [33] as of the reign of Demetrius II. The period was one of constant strife between the political elements aligned behind two branches of the dynasty. Antiochus IV had usurped the throne that belonged to Demetrius I, son of Seleucus IV. This Demetrius had later removed the child Antiochus V, son of Antiochus IV. The adherents of the latter then put forward Alexander Bala, a putative son of Antiochus IV, and with Egyptian aid regained the royal power. Demetrius II, son of the elder Demetrius, in turn invaded Syria and seized the throne from Alexander. Numismatic evidence places the death of Alexander and the accession of Demetrius in 145 B.C.[34] The rule of Alexander was still acknowledged in Babylonia rather late in the year 146/45 B.C., for a tablet is known that bears his name as king and that is dated toward the close of the eighth month of the equivalent Babylonian year.[35] The impression from Orchoi, therefore, belongs either to the reign of Alexander Bala or to the interval of his overthrow by Demetrius II. Whichever was the reigning king of the moment, it was a period of violence when the satisfaction of the mercenary chiefs that supported each rival was of greater importance than the inherited rights of subjects or of cities.

Thus of fifty odd sealings of different years from Orchoi we find the place-name substituted for the ethnikon only in two, both of which mark periods of abnormal political conditions when the abrogation or curtailment of civil rights was of common occurrence. It is significant, furthermore, that on these two sealings the place-name occurs only on impressions of stamps of tax collectors, whereas the ethnikon was retained on the seals of the chreophylax. Rostovtzeff has stated that Ὄρχων and Ὀρχηνοῦ λιμένος are identical, and "must be taken as defining a

---

[33] *Op. cit.*, p. 39, No. 51.   [34] Babelon, *op. cit.*, p. cxxxi.

[35] A. T. Clay, *Babylonian Records in the Library of J. Pierpont Morgan*, Part II (Yale University Press, 1923), p. 87, No. 50.

certain region, a certain territory, that at least of the city of Orchoi and the land assigned to it . . . the fiscal area of Orchoi."[36] In view of the political circumstances that are contemporary with all changes in the use of the city name, whether on seals from Orchoi or on coins of Seleucia, is it not possible to go farther and to suggest that each form of the city name had a political significance in respect to the degree of autonomy under the royal power enjoyed by the polis, and that in particular the use of the ethnikon on an official document indicates that the polis to which the reference applies was to a certain degree the sponsor of the act or function represented by the document? It is in no way assumed that any of the impressions of official seals from Seleucia or Orchoi have a character essentially municipal. The chreophylakes were royal officials, and the system of taxation was administered by the royal treasury. The evidence does point, however, to a use of the polis organization by the royal administration. The seal of the chreophylax of Orchoi bore a royal type, with which was associated the official designation of the polis of Orchoi. The stamps of the tax collectors show the emblem of the royal treasury accompanied by the same reference to the polis as an autonomous unit, but with the two exceptions just cited. These two elements in the official seals attesting the royal power and that of the city are of coördinate significance. It has been stated above that the chreophylakes were originally developed as part of the administration of the city-states, and that in Roman times they were municipal. The only evidence for their royal character during the Seleucid period lies in the use of royal types as one element in the design of their seals. Since, however, these types occupy the principal position in the field, it is reasonable to assume the predominantly "royal" character of the seals. It is suggested that the invariable association of the ethnikon with the royal types on the seals from Orchoi implies that the royal government recognized and clothed with authority an institution that in theory at least was maintained by the administration of the polis. On the stamps of collectors of the general taxes the royal type, the emblem of the treasury, occupies a subordinate position. This, it has been assumed, attested the semiprivate character of the tax farmers. The normal association of the ethnikon with this type symbol

[36] *Op. cit.*, p. 79.

suggests in turn that the royal taxes were regularly collected through the polis. It constituted at least formal recognition of the theoretical autonomy of the city-states within the empire.

Whether such use of the organization of the polis by the royal treasury included a measure of financial support to the city government by a sharing of the taxes is not clear. Some such procedure appears to have been adopted in Ptolemaic Egypt in connection with the tax on the sale of slaves. The tax was collected by the royal government, but the diagramma regulating the tax stipulated that a fee, προπωλητικόν, was to be paid to the city.[37] Westermann has explained the usage by the supposition that the original Ptolemaic diagramma concerning slaves may have been modeled on the Greek city-state laws of Alexandria, and that the fee to the city was carried over into the royal law.[38] Whatever its origin, it appears to presume a certain recognition on the part of the royal government of the rights of the polis to a share in the sources of revenue.

If the association of the ethnikon with the royal types on the official seals and stamps from Orchoi implies for it a certain degree of liberty within the royal administration, the use of the place-name on the tax stamps from Seleucia and the absence of the city name in any form from the seals of the chreophylakes would appear to demonstrate that the latter city under the Seleucid kings had little or no autonomy. The evidence suggests rather that in this, the eastern metropolis, the chreophylakes had no connection, even formal, with the organization of the polis, and that in the administration of the royal taxes the name Σελευκείας has reference only to the geographical area embracing the city and its dependent lands and villages. That the degree of liberty enjoyed by the cities lying within the Seleucid Empire varied in relation to local circumstances is generally acknowledged.[39] That Seleucia, the eastern capital of the empire, should possess a degree of autonomy more restricted than was true of Orchoi, a Hellenized Babylonian city, is quite in accord with contemporary practice. Alexandria and Pergamon, both capital cities, possessed the outward appendages of autonomy, but in practice were ruled by the king with little or no

[37] W. Westermann, *Upon Slavery in Ptolemaic Egypt*, pp. 46–48.   [38] *Ibid.*
[39] M. I. Rostovtzeff, "Syria and the East," *The Cambridge Ancient History*, VII, 177–178.

regard for those rights that had distinguished the autonomy of
the city-states before the establishment of the Hellenistic monarchies.[40] The very fact that they housed important institutions
of the central government must inevitably have curtailed the
liberty of action of the various capital cities. Seleucia, furthermore, was built expressly to serve as a royal city, whereas the
establishment of Hellenic political forms in Orchoi was part of
a general program of the Seleucid kings that aimed at the winning of such previously alien centers to a loyal support of the
dynasty. Both cities owed their constitutions to the dynasty;
in practice neither was free; the dictates of policy, however,
would favor a greater degree of formal liberty for the old Babylonian city than for the new capital foundation. In the light of
the evidence from the two sites and of the contemporary political
circumstances it is assumed, therefore, that the name Σελευκείας
on the tax stamps refers to a fiscal area, and implies for Seleucia
either the absence or a more curtailed degree of autonomy
within the empire than was true of Orchoi. The evidence is
insufficient to determine precisely the relation of the polis of
Seleucia to the royal administration. The fiscal area was undoubtedly coincident with the political boundaries of the polis.
Beyond this relationship it is probable that the city administration was in no way concerned with any of the acts or functions
represented by our various seals and stamps. Such financial
support as was required by the institutions that properly belonged to the polis may well have taken the form of grants from
the revenues of the royal government. In short, I would suggest
that the relationship of Seleucia to the Seleucid Empire was
analogous to that maintained by the Attalids with Pergamon as
revealed by the greater amount of inscriptional and other evidence from that city.[41]

Further evidence of a difference in the relationships of Orchoi
and of Seleucia to the royal government may be adduced from
the manner of portrayal of the various kings on the official seals
used in the two centers. Rostovtzeff has pointed out that at

---

[40] See Rostovtzeff, *op. cit.*, VII, 121–122, and "Pergamon," in same series, VIII, 600–601.

[41] M. Fränkel, "Die Inschriften von Pergamon," *Altertümer von Pergamon*, VIII, 1, 2; cf. M. I. Rostovtzeff, "Pergamon," *The Cambridge Ancient History*, VIII, 600–601.

Orchoi the kings were represented as deified.[42] With the exception of the head of Seleucus assimilated to Zeus on a seal employed apparently just after Seleucus' death [43] the royal portraits on our impressions from Seleucia show the kings as mortal. The deification of Hellenistic monarchs was developed in an effort to harmonize the tradition of liberty held by the city-states with the actuality of incorporation within kingdoms.[44] It is not unreasonable, therefore, to assume that the distinction in the forms of representation of the Seleucid kings on the official seals used in the two cities implies for Orchoi a larger recognition of formal autonomy than was required by the relationship of Seleucia to the dynasty.

PORT DUES

We have now to consider the one impression on which neither royal type nor city name appears.[45] The legend is composed of three lines comprising the word λιμένος, the date, and an incomplete word which is not the city name. Possible restorations of this word will be discussed below. The presence of the date indicates that the impression attests the satisfaction of something due. The absence of the royal type and of the city name that distinguishes this impression from the class as a whole has a definite significance. It must be taken as evidence that the tax division of the royal treasury, whose emblem was the half-anchor, was not concerned with the act which the impression represents. Yet the legend appears to be official. I find an adequate explanation of the characteristics of this impression only in the assumption that it represents the satisfaction, not of a general tax paid into the royal treasury, but of a form of dues collected by and for a special agency. The form λιμένος is the genitive singular of λιμήν, with the primary meaning "harbor."[46] Rostovtzeff has pointed out that in a derived sense the term refers to a tax area, and he so interprets its occurrence on a sealing from Orchoi.[47] It should be noted, however, that when

[42] M. I. Rostovtzeff, "Seleucid Babylonia: Bullae and Seals of Clay with Greek Inscriptions," *Yale Classical Studies*, 3 (1932), 52.

[43] P. 44, impression No. IA3a(1).

[44] W. S. Ferguson, "The Leading Ideas of the New Period," *The Cambridge Ancient History*, VII, 13–22.   [45] No. IC2a(1); see above, p. 64.

[46] Liddell and Scott, *A Greek-English Lexicon*, ed. H. Stuart Jones.

[47] *Op. cit.*, pp. 79–81.

so used λιμήν is always accompanied by a place-name defining the particular tax area, as, for example, λιμένος Ὀρχηνοῦ, λιμένος Μέμφεως.[48] It is difficult, indeed, to conceive of its use in this sense on an official monument unaccompanied by a reference to the particular area involved.

On the other impressions of the class, whether from Orchoi or from Seleucia, the first word of the legend invariably defines the subject matter, "salt," "slaves," "sales tax," "ships." The impressions of the last group which are from Orchoi are similar to the one with which we are concerned in that they all lack the royal type and the city name.[49] If on our impression λιμένος is to be translated "fiscal area," the subject-matter must be expressed by the third word. That is, the arrangement of the legend would be the reverse of the normal form. On the grounds, therefore, that λιμένος with the value "tax area" would require an associated place-name and that its position on the field is one invariably filled by the subject-matter of the legend, its primary meaning, "harbor," has been chosen. This interpretation satisfies the conditions. The subject of the legend is the port; since the impression is concerned with dues paid to an agency other than the treasury, it is assumed that we have here some form of special fee charged by the port for its own uses. The port of Seleucia is not specifically mentioned by the ancient writers. Strabo, however, has stated that the Tigris was navigable from the sea to Seleucia, and Pliny has described a ship-bearing canal that linked the Euphrates basin to the Tigris at Seleucia.[50] The actual remains of the port can be traced today along the eastern extremity of the complex of mounds. Transit trade was the basis for the great wealth of Seleucia, as of the other principal cities of the Hellenistic age.[51] The fundamental policy of the early Seleucid kings was the control of this form of trade to the advantage of the royal treasury.[52] There can be no doubt that the port at Seleucia was carefully developed and controlled by the dynasty; it is extremely unlikely that it was in any way dependent upon the polis. I suggest that the

[48] *Ibid.*, p. 39, No. 51; U. Wilcken, *Griechische Ostraka*, p. 359.
[49] Rostovtzeff, *op. cit.*, pp. 43–44, Nos. 65, 66.
[50] Strabo, xvi. 19; Pliny, v. 26. 90.
[51] W. Tarn, *Hellenistic Civilisation*², p. 220.
[52] Rostovtzeff, "Syria and the East," *The Cambridge Ancient History*, VII, 173–174.

status of the port was that of a detached body directly under the governor-general of the East. The upkeep of the port must have required constant expenditure. It is, therefore, entirely reasonable to suppose that certain dues were exacted by the port to meet such expenses. Dues of this nature would be distinct from charges levied by the royal treasury on goods passing through the port, and the stamp of the port attesting their satisfaction would not be inscribed with the emblem of the treasury, the half-anchor. The name of the city, whether as fiscal area or in reference to the polis, would likewise have no place on the stamp. In short, the character of our impression may be established without reference to a positive interpretation of the fragmentary third line. A definite reading of this word must await the recovery of other impressions with a similar legend. The doubtful restoration given in the catalog, ταμιείου, referring to the treasury of the port, satisfies the requirements, but may not be stressed.

A TAX ON IMPORTED SLAVES

Aside from the impression just discussed relating to port dues the class of official impressions with which we are now concerned has a standard design. This comprises a date, the royal type, the city name, and a formula. It has been stated that the presence of the date signifies that an impression represents the satisfaction of something due. The presence of the type in a secondary position implies that, though it was the royal treasury to which something was due, the actual agent was a semiprivate individual. The place-name of the city refers simply to a fiscal area. The formula defines the commodity upon which something was due. The following formulae occur upon the impressions from Seleucia: ἀνδραποδικῆς | εἰσαγω[γικῶν]; ἀλικῆς; ἀλικῆς | ἐπιτελῶν; ἀλικῆς | ἀτελῶν.

The form ἀνδραποδικῆς has already been discussed. The primary meaning, "concerning slaves," should be retained here. The incomplete term εἰσαγω[ ] may be restored either as εἰσαγωγή, "importation of goods," or as εἰσαγωγικός, "of, or for, importation."[53] It is not possible to determine from the impression whether the longer or the shorter form is to be pre-

[53] Liddell and Scott, *op. cit.*

ferred. Since the formula may be read either ἀνδραποδικῆς εἰσαγωγῆς or ἀνδραποδικῆς εἰσαγωγικῶν, the choice must depend upon the emphasis intended. Does the impression represent a general class of import duties limited in the present instance to a duty on slaves; or was there a general class of regulations governing the commerce in slaves limited in the case of this impression to a duty on imported slaves? On all our impressions of official seals that bear legends it is the first line of the legend that determines the significance of the act or function represented by the seal. If it had been intended to place the emphasis upon import duties, the noun form, εἰσαγωγή, would have been used, but would have occupied the first line to be followed by its limiting term, ἀνδραποδική. Since, however, the principal position is filled by the word ἀνδραποδικῆς, "concerning slaves," by analogy with our other impressions it is reasonable to assume that the succeeding term in some way modifies or limits it. This requires εἰσαγωγικῶν used substantively. The formula might have been written in full, ἀνδραποδικῆς ὀνῆς τῶν ἀνδραπόδων εἰσαγωγικῶν.

Rostovtzeff has suggested another restoration of this legend.[54] He completes the final word as the noun εἰσαγωγῆς and considers it to refer to "the tax paid for an imported slave, a substitute for the ἐπώνιον paid for home-sold slaves." He makes the other term ἀνδραποδικῆς independent as denoting a special tax on slaves.[55] On some of the bullae from Orchoi two impressions occur; one reading ἐπώνιον, the date, the half-anchor, and Ὄρχων; the other, ἀνδραποδικῆς, with the same date, symbol, and place-name. Rostovtzeff identifies the ἐπώνιον as a general sales tax, with ἀνδραποδική as a special, additional, sales tax.[56] An analogy between an import duty, εἰσαγωγή, and the general sales tax, ἐπώνιον, as proposed by Rostovtzeff is attractive. I cannot believe, however, that the satisfaction of two taxes would be attested by the impression of a single stamp. If in the present instance we had to do with two taxes, we should expect to find, as at Orchoi, the use of two separate stamps. The evidence of the impressions from Orchoi does not require an assumption

---

[54] "Seleucid Babylonia: Bullae and Seals of Clay with Greek Inscriptions," *Yale Classical Studies*, 3 (1932), 66, note 12.

[55] *Ibid.*, p. 65.

[56] *Ibid.*, p. 31, No. 20 and others, and p. 65.

that the term ἀνδραποδική used by itself represents a tax. The impressions from that site having this word as a part of the legend are found only in association with those that represent the general sales tax. The latter, however, do occur alone. This circumstance suggests that the ἀνδραποδική was dependent upon the ἐπώνιον. It is important to bear in mind that the term occurs in a variety of senses. Besides its association with the general sales tax at Orchoi and with a tax on imported slaves at Seleucia, ἀνδραποδικῆς is found in connection with an act of registration upon the sale of slaves (καταγραφή) and with what appears to be an act of assessment of the value of slaves.[57] In view of its varied use in association with other terms to express official acts concerned with slaves, it is not likely that it would be employed alone as the name of a particular tax.

Our impression, No. IC1c(1), represents, then, the satisfaction of a tax on imported slaves. It is dated in the year 190/89 B.C. in the reign of Antiochus III. Rostovtzeff infers that the εἰσαγωγή was a "douane intérieure."[58] This can scarcely be taken to apply to an import duty on slaves. A system of local imposts such as Andreades[59] had in mind survives in the modern Orient, where it is applied to the produce of the country that is brought into the cities for sale. It is to some such customs barrier that the passages cited by Professor Rostovtzeff may refer.[60] It must be kept in mind that Seleucia was a seaport to whose wharves came vessels from Arabia and the coasts of Africa and India. The recovery from this site, therefore, of evidence pointing to the collection of import duties at Seleucia is not unnatural. In the absence of evidence to the contrary it is assumed that our impression has reference to a tax paid on slaves imported from abroad.

It is well to summarize at this point the evidence from the excavations with regard to the regulation of the traffic in slaves by the Seleucid government. We have just seen that there was a duty levied on imported slaves. It has previously been shown that the sale of slaves was very probably subject to an act of registration called καταγραφή, and that still another form of

[57] See pp. 141 and 138. [58] *Ibid.*, p. 67.
[59] A. Andreades, "Antimène de Rhodes et Cléomène de Naucratis," *Bulletin de correspondance hellénique*, 53 (1929), pp. 2-3.
[60] Ps.-Aristotle, Oeconomia, ii. 2. 34; Philostratus, *Vita Apollonii Tyanae*, XX, 20.

registration appears to have been provided to settle questions involving the assessed value of slaves. The acts of registration imply the existence at Seleucia of a tax on the sale of slaves, probably similar to that in force at Orchoi.[61] In short, the traffic in slaves was evidently subject to strict control, and the purpose of this control was fiscal.

A well-developed regulation of the traffic for fiscal reasons can adequately be accounted for only on the grounds of its importance. This in turn suggests an extensive use of slaves in Seleucid Babylonia. The evidence is, of course, inconclusive, and it is noted simply as a suggestion.

On the basis of the extant evidence it cannot be determined to which of the Seleucid kings is due the regulation of the slave traffic. Rostovtzeff has pointed out that the series of impressions from Orchoi concerned with a sales tax on slaves opens in 220 B.C., the year in which Antiochus III defeated Molon in Babylonia. At this time Antiochus was in great need of money to pay his troops, and this victory might have thrown a large supply of slaves upon the Babylonian market. Rostovtzeff accepts the possibility that a slave tax may have been introduced by Seleucus I or Antiochus I, but he prefers the assumption that the regulation of the slave traffic was probably due to Antiochus III.[62] The impression from Seleucia attesting the satisfaction of a tax on imported slaves is dated in the reign of Antiochus III, the year of the battle of Magnesia. On the other hand, the form of registration of sales known as katagraphe was in force as early as the reign of Antiochus I. As has been pointed out, the impression bearing this legend was probably concerned with a sale of slaves. The very fact that in the reign of this king we find already established a rather complicated fiscal organization including the katagraphe makes difficult an assumption that the slave traffic was left unregulated for another sixty or seventy years. It should be noted also that there are no grounds for belief that the campaign against Molon was accompanied by extensive enslavement such as usually ensued after a campaign in a foreign country. The principal source for the revolt of Molon, Polybius, emphasizes throughout his account the lack of animosity shown by Antiochus except toward Molon himself.[63]

---

[61] Rostovtzeff, *op. cit.*, pp. 70 and 76–78.
[62] *Ibid.*, p. 69.   [63] Polybius, v. 54.

The troops of the rebel, in large part the regular armed forces of the empire, deserted to Antiochus upon sight, and were escorted back to their stations by officers of the king. When Hermias, the first minister, sought to terrorize the inhabitants of Seleucia, Antiochus intervened for their protection. The later campaign of Antiochus against the Parthians and the Bactrians probably did result in a large influx of slaves on the markets of the empire. These events, however, are not related to the opening of the series of impressions from Orchoi that are concerned with slaves. In the absence of further evidence, I believe that the body of material concerning the rôle played by Antiochus I in the development of the Seleucid administrative system establishes a probability that the regulation and taxation of the commerce in slaves should be assigned to the reign of this king.

THE SALT TAX

The group of impressions having legends which contain the word ἁλική constitutes perhaps the most important body of evidence from Seleucia that concerns the fiscal administration of Seleucid Babylonia. They present, however, several problems that complicate the orderly exposition of their characteristics and of the significance that attaches to these characteristics.

It is necessary first to emphasize the essential unity of the group and its relationship to the general class which forms the subject of this chapter. Each impression bears the place-name of the city, a date, and the symbol of the royal power, regularly the half-anchor. Common to all the impressions of the group is the word ἁλικῆς that occupies the first line of the legend corresponding to the position of the term ἀνδραποδική on the impression discussed just above. Ἁλική is a derivative from ἅλς, "salt," and, like ἀνδραποδική, is formed by the addition of -ικο- to a stem. Its literal meaning is, therefore, "related to or concerning salt." In some instances it was used to denote "salt tax."[64] Its use in Egypt with this meaning has been discussed by Wilcken.[65] Little may be learned, however, from this source beyond the fact that the sale of salt formed a monopoly. Rostovtzeff translates the term variously as "salt monopoly" and as "the salt department of the Seleucid financial administration."[66] Pending the discussion of the value of the impres-

[64] Liddell and Scott, *op. cit.*   [65] *Op. cit.*, p. 141.   [66] *Op. cit.*, pp. 81, 82.

sions on which the word occurs at Seleucia, its literal meaning, "concerning salt," will be retained. The unity of the impressions is further emphasized by the fact that they occur only on bullae, never on flat sealings. These bullae, forty-seven in number, are in large measure incomplete. Ten of them, however, are sufficiently intact to enable one to determine the total number of impressions which each bore. On one of the ten bullae four private seals have been impressed; on the rest, three. None of the forty-seven sealings show the impression of an official seal other than those with which we are now concerned. It appears reasonable to assume, therefore, as common group characteristics that these impressions with the ἀλική legends are not accompanied by other impressions of an official nature, but that three or more private seals were regularly impressed in association with them.

The group of impressions comprises three varieties of formulae apart from the common elements of the legend — the date and the city name. One impression has the single word ἀλικῆς, eleven have the formula ἀλικῆς ἐπιτελῶν, and thirty-five read ἀλικῆς | ἀτελῶν. The formula, consisting of ἀλικῆς, the date, and Σελευκείας, is similar to the legend found on impressions from Orchoi: ἀλικῆς, the date, and Ὄρχων.⁶⁷ The terms ἐπιτελῶν and ἀτελῶν occur only on the impressions from Seleucia. They are the genitive plurals of ἐπιτελής and ἀτελής, respectively, with the general meanings "subject to tax" and "free from tax" or "untaxed."⁶⁸ The question of the particular values represented by the two words in their present context is somewhat involved. There is no doubt that ἀτελής was used in reference to both persons and things. Rostovtzeff has questioned the possibility of using ἐπιτελής in reference to persons; he states that in the Hellenistic period the term is found applied only to things.⁶⁹ With both ἐπιτελῶν and ἀτελῶν as they occur on the impressions from Seleucia, he would supply ἀλῶν. In so doing he assumes that at Seleucia two kinds of salt were recognized, one subject to tax, the other free of tax. This assumption presents certain difficulties. In the first place, there is, I believe, no evidence that certain kinds of salt were exempted from taxation in Seleucid Babylonia or in other parts of the Hellenistic east.

---

⁶⁷ Rostovtzeff, *op. cit.*, p. 42, Nos. 62–64.
⁶⁸ Liddell and Scott, *op. cit.*   ⁶⁹ *Op. cit.*, p. 86.

On the contrary, as Rostovtzeff has pointed out elsewhere, the evidence is clear that in the Seleucid Empire and in certain other of the Hellenistic monarchies the taxation of salt constituted one of the most important sources of revenue.[70] That the purchase of a certain quantity of salt was compulsory for each consumer in Syria is suggested by the narratives concerning the efforts of Demetrius I to conciliate the Jews.[71] Rostovtzeff believes that this obligation to purchase taxable salt extended throughout the Seleucid Empire.[72] Though there has been little direct evidence about the administration of taxes in the empire, a good deal is known regarding the system of taxes enforced in Palmyra.[73] This center had formed part of the Seleucid Empire, and it is generally recognized by scholars that the traditional fiscal usages of the Palmyrenes were inherited from the Seleucid administration.[74] An examination of Chabot's translation and restoration of the Greek and Aramaic texts dealing with the regulation of the salt traffic establishes the fact that at Palmyra exemption from the salt tax was unknown. It has been pointed out above (p. 180) that the seal impressions from Orchoi which are concerned with salt have the word ἁλικῆς, unaccompanied by references to liability to or exemption from a tax. There was, therefore, no exemption from the salt tax at Orchoi. It is difficult to see how certain kinds of salt might have been tax-free in Seleucia and subjected to a tax in the neighboring city of Orchoi. In short, the general evidence from other sources renders difficult the interpretation of ἐπιτελής and ἀτελής as having reference to salt. The relation of the ἁλική impressions to one another in respect to their provenances and their chronological sequence is likewise opposed to this suggested interpretation. On the other hand, the requirements of the evidence, whether general or local, are met by the alternative translation of ἐπιτελῶν and ἀτελῶν as having reference to persons, i.e., "[those persons] subject to tax" and "[those persons] exempt from tax." The negative objection to this translation of ἐπιτελής, that its use

[70] *Op. cit.*, p. 82; cf. H. Blümer, "Salz," Pauly-Wissowa, *Real-Encyclopädie*, Zweite Reihe, I, 2075.

[71] Josephus, *Ant. Jud.*, xiii. 2. 3; I Macc., x. 27–29.

[72] *Op. cit.*, p. 82, note 9.

[73] J. B. Chabot, *Choix d'inscriptions de Palmyre*, p. 23.

[74] Rostovtzeff, *op. cit.*, p. 76; cf. Léon Legrain, "Tomb Sculptures from Palmyra," *University of Pennsylvania Museum Journal*, 17–18 (1926–27), 325.

in the Hellenistic period as referring to persons is not known, naturally cannot be considered conclusive. The full and literal sense of our three varieties of impressions concerned with ἁλική may, therefore, be rendered as follows: "To attest the satisfaction of that due the treasury in respect to salt for the year . . .," with the addition in one case of "in respect to those subject to the tax," in the other, of "in respect to those exempt from the tax."

It will be fitting at this point to consider the provenances of these impressions and the chronological relation of the three varieties of legend. The one impression, No. IC1a(1), that has the simple form ἁλικῆς alone is also the earliest in our series. It bears the date 26 A.S., equivalent to 286/85 B.C., in the reign of Seleucus I, with Antiochus associated, and was found on the surface of the mounds. The impressions that have the formula ἁλικῆς | ἐπιτελῶν total eleven, Nos. IC1a(2)–(12). Of the eleven six are from the surface and five were found in a room of the Great House, a part of Archive A.[75] On one of the latter group the date is missing; the four remaining are dated in 229/28, 208/07, 197/96, and 191/90 B.C. The first date falls in the reign of Seleucus II; the others come in that of Antiochus III. There are thirty-five impressions with the legend reading ἁλικῆς | ἀτελῶν, Nos. IC1b(1)–(35). One of these, No. IC1b(1), was found on the surface and is dated in the year 214/13 B.C. The other thirty-four were found together in another room of the Great House, Archive B, and range in date from 188/87 B.C. in the reign of Antiochus III to 153/52 B.C. in the reign of Demetrius I.

It is important to bear in mind the salient facts with regard to the two archives. The Great House was a private residence, the home, apparently, of a family of wealth and importance in the city. The earliest phase of this structure was approximately coincident with the period of Seleucid control of Babylonia, more exactly, from some time after 294 B.C. in the reign of Seleucus I to a point in the reign of Demetrius II, not after 141 B.C. The two archives belong to this period. They appear to have been destroyed at the same time by a fire that caused considerable damage to the structure itself. The fire, indeed, may be said to have terminated this particular occupation of the Great

---

[75] The architectural associations of the sealings are discussed in detail above, pp. 10–14.

House (Level IV). The contents of Archive B suffered less damage than did those of Archive A, and there is reasonable assurance that practically all the sealings originally contained in it have been recovered. The legend-bearing impressions found in Archive B comprise the one variety reading ἁλικῆς | ἀτελῶν. They form an annual series for a period of thirty-six years from 188/87 through 153/52 B.C., broken only by the loss of the impressions for the years 186/85 and 171/70 B.C. Archive B, therefore, appears to have been concerned solely with documents that involved some form of exemption from the ἁλική. It is possible that impressions for one or two years at the opening or close of the series are missing. The nearly complete condition of the series, however, makes reasonable an assumption that Archive B was opened not prior to 189 and was closed by 151 B.C.

From Archive A there was recovered a much larger mass of sealings than was found in Archive B, and there is no question but that it contained originally a much greater number of documents. Unfortunately, however, the destruction was so thoroughly accomplished that comparatively few seal impressions have been preserved. Those that have survived have established the fact that this archive was already open at a date late in the reign of Seleucus I and continued in use to the time of its destruction during the reign of Demetrius II. Though Archive A was somewhat general in character, as demonstrated by the presence in it of scattered impressions representing transactions in slaves and the satisfaction of some form of harbor dues, the fact that only the impressions reading ἁλικῆς | ἐπιτελῶν recur in it suggests that this archive was principally concerned with documents that involved some form of liability to the ἁλική. Again, the fact that the ἁλική impressions in Archive A are distributed over a wide period of time, taken in conjunction with the annual series of impressions in the better preserved Archive B, establishes presumptive evidence that before its destruction Archive A contained a similar complete series.

It is important to consider the significance of the chronological relationship of the two series of ἁλική impressions from the archives. Though Archive A contained a number of impressions that belong to the thirty-six-year period covered by Archive B, all the impressions in Archive A reading ἁλικῆς | ἐπιτελῶν precede those with the legend ἁλικῆς | ἀτελῶν in

Archive B. Owing to the incomplete character of Archive A this relationship might be considered one of chance. However, since Archive B, although complete, contains no impressions reading ἁλικῆς | ἐπιτελῶν, and since none with the legend ἁλικῆς | ἀτελῶν has been found in Archive A, a presumption is established that the two series are mutually exclusive. The relationship of the two archives may be summed up as follows. The owners of the Great House during its first phase possessed a general archive. It served principally to house a series of documents concerned in some way with salt on which a tax had been paid. About 188 B.C. these transactions in salt were subjected to a change. The old series ceased, and in a new archive created especially for the purpose were filed annual documents concerned with salt on which no tax had been required. After about thirty-six years this file was closed. The general archive meanwhile continued to receive accretions of other sorts of documents until about 141 B.C., when both the open and the closed files were destroyed.

It has been stated above that the impressions which bear the three varieties of legends concerned with salt occur only on bullae. We must now consider the nature of the documents that were contained in these bullae and the function of the person or institution that impressed on them the official stamp. Practically nothing is known of the administration of the salt tax in the Seleucid Empire. It becomes necessary, therefore, to outline the various possible forms that this administration might have taken. Either there was a monopoly on the sale of salt or its sale was free. Taxes may have been collected at one or more of the different stages in the commercial handling of salt. There may well have been two varieties of salt on the Babylonian market, one imported, and the other local. In this region today the cheaper grades of salt are collected from lands which have been subjected to flooding by certain of the rivers which carry the mineral in solution from salt beds in the mountains to deposit it upon the alluvial plain. This is especially true of the Diala, in the Hellenistic period called the "Gyndes," that enters the Tigris just above Seleucia. Good rock salt is quarried in the mountainous areas to the north, the best coming from just north of Lake Urumia in ancient Media Atropatene. The first handlers of salt may, therefore, have been either producers or importers. A tax may have been collected from such individuals before sale, or upon sale by producer or importer to wholesaler, by wholesaler to retailer, or by retailer to consumer. It is possible, indeed, that more than one of these transfers was taxed.

The bullae on which the impressions concerned with salt occur possess two characteristics that are of value for a determination of the manner of collection of the salt revenues in the Seleucia area. These bullae, forty-seven in number, show a considerable variation in their inner diameter; it follows that the documents contained in them differed in length. These annually recurring documents were concerned with a single subject — the satisfaction of the ἁλική — and they were all of coördinate value. The difference in their length indicates that their contents were not similar. Business documents in ancient times even more than today followed a stock phraseology; only unusual circumstances would cause a departure from the standard form. The variation in the size of the bullae affords, therefore, satisfactory evidence that the transactions which they represent were not routine. A series of simple receipts for payments would constitute routine transactions. The references to the satisfaction of the ἁλική in Egypt illustrate the monotonous phraseology of receipts.[76] A series of contracts of purchase or sale would tend to differ in length of content only to the extent that some of them involved unusual conditions. Written contracts covering the retail sale of salt, if such existed, undoubtedly were of uniform phraseology. Similar contracts between retail and wholesale merchants likewise would not be expected to show an appreciable variation. On the other hand, purchases in the form of annual contracts between a wholesale merchant and importers or producers of salt frequently would involve additional details with regard to qualities as well as to places and times of delivery that would not occur in smaller transactions between merchants in the market or between merchants and consumers. Such additions would result in documents of unequal length. The evidence of the variation in the sizes of the series of bullae may be said, therefore, to be definitely opposed to an assumption that the documents originally associated with the bullae were receipts, or were routine retail contracts of purchase or sale. Rather, the evidence suggests that these documents

---

[76] See Wilcken, op. cit., p. 141.

comprised contracts on the part of a wholesale merchant in salt for the purchase of a year's stock of his commodity from producers or importers.

The second characteristic of the bullae that is germane to the discussion consists of the number of impressions of private seals that occur in association with the impression of the official stamp. It has already been pointed out that normally three, but occasionally four, private seals appear to have been impressed on this class of bullae. To what classes of individuals may these seals have belonged? In the first place, it should be noted that the seals of the successive owners of the archives would not be found on bullae from their archives.[77] The private seals must, therefore, have belonged to the opposite parties to the various transactions represented by the documents or to witnesses to the transactions. As the impression of the official stamp on the bullae attests the satisfaction of something due the treasury in connection with salt, so the documents within the bullae formed the records of transactions that involved the satisfaction of the tax. If the ἁλική formed a monopoly in the sale of salt, the documents constituted receipts given by the monopoly to the archive owner. If, however, the ἁλική was collected in connection with a transfer of salt in commerce, that is, if it was a sales tax, the documents were contracts of purchase and sale. If the documents were receipts from the salt monopoly, the official stamps represent the monopoly and the impressions of private seals, the witnesses to the transactions. On the basis of the alternative supposition that the documents were private contracts, the owners of the archive whose seals do not appear formed one party to the contracts, and the private seal impressions are those of the other parties, together with the witnesses. This supposition presumes that the impression of the official stamp on each bulla represents a tax collector who was present at the consummation of the contract in order to attest the satisfaction of the ἁλική. The circumstances would be somewhat analogous to those surrounding the collection of the slave tax in Ptolemaic Egypt.[78] The significance of the impressions of private seals on these bullae is this, that the existence of a monopoly would require the assumption that three or four witnesses were needed in the case of the purchase of salt from the monopoly,

[77] See pp. 7–9. [78] See p. 141–142.

whereas if the salt tax was collected in connection with a private contract of purchase or sale the private impressions signify that the two parties to each contract were normally accompanied by two witnesses. The one bulla having the impressions of four private seals may be explained by the supposition that in this particular year the owner of the archive entered into contract with two associated individuals, both of whom affixed their seals in addition to the two witnesses. The employment of witnesses to written contracts of sale was, of course, the regular procedure in both the Babylonian and the Hellenistic periods. On cuneiform tablets the number of witnesses appears to vary considerably, possibly in relation to the importance of the contract. Three witnesses are mentioned in the Avroman parchments and in the documents from Doura-Europos.[79] On the other hand, in transactions such as the purchase of salt from an official monopoly or the payment of an excise tax by producers or importers it is doubtful whether witnesses would be required; certainly the number of witnesses, three or four, is excessive. This evidence afforded by the impressions of private seals on the series of bullae suggests the following conclusions: It may be said to refute entirely an assumption that the documents of the bullae represent receipts given by tax collectors to the first handlers of salt before sale, that is, producers or importers. It is definitely opposed to an assumption that the documents represent receipts given by a salt monopoly to purchasers of salt. It favors only the one interpretation, that the documents were contracts of purchase or sale in connection with which a tax was collected.

The two characteristics of the bullae, the variation in their size and the number of the impressions of private seals, agree in the evidence they afford regarding the significance of the term ἁλική as employed in Seleucid Babylonia. Though it is indirect, the relatively large number of objects that supply the data establish the serious character of the evidence. It affords a reasonable hypothesis supported by all the extant facts upon which to base the further consideration of the material. It is assumed, in brief, that a monopoly in the sale of salt did not

[79] E. H. Minns, "Parchments of the Parthian Period from Avroman in Kurdistan," *The Journal of Hellenic Studies*, 35 (1915), p. 22; F. Cumont, *Fouilles de Doura-Europos*, p. 286; M. I. Rostovtzeff and C. B. Welles, "A Parchment Contract of Loan from Doura-Europos on the Euphrates," *Yale Classical Studies*, 2 (1930), 32.

exist, and that a tax was collected upon its sale. Though, of course, it is possible that a sales tax on salt was levied upon more than one turnover, the bullae are concerned solely with transactions that were wholesale and were certainly not of a routine nature.

Rostovtzeff has suggested that a royal monopoly in the sale of salt existed in the Seleucid Empire as well as in other contemporary kingdoms.[80] As has been stated above, there does appear to have been some form of monopoly in Ptolemaic and Roman Egypt.[81] However, this fact may scarcely be used as an argument for the existence of a similar institution in the Seleucid Empire. The closely knit population of Egypt, accustomed long before the Hellenistic period to an exacting discipline, lent itself to the intense organization of the whole economic structure such as we find under the Ptolemies. It is very doubtful whether the distinctively disunited and frequently turbulent character of the groups comprising the Seleucid Empire would have permitted a similar organization of this kingdom. The enforcement of a monopoly is difficult under any circumstances. In Babylonia at the present time numerous salt deposits left by the rivers are freely worked by the peasants. There is no reason to doubt the existence of such deposits at an earlier period. The policing of all salt beds under these circumstances would have entailed great expense. In fact, it has always proved impracticable to tax an agricultural population in respect to any local produce, including deposited salt, that is actually consumed by them. It would be essentially the consumption of salt by the town and city populations that would serve in Babylonia to make of this commodity an important source of revenue. The fact that the surplus produce of the country is without value unless it can be transported into the towns has led to the practice, common in both the ancient and the modern Orient, of erecting local customs barriers at the entrance to such centers of population, where an *octroi* would be levied on the produce either before or as a part of its sale. Reference has been made to the existence of such barriers in Parthian Babylonia. Control of produce of

---

[80] "Seleucid Babylonia: Bullae and Seals of Clay with Greek Inscriptions," *Yale Classical Studies*, 3 (1932), 82.

[81] Wilcken, *op. cit.*, p. 141; M. Rostowzew [= Rostovtzeff], *Geschichte der Staatspacht in der römischen Kaiserzeit*, p. 83.

all kinds for purposes of taxation is relatively simple only as the goods arrive on the market. The collection of a government's share in the harvest as practiced in the Orient may be cited as an exception. The exception is more apparent than real, for in this case the tax is collected only when the produce has been brought to a centrally located threshing floor that cannot be concealed, where it is subject to division also between peasant and landlord. As in the case of a sales tax, the tax collector has to do with a transaction between two or more opposed parties.

Important evidence germane to the discussion is furnished by the fiscal laws of Palmyra.[82] Among the taxes enumerated are those on farm produce brought into the city for sale. The wording of the law reflects the existence at Palmyra of an octroi similar to that evidenced by the local customs barriers of Parthian Babylonia. That is, we find the system of octroi taxation in two important areas, each of which represented a distinct cultural background, but both of which were formerly a part of the Seleucid Empire. In neither may we assign the inherited fiscal organization to the influence of any other great power such as Ptolemaic Egypt or Rome. It is, of course, an established fact that one of the fundamental policies of the Seleucid dynasty was the organization of cities throughout the empire. To these cities became attached the greater part of the surrounding agricultural lands that were not actually royal fiefs. These circumstances suggest that one of the principal sources of revenue in the Seleucid Empire may well have been the taxation of country produce as it was brought into the towns for sale. As a part of such produce I would include salt.

It should be noted that the decrees from Palmyra in no way indicate that a monopoly upon the sale of salt had ever existed in that territory. There were important local salt beds, and their produce was brought into the city for sale. The inscriptions dealing with the decrees are fragmentary. Dessau and Dittenberger both restored the Greek version to read that the tax on salt was paid by the merchants after purchase from importers or producers.[83] Chabot bases his conclusion largely on the Aramaic version and holds that the tax was paid by importers

---

[82] See p. 181.

[83] Dittenberger, *op. cit.*, No. 629, ll. 93; H. Dessau, "Der Steuertarif von Palmyre," *Hermes*, 19 (1884), 486.

or producers before sale. With regard to the producers of local salt I quote Chabot:[84] "Le propriétaire des salines était tenu de la faire mesurer par le fermier [the tax farmer], et de payer la taxe avant de le mettre en vente." I understand by this that the salt was measured and taxed not at the salt beds away from the city, but at the city gates. Whichever restoration is correct, whether at Palmyra there existed an excise or a sales tax on salt, a monopoly was clearly unknown.

A comparison of the impressions dealing with salt with those concerned with imported slaves affords further evidence against an assumption that there existed in Seleucid Babylonia a monopoly upon the sale of salt. In both groups the principal word of the legends, ἁλικῆς, ἀνδραποδικῆς, is formed in the same manner. Both varieties have the same symbol, the half-anchor, occupying a similar position on the field. It follows that both sets of impressions represent a single government office within the treasury. Owing to the absence of an essential distinction between the two varieties of impressions, if the ἁλική stamp is taken to represent a monopoly in the sale of salt, ἀνδραποδική must logically be assumed to stand for a monopoly in the sale of slaves. The latter supposition could be supported by no evidence, either direct or by analogy. Since in all other examples from Orchoi and Seleucia the half-anchor appears only on stamps that attest the satisfaction of some form of tax, usually in connection with a sale, and since this symbol is absent from the two varieties of impressions that refer to imposts other than taxes, the λιμένος stamp from Seleucia and those from Orchoi reading πλοίων Εὐφράτων,[85] it is only reasonable to assume that the ἁλική impressions likewise refer to a tax rather than to sales by a monopoly.

It will be well to discuss at this point the ownership of the archives to which the impressions dealing with salt belonged. It may not be assumed that the archives belonged to a public office of registration. Aside from the private nature of the house the character of the documents is hostile to this supposition. A wide variety of subjects would be represented in an office of registration, and numbers of documents pertaining to one subject would occur in the same year. The series of single

---

[84] *Op. cit.*, p. 32.
[85] See p. 173 and Rostovtzeff, *op. cit.*, pp. 43–44, Nos. 65, 66.

annual documents referring to salt make the assumption impossible. We must reject, likewise, the view that the inhabitants of the Great House were tax contractors over a succession of generations. In the first place, one would not expect to find impressions of their official stamps on bullae filed in the archives of such contractors. This follows from a consideration of the essential purpose served by bullae.[86] The assumption is rendered untenable by the occurrence in the archives of but one document in each year. Each tax contractor would have occasion during the year to stamp numbers of documents dealing with salt. Illustrations of this fact are impressions that occur on different bullae, IC1a(8) and (9), each dated in the year 193/92 B.C. One of these was found in Archive A; the other, on the surface. There remains but the alternative that the successive owners of the archives and of the Great House were private individuals, parties to the transactions of which the archives formed the record. In other words, the archives belonged to a family.

Were the archives a commercial or simply a household record? Do they represent receipts for salt purchased for household consumption, or have we to do with a merchant family, dealers in salt on the Seleucia market during the third and second centuries B.C.? Rostovtzeff has suggested that the series of bullae from Seleucia represent a set of household receipts.[87] The characteristics of the bullae, however, do not appear to support the hypothesis. It has already been pointed out that considerable variation existed in the length of the documents originally contained in the bullae. Transactions such as purchases for home consumption would involve only routine receipts, the form of which would not vary sufficiently to produce appreciable differences in the length of the papyrus or parchment upon which they were written. Again, it has been shown that the presence of the seals of witnesses on the bullae is opposed to an assumption that they encased routine receipts.[88] Among the impressions of private seals a number represent the portraits of Seleucid kings and queens. These can be adequately explained only by the supposition that they belonged to personal stewards of the royal family.[89] If receipts for household purchases by a private family had required the assistance of witnesses, one would not

[86] See pp. 7–9.
[88] See pp. 186–187.
[87] *Op. cit.*, p. 85.
[89] See Chapter VI.

expect to find among them personages of this class. The character and size of the Great House and the wealth of its owners render difficult an explanation of the archives as a household file. The archives were maintained in a formal way in rooms devoted exclusively to this purpose. The salt consumed by such a household and the receipts for the relatively petty tax obviously would have been inconsequential to a family of the position indicated by the evidence, and would in no way have justified the maintenance of such elaborate archives. Further proof is afforded by the two sets of formulae, "subject to tax" and "exempt from tax." If, as Rostovtzeff has suggested, the formulae apply to salt rather than to persons, and if the series of documents were the records of household purchases of salt, we have the situation that for the period covered by Archive A the family purchased exclusively salt that was subject to the tax, and then for a period of thirty-five years, represented by Archive B, bought only salt that was exempt from the tax. If, however, the formulae refer to persons, and if the bullae are taken again to represent a household file, it must be assumed that, after having paid the tax each year during the period covered by Archive A, for a succeeding period of thirty-five years this wealthy family was permitted to purchase its domestic supply of salt without payment of the tax. The second hypothesis is less unreasonable than the first, but both are strained. It must be kept in mind that, although the two formulae as found on the bullae in the archives are mutually exclusive in time, in Seleucia as a whole both might be found in regular occurrence each year. Whatever the interpretation of the two formulae may be, the use on official stamps of the phrase "subject to tax" implies the simultaneous existence of a state of exemption from tax in respect to the same commodity; the converse condition holds equally true. The fact that the formulae in the archives are strictly separated in time, one immediately succeeding the other, constitutes an exceptional condition that requires a reasonable explanation.

The significance of the separation in time of the two sets of bullae is heightened by a survey of the political circumstances that dominated the point of separation. The earliest document in Archive B, that is, of the series marked by the use of the phrase "free of tax," is dated in the year 188/87 B.C. Since the Babylonian calendar opened with the month Nisan, which generally coincides with our April, the date of the document may be placed between April, 188, and March, 187 B.C. In the year 188, after the signing of the peace with Rome by which the Seleucid Empire was obligated to the payment of a crushing indemnity, Antiochus III undertook a campaign into Persia in the hope of regaining there what he had lost in the west. He is supposed to have left Antioch for the east in the late summer or autumn.[90] It is to be presumed that Seleucia was the base from which the Persian expedition was organized. The latest mention in cuneiform of Antiochus III as king is dated in the year 125 A.S., with no month named.[91] On the basis of the Babylonian reckoning this is equivalent to the period between April, 187, and March, 186 B.C., approximately. The earliest extant tablet dated in the reign of Seleucus IV after the death of Antiochus is of Tammuz 11, in 125 A.S.[92] This date falls toward the end of July, 187 B.C. It follows that Antiochus was killed between April and July, approximately, of this year. A campaign in the hill country of Persia could not have gotten under way much before April. It would appear, therefore, that Antiochus had his headquarters in Seleucia from the autumn of 188 into the spring of 187, during the latter half of the year in which Archive B was opened. At this time not only had the treasury been drained by the war with Rome and the subsequent preparation of the first payment on the indemnity, but, in addition, Antiochus must have stood in bitter need of cash with which to sustain the new campaign into Persia. It is obvious that this was not a moment when any form of exemption from taxation would have been accorded.

At this point we should consider the significance of the three forms of legends that have to do with salt. At Orchoi there occurs only the simple form ἁλικῆς, and the earliest impression from Seleucia, No. IC1a(1), is similar. The terms "subject to tax" and "free of tax" represent a situation that arose in the Seleucia area and was not general throughout Babylonia. It

---

[90] A. Bouché-Leclercq, *Histoire des Séleucides*, I, 223; B. Niese, *Geschichte der griechischen und makedonischen Staaten*, III, 88; Alfred von Gutschmid, *Geschichte Irans*, p. 39.

[91] J. Strassmaier, "Zur Chronologie der Seleukiden," *Zeitschrift für Assyriologie*, 8 (1893), 110.

[92] Clay, *op. cit.*, Part II, pp. 12 ff.

has been shown that both forms were contemporary in Seleucia although mutually exclusive in time as they are found in the archives. In explanation of the occurrence of the three forms at Seleucia I offer the following hypothesis. The simple form found in Orchoi and in the early Seleucid period at our site represents the ἁλκή as generally administered. The other two forms constitute evidence of a practice possible only in an important financial as well as political center such as Seleucia, namely, the advance of cash to the royal treasury on the part of important merchants in anticipation of taxes. The formula ἁλικῆς | ἐπιτελῶν represents the current payment of the ἁλική; the phrase ἁλικῆς | ἀτελῶν impressed on a document attested that the transaction involved salt on which the tax had been paid in advance. This appears to provide the most satisfactory interpretation of the occurrence of the three forms at Seleucia, but not at Orchoi, and of the maintenance of the two archives in the Great House. I suggest that the owner of the house, a merchant in salt, made an advance to the treasury to meet in part the needs of the Persian campaign of Antiochus. Archive B was the record of transactions in salt that had been rendered free of tax in order to amortize this advance. These records would naturally be separated from the larger and general business archive of the firm, Archive A. The action of this particular merchant in no way constituted an exceptional occurrence, such as was perhaps the well-known incident of the payment by Hermias of the army of Antiochus III during the Molon rebellion.[93] The existence of one or the other of the two formulae from as early as the reign of Seleucus II, for instance, No. IC1a (2), indicates that such anticipatory payment of taxes was a recognized and regularly recurring practice. Its development may, of course, go back to some period of extraordinary strain upon the cash resources of the government.[94] Our evidence concerns salt; whether or not transactions in other commodities formed the basis for similar advances cannot be determined. Salt, a staple article *par excellence*, whose consumption never shows great variation, has been, of course, a favorite security for loans

---

[93] Polybius, v. 40.

[94] Seven of eight impressions dealing with salt which were found on the surface represent current payments of the tax. The anticipation of taxes, therefore, though a recognized practice, was resorted to, as with us today, with relative infrequency.

in many countries and periods. That the practice was not known at Orchoi or during the earlier years at Seleucia is to be expected; its normal occurrence would require the existence of accumulated capital beyond what was required by the regular channels of trade. It implies the existence of merchant-bankers.

It will be well at this point to recapitulate the argument with regard to the significance of the term ἁλική as employed in Seleucid Babylonia. We have already considered the evidence afforded by the character of the Great House, its size, and the wealth implied; by the formality of the organization in that house of two distinct archives; by the variation in the size of the bullae found in the archives; by the number of the private seals that had been impressed upon the bullae; and, finally, by the significance of the distinct formulae used to express the ἁλική and of the occurrence of these formulae in the archives in relation to the contemporary political and financial situation. On the basis of these factors it appears that there is no evidence for the existence of a monopoly upon the sale of salt; rather the ἁλική comprised a sales tax levied upon wholesale transactions. Normally this tax was paid upon the completion of particular transactions. But in Seleucia, on terms undoubtedly at least as favorable to the individual as to the government, the practice was recognized of cash advances to the treasury, which were liquidated as well as secured by a waiving of the tax over a stipulated period.

It has been stated that the salt tax was levied on wholesale transactions. It is possible to advance a step farther and to propose that it was collected on the first commercial turnover of salt. The handling of a commodity such as salt in the Orient today proceeds normally through three turnovers: producer or importer to wholesale merchant, wholesaler to the retail grocer, and retailer to the consumer. It is unlikely that in Seleucia there were recognized two categories of wholesale merchants through whose hands salt passed before it reached the retailer. In the transactions with which the archives are concerned the owners of the house must have been the buyers. This is indicated by the single transaction each year recorded by the archives. Single contracts for the supply of goods for a whole season constitute in certain instances reasonable business practice, whereas one sale per year would be most improbable. As buyers the house owners could not have been importers or producers. That they were not retail merchants buying from wholesale firms can be demonstrated on several grounds. It has already been stated that the variation in the length of the documents which the bullae encased argues that the transactions were not routine. They must have involved details that could not be adequately expressed by the formal phraseology of routine contracts. A contract on the part of a wholesale merchant with a producer to supply salt sufficient for the commerce of one year satisfies this condition; purchases by a retailer from a wholesale merchant would not be expected to show a perceptible variation. That a retailer would purchase on one contract a year's supply of salt is extremely unlikely; the capital involved would be excessive. The investment of large capital in a retail business is, of course, a very recent development in commerce. The wealth of the archive owners as evidenced by both the character of the house and the single purchase each year permits of only one conclusion: the firm were wholesale merchants on a large scale. Since they were the buyers, the opposite parties were necessarily the first handlers of salt, producers or importers, and the tax, therefore, was levied on the first turnover.

The collection of a tax on the first exchange of the commodity concerned was, perhaps, the normal procedure in the Seleucid Empire. Reference has already been made to the significance of the system of "octroi" taxation in Parthian Babylonia and to that of the Palmyrene usage. At Palmyra producers of salt brought their goods to a particular place, under the supervision of the tax farmer, where they were sold to merchants. As has been stated, owing to the incomplete condition of the texts a difference of opinion exists whether the tax was paid by the producers or the merchants. There may be a question also whether in a relatively small center such as Palmyra there was a category of wholesale merchants between producer and retailer. The evidence, however, does demonstrate that the tax was collected either prior to or upon the first turnover, probably the latter. In adopting this practice the Seleucid dynasty followed a natural principle. In the various commercial turnovers of commodities in countries such as Babylonia, Mesopotamia, and those of the western part of the empire at least the one point at which control by the government revenue service could have functioned both adequately and economically was upon the first arrival of commodities in the various cities and organized towns. The practice in the eastern satrapies cannot well be judged, owing to our lack of knowledge about the relation between city and country in the economic organization.

It has been assumed that the archive owners, that is, the buyers, paid the tax. In Ptolemaic Egypt the seller appears to have been responsible for the act of registration, and the buyer regularly paid the tax.[95] That a similar practice prevailed in Seleucid Babylonia is demonstrated by the uniform appearance of the stamp of the tax collector on our series of bullae. It has been shown that, in contrast with the documents they encased, the bullae bore only such impressions as the filing and accounting practice of an archive owner might require.[96] In the present instance, if the tax had not been paid by the buyer, the bullae in his archive would not have borne the stamp of the tax collector.

In this connection it should be noted that the absence of the impressions of seals of registration from the bullae that bear the ἁλική legends does not prove that the documents encased by the bullae were not registered. It does indicate that the archive owners, who had satisfied the tax, had not paid in addition a fee of registration. On two of the three bullae from Orchoi that are concerned with the salt tax occur impressions of what appear to be official seals of registration.[97] It is probable that in these instances one individual had paid both the tax and the registration fee, an unusual condition. The material from Seleucia demonstrates the existence of a complicated system of regulation of business by the government through forms of fiscal registration. Since the salt tax appears to have constituted a major source of revenue[98] and was definitely a sales tax, the evident importance attributed to registration by the financial adminis-

[95] Westermann, *op. cit.*, pp. 9–14 and 42.
[96] See pp. 7–9.
[97] Rostovtzeff, *op. cit.*, pp. 42–43, Nos. 62–64; cf. p. 82.
[98] Josephus, *Ant. Jud.*, xiii. 2. 3, and I Macc., x. 29, both contain accounts of a letter supposed to have been written by Demetrius I to the High Priest of the Jews seeking his support and promising the remission of taxes. The salt tax is singled out for particular mention. This clearly indicates the importance of the tax, although I cannot follow those who see in these references evidence for a compulsory consumption of salt.

tration argues strongly that the ἁλική was accompanied by an act of registration.

As we have seen, the ἁλική was functioning at Seleucia as early as 286/85 B.C., although the earliest example of the use of the formula "subject to tax" or "free of tax" dates from 229/28 B.C. The earliest impression belongs to the period when Antiochus I ruled in the east while Seleucus Nicator was busy consolidating his position in the west. The second date falls in the reign of Seleucus II. The organization of the salt tax as it functioned in Seleucid Babylonia as a whole must be credited to either Seleucus I or Antiochus I. The fact that no impressions have been found that belong to the period before Antiochus was sent to Seleucia, that is, prior to 293 or 292 B.C., does not prove, of course, that the salt tax was organized after that date. The political conditions to which the empire in general and Babylonia in particular were subjected in the decades prior to 293 and succeeding 280 B.C. do, however, suggest that it was Antiochus rather than his father who was responsible for the organization of the revenue service in the east.

CHAPTER VI

SEALS OF PRIVATE AGENTS OF ROYALTY

REFERENCE has already been made to a class of impressions that appear to bear the portraits of members of the Seleucid dynasty, both men and women, but that do not have the normal characteristics of official seals.[1] These impressions, with one exception, No. IIA2x(6), were found in the archives of the Great House, and must be assigned to the third and second centuries B.C. It was pointed out that in this period private individuals would not have employed their portraits as seal types. Beyond this general consideration the evidence afforded by the objects themselves offers a basis for their interpretation.

The impressions in question total thirty-one, of which thirteen represent women and eighteen, men. On twelve of the eighteen impressions it is clear that the men are represented as wearing the diadem; on three there are traces that suggest a diadem; one may show either a diadem or a wreath, one either a helmet or a kausia, and one the elephant scalp headdress of Alexander the Great and Demetrius II. The greater number of the eighteen impressions reveal a distinct effort at portraiture. This is true of the one impression on which it is difficult to distinguish whether the headdress is a diadem or a wreath. There can be no supposition that these impressions represent deities. The female heads or busts have been executed in a more conventionalized manner. But, on the other hand, not one displays a symbol or other characteristic that would suggest the interpretation of this group as representations of female deities.[2] It would be possible to assume that the portrayal of female forms, considered apart, is a representation of private women. However, in view of the fact that the impressions of male heads portray royalty, a like interpretation is required of the group of female heads and busts. That is, we cannot assume a condition

---

[1] See pp. 29–30. In the catalog they occupy pages 65–73.
[2] See No. IIIA1d(6), p. 83, a female head with which is associated a crescent. The representation here is of a deity, probably Artemis.

that involved a frequent occurrence of the portraits of women as seal types and the absence of a corresponding use of the portraits of men in private life. On the basis of the evidence all this class of impressions must be taken to represent royalty, in other words, members of the Seleucid dynasty.

The characteristic of size is of significance for the interpretation of these impressions. Those showing the portraits of men have an average size of $12^+ \times 9$ mm.; those representing women, $11^+ \times 8.5^+$ mm. Only one is fairly large, 16×14 mm. The impressions that have royal portraits as types, but that have been classed as official, are all incomplete. Their incomplete dimensions give an average of $22^+ \times 22^+$ mm. None when complete had a short diameter of less than 20 mm. On the basis of size, therefore, the class of impressions under consideration is entirely distinct from impressions of official seals. On the other hand, the average dimensions of the class correspond closely to those of normal private seals.

The quality of engraving represented by the class is rather uniform and is consistently superior to the average quality shown by the impressions of private seals. It falls short, however, of the best workmanship displayed by private seals and of the average maintained by the official seals. The quality of the impressions renders impossible an assumption that they represent the personal private seals of royalty. Such seals would be characterized by superior engraving.

It has been stated that, with one exception, the impressions of royal heads were found in the archives of the Great House. Two of them occur on bullae alongside stamps attesting the satisfaction of the salt tax, No. IIA1m(1) with No. IC1b(21), No. IIB1b(1) with No. IC1b(10). The impression bearing the jugate heads of Cleopatra and Alexander Bala, No. IIA1q(1), is associated with No. IA1d(1), concerned with a transaction in slaves. All the impressions are on incomplete fragments of bullae or on single appended sealings. Since the archives were concerned chiefly with commerce in salt, it would appear that these impressions were in some way related to transactions in this commodity. Additional evidence that they were not official is afforded by the fact that the portraits do not occur on some complete bullae that are characteristic of those concerned with salt, but are found on others. It has been pointed out that this class of bullae regularly show the impressions of three small seals beside the impression of the tax stamp. If the impressions of royal portraits were official, that is, if they represented some department of state, they would occur on all the bullae belonging to one essentially homogeneous series. The provenance of the impressions serves again to confirm the fact that they do not represent personal seals of members of the royal family. The archives were of a definitely commercial character with which members of the dynasty would not be concerned in a direct personal way.

The evidence concerning this class of impressions may be summarized as follows. They have as types portraits of members of the Seleucid royal family. They represent neither seals of departments of state nor the personal seals of royalty. They are in some way connected with the commercial transactions in which the owners of the archives were engaged. An interpretation that appears to meet these conditions in a satisfactory manner is afforded by an assumption that the impressions were made by seals of personal business agents of the royal family. This interpretation explains the use of the royal type on seals that by reason of their size and the quality of execution appear to have been employed by private individuals of no exalted rank. Individual members of the Seleucid dynasty must have had various sorts of personal agents, stewards who managed their private affairs. So far as a record has been preserved, the principal source of private income for the royal family was that derived from estates in various parts of the empire. That members of the dynasty, including women, held such lands individually is made evident by inscriptions dealing with royal holdings in both Asia Minor and Babylonia.[3] The activity of royal stewards in Seleucia throughout the period from the reign of Seleucus I to that of Demetrius II as attested by the class of impressions under discussion can best be explained by the supposition that these men were in charge of royal estates in Babylonia. In the consideration of the salt tax it has been shown that the small seal

[3] Theodor Wiegand, *Milet, Ergebnisse der Ausgrabungen und Untersuchungen seit dem Jahre 1899* (Berlin, 1928), VI, 36; W. Dittenberger, *Orientis Graecae Inscriptiones Selectae*, No. 225; C. F. Lehmann-Haupt, "Sprechsal: Noch einmal Kassû," *Zeitschrift für Assyriologie*, 7 (1892), 330–332; cf. W. Westermann, "Land Registers of Western Asia under the Seleucids," *Classical Philology*, 16(1921), 12–19; M. I. Rostovtzeff, "Syria and the East," *The Cambridge Ancient History*, VII, 167.

impressions on the bullae, which include those with the royal portraits, represent the sellers of the salt to the owners of the archives, together with the witnesses to the contracts. The occurrence of extensive salt beds on estates in present-day Babylonia argues for a similar condition in ancient times. It is held by some writers that the subjects of the Seleucid kings were compelled to purchase a certain amount of salt annually.[4] Whether or not this is true it will be generally granted that salt played a much more important rôle in the domestic economy of ancient than of modern times. In the absence of systems of refrigeration salt was the common preservative for all foodstuffs. It is entirely reasonable to assume that the presence of salt beds added to the value of estate holdings, and that, consequently, some of the royal estates in Babylonia included in their products the supply of salt for the Seleucia market. It must be kept in mind, of course, that the royal estates were not the sole local producers of salt. That such was not true is demonstrated by the fact that the archives contained bullae concerned with salt on which the impression of the seal of a royal steward does not occur. The royal family personally no more than the state officially established a monopoly in the supply of salt. The revenues derived from the estates were based apparently on production and sale in a competitive market. Whatever the means employed by the dynasty to obtain possession of their domain, whether by inheritance from the Achemenids or by confiscation of private or temple lands, there is no evidence of a distinction in business practice between the royal estates, once they were acquired, and those privately owned.

The fact of the acquisition of lands in Babylonia by the royal family is well established by cuneiform texts. Lehmann-Haupt has discussed an important tablet that deals with a gift of grain, lands, and other goods by Laodice, wife of Antiochus II, to temple corporations.[5] Antiochus is represented as having given to his wife and their sons lands that formed a part of the royal estates, as Lehmann-Haupt translates, "die Saatfelder des eignen Palastes." These lands, along with other goods, Laodice in turn made over "an die Babylonier, Borsippäer, and Ku-

---

[4] M. I. Rostovtzeff, "Seleucid Babylonia: Bullae and Seals of Clay with Greek Inscriptions," *Yale Classical Studies*, 3 (1932), 82, 85.

[5] *Loc. cit.*

thäer," a phrase which refers, apparently, to temple communities around Babylon. We are not concerned here with the motives that led to this double transfer, but only with the fact of the existence of royal estates in Babylonia owned by individual members of the royal family. This same Laodice is represented in an inscription from Asia Minor as a purchaser of lands from her husband.[6] This individual ownership rather than the retention of the estates by the head of the royal house in each generation is emphasized by our impressions. The two instances of the occurrence of jugate heads, Nos. IIA1q(1) and IIA1s(2), must be taken as evidence of joint ownership of estates by the king and queen. The normal practice, however, appears to have provided for the ownership of revenue lands by the individual princesses of the Seleucid line.

It is instructive to compare the tablet published by Lehmann-Haupt with one in the British Museum first published by Strassmaier and more recently translated and discussed by Sidney Smith.[7] I quote a part of Smith's translation:

". . . in the 37th year, Antiochus [the First] and Seleucus [his son]. In the month of Adar on the 9th the governor of Akkad and the town magistrates of the king who went to Sapardu in the 36th year to the king returned to Seleucia, the royal city on the Tigris. They wrote (?) their rescripts to the Babylonians. In Teshri on the twelfth they brought the Babylonians out to Seleucia. In that month the governor of Akkad acquired the seed-land which they gave in the 32nd year according to the king's wish for the food supply of the inhabitants of Babylon, Borsippa and Kuthah, and the oxen, sheep and everything whatever which in the towns and cities according to the king's wish unto the Babylonians they gave, for the king's household. In that year a quantity of bricks for rebuilding E.SAG.ILA were made above and below Babylon . . . with sun dried brick in . . . . There was a famine in Akkad. The people hired their children for silver. The people died of hunger. In that year there was much scabies in the country. They paid current prices in Babylon and the cities in copper coins of Greece. . . ."

The importance of the account for our immediate purposes lies in the sentence which relates that the governor of Akkad acquired for the king's household certain lands and cattle that had previously been given to the people of Babylon, Borsippa,

---

[6] Wiegand, op. cit., VI, 36.

[7] J. Strassmaier, "Neue babylonische Planeten Tafeln," Zeitschrift für Assyriologie, VI (1890), 234; S. Smith, Babylonian Historical Texts, p. 150; cf. C. F. Lehmann-Haupt, "Hellenistische Forschungen," Klio, 3 (1903), 491.

and Kuthah. Let me quote first Smith's comment on the passage:[8] "The satrap had to send orders to the Babylonians which entailed the removal of the civilian population [By this Smith refers to the non-priestly population.] to Seleucia; it is not clear whether this was due to the difficulty of feeding the population during the prevalent famine, for military or other reasons. He also had to commandeer the land and cattle distributed amongst the people five years earlier; the wretched inhabitants were left to die of starvation and disease. In a few years the good which Seleucus had done in Babylonia by pursuing Alexander's policy was effectively undone." Mr. Smith connects the famine with the acquisition of lands and cattle by the governor, and the latter with the general military or economic situation. In the reference to the cattle and other things "which in the towns and cities according to the king's wish unto the Babylonians they gave," he appears to assume that "Babylonians" is synonymous with "inhabitants of Akkad." For the famine was "in Akkad"; it was general. I take it rather that the distribution of goods in the thirty-second year and their recovery in the thirty-seventh year applies only to the inhabitants of Babylon, Borsippa, and Kuthah.

It should be noted that in the tablet published by Lehmann-Haupt these three names are again associated in a gift to the temples. The "they" who are the givers of the distribution in the thirty-second year refers to the people of "the towns and cities." The distribution was intended for the mass of people who had become dependent upon the temple communities. The removal of a great number of these people to Seleucia, apparently the greater part of the population, resulted in an excess of land and cattle around the old centers. The emigrants must have been provided with a means of livelihood in and around the new city. They certainly were not brought to the capital city to starve or to beg. Was it not true of ancient as of present-day cities in the Orient that a considerable part of the population was actually engaged in agriculture, cultivating fields and gardens within an area of two hours' walk from the edge of the city proper although living within the walls? It is not possible that the enormous population of Seleucia was able to support itself by trade and industry alone. It is entirely reasonable to assume

[8] *Op. cit.*, p. 153.

that the "Babylonians" transferred to the new site were to a large extent intended to supply the city with food and to serve as customers to the Greek tradesmen. To them must have been assigned garden, grain, and grazing land on the outskirts of Seleucia.

The text states that in the thirty-second year the governor of Akkad re-acquired the lands and cattle around Babylon "for the king's household," in the Babylonian "bît sărri." In view of the context it must be assumed that the governor's act was connected with the previous transfer of the people to Seleucia; it offset a corresponding grant of lands and cattle upon their arrival at the new site. The phrase "for the king's household" would not have been employed if the purpose of the governor had been to "commandeer" goods for the state, for military or economic reasons. The phrase implies that they were destined for the king personally, not as the head of the state. I think it reasonable to assume that the lands around Babylon vacated by the emigrants became royal estate. It is probable, therefore, that these emigrants had been settled on royal land around Seleucia. The acreage so taken up by the new settlers became city land. It is clear that Antiochus was far from wrecking the policy of Alexander, as Smith suggests. The tablet describes a simple settlement of people from an overcrowded center to a more favorable site, accompanied by the necessary transfer in the title of lands and goods that could not well be moved. The reference to the "famine in Akkad" is unrelated to the account of the transfer. The reconstruction of ESAGILA is the second item in the record of an effort on the part of Antiochus to rehabilitate Babylonia, which had suffered severely during the temporary occupation by Antigonus. The account is important for an appreciation of the rôle played by Antiochus in the establishment of the Seleucid Empire. Of immediate significance are the reference to royal estates near Babylon on the Euphrates and the implied reference to other royal lands around Seleucia on the Tigris.

The tablet from the British Museum pictures the acquisition of royal estates around Babylon; that published by Lehmann-Haupt may well represent the return of these same lands to the temple communities by Laodice, who was the daughter of Antiochus I as well as his daughter-in-law. The later tablet is incomplete. In describing the original gift of the lands by Antiochus II to Laodice it reads: "Antiochus the king [the Second] had effected a favorable enactment. All that Antiochus his father [the First] and Seleucus his grandfather . . . the grainfields of his own palace. . . ." I suggest that in its original form this account refers — in respect to a part of the estate near Babylon inherited by Antiochus II — to the real property acquired by Antiochus I in exchange for the land around Seleucia donated by him for the settlement of the Babylonians. The return of the properties by Laodice in no way presupposes an act of restitution. During the wars of the Diadochi the temples suffered along with the rest of Babylonia. As Sidney Smith has stated elsewhere in the work cited: "It may be noted here that the ruin of Babylon is to be attributed to the savagery of Antigonus; the founding of Seleucia on the return of Seleucus was due to the necessity of finding accommodation for the people, and not from any desire to destroy the ancient city."[9] The work of Antiochus in Babylonia while Seleucus was occupied in the west, as well as after the death of his father, was one of reconstruction. By the reign of Antiochus II this must have borne fruit. The reconstruction of the temples in part, at least, would be followed by an increase in population that would again require the lands left vacant by the emigrants of the previous generation. Whether this population would continue to contribute to the private revenues of the dynasty or whether, as in an earlier age, the temples were to become their overlords must have been a matter of prime policy to the priesthood. What may have been the motives of Laodice in her gift and what she secured in return do not concern us. Her act was in any case a recognition of economic necessity.

The existence of a class of seals representing personal agents of the royal family would have to be assumed even in the absence of proof. In all the Hellenistic monarchies the ruling families were active in the development of sources of personal revenues. The individuals who managed their private business would not, in most cases, be a part of the administrative bureaucracy; yet they must have possessed greater powers than did the stewards of private individuals. The apparent commingling of state and private transactions on the part of high officials in Ptolemaic

[9] *Op. cit.*, p. 136.

Egypt, as witnessed by the correspondence of Zeno, cannot be taken as characteristic of Hellenistic practice.[10] Actually the letters prove no confusion in the theory of administrative organization, but only a tendency on the part of powerful officials to make use of their positions for personal advantage. The number of private agents of the royal family in each country must have been large. Inevitably there would develop a type of seal that would establish the authority of these stewards and yet serve to distinguish them from officials in the state administration.

In this connection one should note the occurrence in other parts of the Hellenistic world of seal impressions and gems which bear the portraits of rulers, but which do not appear to have an official character. J. G. Milne has described a group of sealings now in the Royal Ontario Museum that belong to the Ptolemaic period in Egypt.[11] In form these objects correspond approximately to the "appended sealings" from Seleucia.[12] Among the seal impressions to be found on them are a number of portraits of members of the Ptolemaic royal family, kings, queens, and in some instances family groups. The size ranges from 20 × 14 mm. to 8 × 6 mm. The quality of engraving represented by the impressions varies considerably and for the most part is not consistent with that to be expected in personal seals of royalty. None show legends. In all their characteristics these impressions appear to be similar to the corresponding group from Seleucia. Milne has suggested that the seals by which they were made were official. However, in view of the new evidence it appears reasonable to classify them as of private agents or of stewards of royalty. Additional examples of this class of seals may be found in Furtwängler's standard work on antique gems, to which reference has repeatedly been made in the catalog. Disregarding the numerous portrait seals of Roman times one finds a large group of gems of the Hellenistic period that bear the likenesses of royal personages. Some of this group have dimensions that permit of their classification as official seals. Thirteen, however, are comparable in size as well as in motif to the class of impressions from Seleucia and represent, I believe, seals of

---

[10] M. I. Rostovtzeff, "Ptolemaic Egypt," *The Cambridge Ancient History*, VII, 120, 135.

[11] *The Journal of Hellenic Studies*, 36 (1916), 87.

[12] See pp. 2–3 and 9–10.

private agents of royalty. The size varies from 10.5 × 9.5 to 19 × 18 mm., with average dimensions of 16.8 × 14 mm. The design of each represents a man's head or bust accompanied by one of the distinctive insignia of royalty, usually the diadem. The quality of the execution is good without being remarkable.[13] Furtwängler shows also a number of Hellenistic gems which bear the portraits of women and which in style, execution, and size resemble closely the corresponding group from Seleucia. A conclusive determination of their significance, whether they represent royal ladies or private individuals, is beyond the scope of this discussion. It would depend, of course, upon the date and the provenance of each gem in relation to the period in which one might expect the use of the portrait as a seal design on the part of private individuals.[14]

[13] A. Furtwängler, *Die Antiken Gemmen*, Pl. 31, Nos. 16, 19, 20; Pl. 32, Nos. 4, 8, 10, 12, 13, 22, 24, 28; Pl. 33, Nos. 12, 21.

[14] Professor A. E. R. Boak has kindly called to my attention the fact that the expedition of the University of Michigan excavating Dimê in the Fayûm has found impressions of official seals which bear the portraits of Roman emperors, sometimes unaccompanied by legends. The seals were apparently small. This material will be published shortly by Professor Boak.

CHAPTER VII

NOTES ON THE ICONOGRAPHY OF THE IMPRESSIONS

IN THE catalog of impressions the basis for the identification of certain representations of royal personages was omitted for the sake of brevity. Four of these impressions, Nos. IA3a(1), IA3c(1), IA3o(1), and IA3o(2), are of official seals, and one, No. IIA1a(1), is of the seal of a royal steward. Nos. IA3a(1) and IIA1a(1) have been described in the catalog as likenesses of Seleucus I. The identification will now be discussed. No. IIA1a(1) represents an aged man with beard and mustache and wearing a diadem. No. IA3a(1) has been partly obscured by the superimpression of another seal; only the front of the head may be distinguished. The nature of the headdress cannot be determined. A beard and mustache are clearly shown. These features and the line of the forehead, the eyebrows, and nose are closely similar on both impressions. The fact that one has been made by an official seal and the other by that of a steward creates a difference in the quality of the execution. There can be no doubt, however, that both represent one individual. No. IA3a(1) occurs on a bulla alongside two other impressions of official seals that have portraits as types. One, No. IA1b(1), is a characteristic portrayal of Antiochus I; the other, No. IA1c(1), the portrait of a young man, has been obscured, and the presence or absence of a diadem cannot be determined. The second likeness of Seleucus, No. IIA1a(1), is found on a bulla that carries in addition the impress of a private seal.

Impression No. IA3a(1) is closely related to the "head of Zeus" on early coins of Seleucus I.[1] The attribution to Zeus is based on the presence of a laurel wreath. However, the features — the forehead, the nose, and especially the eye — are those of our impressions. The form of the beard and the mustache is also similar. On certain coins of Antiochus I appears a portrait that is considered to represent the best-known likeness of

---

[1] G. F. Hill, *Catalogue of the Greek Coins of Arabia, Mesopotamia and Persia*, Pl. XXIII, 2; E. Babelon, *Les Rois de Syrie, d'Arménie et de Commagène*, Pl. III, 2–4.

Seleucus I.[2] He is shown without beard or mustache, wearing the diadem, and horned. The features of Seleucus on these coins, however, are essentially those portrayed on our impressions. I find a striking resemblance between this portrait of Seleucus and the particular "Zeus heads" on other coins of Seleucus. On a copper coin of Antiochus I issued in Greece the obverse shows a bearded and laurel-crowned head that approximates again the features of Seleucus I.[3] I think there can be no doubt that the coins of Seleucus which have been cited and the coin of Antiochus struck in Greece were intended to represent either Zeus with the features of Seleucus or Seleucus with those of Zeus. It should be kept in mind that the likeness of Seleucus that shows him with horns as well as the diadem was intended to portray him as both god and king. Our small impression, No. IIA1a(1), depicts Seleucus as an old man, king but without attributes of divinity. This is in keeping with the purpose served by the seal. The impression suggests that Seleucus actually wore a beard in his old age. Babelon has remarked that Seleucus II, Antiochus IV, and Demetrius II must all be presumed to have grown beards for the purpose of furthering their assimilation to deities.[4] The same conjecture holds true for Seleucus I. On our other impression, No. IA3a(1), made by an official seal, the presence or absence of a laurel wreath cannot be determined. In view of the close similarity between this representation and those of Seleucus-Zeus on the coins it is probable that the laurel wreath was present, and that the seal portrayed Seleucus as Zeus. The god Seleucus of our impression and of the coins is naturally mature without, however, definite indications of old age. In this respect there is a sharp contrast between the two impressions.

The portrait of the aged Seleucus as king requires the assignment of impression No. IIA1a(1) to the closing years of his reign, but a few years prior to 280 B.C. Impression No. IA3a(1) must be dated within somewhat broader limits. We may disregard for the moment a consideration of the dates on the coins and of the chronology for the apotheosis of Seleucus. As has been stated, the impression is accompanied by two others of

[2] F. Imhoof-Blumer, *Monnaies grecques*, Pl. H, 10; idem, *Porträtköpfe*, Pl. III, 8; cf. idem, *Monnaies grecques*, p. 424; Babelon, *op. cit.*, p. xiv.
[3] Babelon, *op. cit.*, Pl. V, 9.   [4] *Op. cit.*, p. cxlvii.

official seals, one a portrait of Antiochus as a mature man, the other a representation of a youth. The latter as the type of an official seal associated with representations of Seleucus and Antiochus must be identified as a portrait of a son of Antiochus. It will be shown below that the choice is limited to Seleucus, the elder son of Antiochus, rather than to the younger, later to become Antiochus II. On cuneiform tablets the young Seleucus is first mentioned as co-ruler with his father in 32 A.S.; the latest tablet with his name falls in the year 49.[5] This provides a range of eighteen years after the death of Seleucus I during which the portrait of this prince may have been employed as the type of official seals. It cannot be presumed that this would have been done before the death of the grandfather. On the other hand, seals distinguished by a representation of Seleucus I may well have been continued in use after his death, especially if the god-ruler was portrayed. In all probability the founder of the dynasty was so honored for but a few years after his death, when his types were entirely superseded by those of Antiochus. It is perhaps safe to assign the bulla and its impressions to the period between 280 and 275 B.C. This does not, of course, fix the date for the fabrication of the seals themselves; the signet which bore the portrait of Seleucus I may have been in use for some years prior to his death.

Even though, as appears probable, the seal type portrayed him as the god-ruler, our inability to fix a precise date for the seal itself renders it of little value in a study of the apotheosis of Seleucus. If, however, the features portrayed on our two impressions representing Seleucus I are, as I believe, identical with those of the Zeus head on the coins, certain considerations present themselves with regard to the period within which the deification of the Nicator was promulgated. If the coins record some form of assimilation of Seleucus to Zeus, the chronological sequence of the coins should throw light not only upon the date for the apotheosis but perhaps upon the manner of development of the concept itself. Among the obverse types that display a Zeus head with the features of Seleucus is one that antedates the assumption of the royal title in 306 B.C.[6] This is indicative

[5] J. K. Beloch, *Griechische Geschichte* [2], IV, 2, 199.
[6] Hill, *op. cit.*, p. 192, No. 64; Pl. XXIII, 3; cf. B. Niese, *Geschichte der griechischen und makedonischen Staaten*, I, 321; Diodorus Siculus, *Bibliotheca Historia*, xx. 53. 4.

of an effort on the part of the new ruler to establish his authority through the claims of divinity before he dared demand obedience as king. Indeed, it would be interesting to determine whether the action of Antigonus in proclaiming himself king, a move which Seleucus was obliged to follow, interrupted a program on the part of the latter that had not contemplated such a direct answer to the perplexing question of a satisfactory basis for world rulership. The wide variety in the obverse types during his reign suggests a hesitation, even the lack of a fixed program, on the part of Seleucus and his advisers. Two of these types should be noted. Both are acknowledged portraits of the beardless Seleucus; on one the head is covered by a helmet, to which are fastened horns, traditionally symbols of divinity; on the other the horns are attached directly to the head, which is encircled by a diadem.[7] It is the latter of these two portraits that so closely resembles the features of our two impressions.[8] Without doubt Babelon is correct in his assumption that these types were adopted by Seleucus in response to the appearance on the coinages of Ptolemy and Lysimachus of Alexander heads with the horns of Zeus Ammon.[9] But the horns associated with the representations of Seleucus are not those of Zeus Ammon; they indicate divinity, but suggest no assimilation to Zeus. The two types of heads showing the features of Seleucus, one bearded and laurel-crowned, the other horned, appear to represent two distinct approches to an apotheosis of the ruler. In contrast to the hesitant advance on the problem suggested by these two concepts, the two types of Seleucus that show him with the horns of divinity indicate a progression in a definite program. The appearance of the horns as an ornament on the helmet prepares the way for the portrayal of Seleucus with these symbols attached to the head itself. There is need for a new study of the coin types of Seleucus and Antiochus on the basis both of their sequence in time and of the particular areas in which they were intended to circulate. The apotheosis of the Seleucid royal family clearly was not attained by a regular progression. It was influenced not only by contemporary foreign events but by varying degrees of resistance within the empire.

[7] Babelon, *op. cit.*, Pl. I, 14; F. Imhoof-Blumer, *Porträtköpfe*, Pl. III, 8.
[8] See p. 210.
[9] Babelon, *op. cit.*, p. xix.

Mention has already been made of a seal impression associated on a single bulla with representations of Seleucus I and Antiochus. This impression, No. IA1c(1), bears the portrait of a young man. Owing to smearing, the presence or absence of a diadem cannot be determined. The size and quality, however, point to the official character of the seal. The features suggest those of Seleucus I, but with certain distinctions that are more characteristic of portraits of Antiochus II. That Antiochus I had a son Seleucus older than Antiochus II, who met his end before the death of his father, has long been known from inscriptions and cuneiform tablets as well as from references in minor classical authors.[10] Further evidence regarding this prince is furnished by models of coins from Seleucia that bear the portrait of Antiochus I on the obverse, but on the reverse show the legend βασιλέως Σελεύκου.[11] This younger Seleucus exercised royal power as co-ruler with his father. The cuneiform texts join his name to that of his father as co-ruler for a period of eighteen years. It is only after 266 B.C. that he is definitely replaced by his brother, Antiochus II.[12] Since our impression has associated with it those bearing the representations of Seleucus I as well as of Antiochus I, and since it is unlikely that the seal types of the Nicator would persist for almost twenty years after his death, adequate ground is afforded for the assignment of the portrait to the younger Seleucus. The identification is supported by the evident relation of the features portrayed to those of both Seleucus I and Antiochus II, the grandfather and the brother.

Adequate account has not been taken of the importance of the young Seleucus in the early history of the Seleucid dynasty. After the death of Seleucus I Antiochus was occupied for some years with the preservation and the organization of the provinces in the west, Syria and Asia Minor. The seal impression and the coin models from Seleucia supplement the literary evidence to indicate that the prince Seleucus ruled the east, thus perpetuating the arrangement made by his grandfather for the residence

---

[10] W. Dittenberger, *Orientis Graecae Inscriptiones Selectae*, I, 220, 246; J. Strassmaier, "Zur Chronologie der Seleukiden," *Zeitschrift für Assyriologie*, 8 (1893), 108; Trogus Pompeius, *Prologus*, 26; John of Antioch in C. Müller, *Fragmenta Historicorum Graecorum*, IV, 558, fragment 55.

[11] See pp. 247–248, Nos. IVa(1) and IVa(2).

[12] Strassmaier, *loc. cit.*

of the heir-apparent in Seleucia. The passage from John of Antioch, already cited, suggests at least the threat of a revolt on the part of the prince against Antiochus. The coin models with their legend "King Seleucus," unaccompanied by the name of Antiochus, support this possibility.

It remains to consider the basis for the identification of two other portraits on official seal impressions, Nos. IA30(1) and (2).[13] It has been assumed that they represent Timarchus and his brother Heracleides. The evidence, however, is indirect, and the characteristics of the impressions include elements that are perplexing.

There can be no question that the impressions are of official seals. Although incomplete, they are among the largest that have been found at Seleucia. The quality of engraving displayed is superior to that of any of the other impressions that are known to have an official character. The two impressions occur on a single bulla, along with four small impressions of private seals. In respect to their occurrence and associations they appear to be similar to seals of registration. No legend is visible on them. However, they are incompletely impressed, and the presence or absence of legends on the seals with which they were made cannot be determined. The bulla on which the impressions occur was found definitely below the floor of a room in Level III of the Great House. It belongs to a late date in the occupation of Level IV. Since this level approximately coincides in time with the extent of Seleucid rule in Babylonia, the impressions must be assigned to one of the later reigns. The private seals impressed on the bulla possessed designs that are common on sealings of the Seleucid period, but that are not found on those of Parthian times. The portraits themselves are of the best Greek workmanship, and the features of the two individuals are distinctly Western, not Oriental. In short, the evidence requires the designation of these impressions as of seals of departments of state within the Seleucid Empire. The portraits as the types of official seals must represent men who exercised dominion over that part of the empire which included Seleucia toward the close of the period of Seleucid control of Babylonia.

Over against these conclusions must be set certain characteristics of the impressions that render them distinctive. As a

[13] See p. 209.

rule the portraits of rulers that appear on the other seals of departments of state included in the catalog [14] show them with divine or royal attributes. A diadem, laurel wreath, or radiate crown may be distinguished on all that have not suffered through overimpression or wear. The two portraits under consideration, however, represent men, one wearing a petasos-like hat or kausia, the other bareheaded. Neither wears the diadem. Again, both on the seals and on their coinages the Seleucid kings are shown with heads turned right; on the two impressions the heads face left. These characteristics force the conclusion that the portraits do not represent members of the Seleucid dynasty.

It is evident that for the identification of the portraits one is limited to the small group of rebels against the authority of the dynasty in the eastern provinces, individuals who exercised for a period the substance of royal power before they dared openly proclaim themselves king. Years ago Percy Gardner remarked that coins of Antiochus II issued in Bactria shortly prior to the revolt of Diadotes show on the obverse the features of the latter, although the formal representation is of the king. That is, the revolting governor prepared the way for his open assumption of power by accustoming the public to the presence of his portrait on official monuments.[15] The two recorded instances of revolt against the Seleucid power that affected Babylonia before its occupation by the Parthians are those that concern Molon and Timarchus. Molon made himself independent about 220 B.C., almost eighty years before the close of occupation of Level IV of the Great House. The evidence of the provenance of the impressions is, therefore, against an attempt to associate them with this effort of Molon. Further adverse evidence is afforded by the fact that Molon entered Babylonia from his own provinces to the east only after he was a proclaimed rebel.[16] Documents issued under his authority in Seleucia would show him with the attributes of royalty. The revolt of Timarchus took place some time between the death of Antiochus IV about 164 B.C. and his own overthrow by Demetrius I in 160 B.C. At the time of his revolt he was satrap of Babylonia and in control of Media farther east.[17] In respect both to its date and to its place of

---

[14] Pp. 44–47, Nos. IA3a(1) to IA3m(1).
[15] P. Gardner, *The Seleucid Kings of Syria*, p. xvi.
[16] Polybius, v. 41.   [17] Niese, *op. cit.*, III, 247.

origin, therefore, the revolt of Timarchus satisfies the conditions imposed by the impressions. In his attempt Timarchus was aided by his brother, Heracleides.[18]

The exact relationship of this brother to the revolt is not stated by our extant sources. As finance minister under Antiochus IV, as well as at the moment of the revolt, he must have been possessed of wide authority. We know, further, that he personally managed the successful movement to overthrow Demetrius in favor of Alexander Bala.[19] The contemporary use of the two portraits as seal types requires an assumption that two individuals shared in some degree the powers of state. On the evidence of his coins Timarchus alone became king in name.[20] Whatever may have been the status of Heracleides in the movement, it was but natural that Timarchus as the elder brother should assume the diadem.[21] That the sources show Heracleides to have been banished, whereas Timarchus was killed, has little significance. There is no evidence that the younger brother fell into the hands of Demetrius. The rôle played by Heracleides in the movement of Alexander Bala proves his continued hostility to Demetrius. If, as the evidence appears to require, the two portraits are identified as Timarchus and Heracleides, it must be assumed that the latter, at least in the organization of the revolt and at its outbreak, was actively associated with his brother. We know from the evidence of Diodorus Siculus that Timarchus, anticipating his open rebellion, had collected a great army in Media ostensibly in the service of the state.[22] It is quite possible that in his capacity as finance minister for the empire Heracleides in similar manner had arranged in advance of the outbreak for the accumulation of important funds in the treasury at Seleucia. It is assumed, therefore, that our impressions belong to the period just prior to the actual outbreak of rebellion, or shortly after the event, before there had been opportunity to prepare new seals of state that would represent Timarchus as king.

The question will be raised whether one of the portraits on the bulla resembles the features of Timarchus as found on the

---

[18] Appian, *Syriaca*, viii. 45, 47.   [19] *Ibid.*
[20] Babelon, *op. cit.*, p. 89, No. 702.
[21] See Hans Volkmann, "Demetrius I. und Alexander I. von Syrien," *Klio*, 19 (1925), 392.   [22] xxxi. 27.

obverse of his coins. So far as I am able to determine, neither of the portraits approximates those on coins assigned either to Molon or to Timarchus. Indeed, they resemble none of the heads that appear on the Seleucid coinage. There is no adequate reason, however, to assign the portrait on the coins of Timarchus to the usurper. The revolt became overt after Demetrius I had murdered the *de facto* king Antiochus V, youthful son of Antiochus IV. The portrait of Antiochus V is well known from his coins. There is to me a remarkable resemblance between the so-called portrait of Timarchus on his coins and that of Antiochus V. The sole difference of significance lies in the age; the coins of the former show a mature face whereas on those of the latter the expression is youthful. Since the revolt was crushed by Demetrius within a year, the coins of Timarchus represent his first issues. I suggest that in these issues he intentionally preserved as obverse type a portrait that would not represent a break with the legitimate coinage. Diadotes, the revolted satrap of Bactria, though giving to the portrait of Antiochus II his own features, retained on the coins of successive issues the formal appearance of both the obverse and reverse types of his legitimate predecessor. Babelon has remarked in this connection: "pour faire accepter plus facilement leurs espèces dans les transactions commerciales, les satrapes devenus rois ont dû reproduire les types monétaires en vogue dans leurs pays respectifs au moment de leur revolte." [23] Coins unlike seals of state employed on domestic commercial documents must necessarily have been acceptable to people beyond the limits of the power that had issued them. If Timarchus had been able to maintain his position, his later coins without doubt would have borne his real likeness. The retention on his first issues of the features of the legitimate king whom he succeeded was but part of a prudent fiscal policy.

The impression which has been regarded as representing the portrait of Timarchus requires special consideration. It is distinguished from the other by the petasos-like hat or kausia. A coin model from Seleucia has as obverse type a male bust shown with a similar hat worn over the diadem.[24] The features have become partly obscured. So far as they may be distinguished, one remarks a certain resemblance to the portrait on

[23] P. lix.   [24] See pp. 249–250, No. 7a(1).

the seal impression, but it is not possible to make a definite identification. The model, however, represents a king recognized in Seleucia during the period prior to the Parthian conquest. The petasos or kausia never appears on the Seleucid coinage. Its use is characteristic of the coins of Antimachos of Bactria, who reigned during the first half of the second century B.C., that is, just prior to the period of Timarchus. Other Bactrian kings appear in helmets having the shape of a kausia.[25] On the coins of contemporary Hellenistic monarchs in the west this form of hat is rarely seen. Genthios, king of Illyria, is shown with the petasos and no diadem.[26] In spite of the strength of the Macedonian tradition among the successors of Alexander the evidence of the coins suggests that use of the kausia as royal headgear was common only in the newer kingdom of Bactria. The reverse type of the coin model consists of the figure of the young Hercules standing and crowning himself with his right hand while the left holds the usual lion-skin and club. This type is unknown to Seleucid coinage. It does occur, however, on Bactrian issues that are either contemporary with the period of Timarchus or antedate it by a few years.[27] Both Gardner and Babelon long since remarked the use on a tetradrachm issued by Timarchus of a reverse type common to Eucratides of Bactria.[28] This Eucratides ruled in Bactria at the time that Timarchus as governor of Babylonia and Media was preparing his revolt. The Bactrian coinage at its best represents a higher form of the engraver's art than do the best specimens among the Seleucid issues. In this connection it may be noted that the two seal impressions with which we are concerned display an execution superior to that of our other impressions of official seals. The gems by which they were impressed were clearly not cut by the engravers responsible for the seals of the legitimate government employed at Seleucia.

It is important to bear in mind the political situation in the east at the moment of the revolt of Timarchus. To the north

[25] S. W. Grose, *Catalogue of the McClean Collection of Greek Coins*, Fitzwilliam Museum, III, 408, No. 9689.

[26] Imhoof-Blumer, *Porträtköpfe*, p. 72, No. 18.

[27] Grose, *op. cit.*, III, 410, No. 9705; 407, No. 9687.

[28] Gardner, *op. cit.*, p. 50, No. 2; Babelon, *op. cit.*, p. cxv; cf. G. Macdonald, "The Hellenic Kingdoms of Syria, Bactria and Parthia," *The Cambridge History of India* (Cambridge, 1922), I, 457.

and east of the satrapies that had been entrusted to him were the kingdoms of Armenia, Parthia, and Bactria, which had won their independence during the previous century. As Niese has pointed out,[29] after the death of Antiochus IV the control over all the remaining provinces in the east was but nominal. Bactria had early expanded into a great power. But now the hitherto obscure kingdom of Parthia under the able leadership of Mithradates I became a center of aggression. Eucratides of Bactria lost two of his provinces.[30] Mithradates was next to turn on Media, inaugurating in the west a series of campaigns that finally brought the Parthians to the Euphrates. The Seleucid dynasty now ruled little more than the province of Syria. The Parthians represented an element foreign to both Greeks and Iranians. With the loss of Seleucid prestige and the gradual disappearance of effective control of the great trade routes from Central Asia to the Mediterranean, it was inevitable that the conservative elements in the east should seek some political realignment that would offset the Parthian threat to Greek and Iranian economic and political security. There is evidence that somewhat later the Greek commercial aristocracy of Seleucia at least turned to the Arsacid dynasty for the protection of the vital arteries of trade. It is but natural, however, that in the beginning the Parthians should have been feared as upstarts and barbarians. Our classical sources have pictured the revolt of Timarchus from the point of view of the western world as the attempt on the part of two ambitious men to take advantage of a moment of weakness when the Seleucid Empire was torn by dynastic strife. Nothing may be learned from these sources of the relations of Timarchus with Bactria. By chance Diodorus Siculus has mentioned the alliance concluded by Timarchus with the king of Armenia, apparently arranged before the open outbreak.[31] In view of the political situation, the weakness of Syria and the growing aggressiveness of Parthia, it would appear reasonable that Bactria especially would favor the organization of a strong military power just to the west of Parthia, with whom she would seek to be on the friendliest terms. Without specific evidence, indeed, the political circum-

[29] *Op. cit.*, III, 284.
[30] G. Rawlinson, *The Sixth Great Oriental Monarchy*, p. 75.
[31] xxxi. 27.

stances of the moment would justify the recognition of the revolt of Timarchus as the expression of political and economic policies much wider than the measure of personal ambition; Timarchus should be viewed not as an instigator but as an instrument. Specific evidence to a degree, at least, is provided by the three official documents from Seleucia, the two seal impressions and the coin model. These objects belonged to a government that became established at Seleucia, and they definitely express a relationship between this government and that of Bactria. The assignment of the three documents to the revolt of Timarchus appears to be required by their mutual relationship, by the provenance and the execution of the impressions, and by the relation of the types of both model and impressions to those of Bactrian coins. Specifically I would suggest that in the development of his effort Timarchus was intimately associated with and, to a degree, was dependent upon the Bactrian power.

CHAPTER VIII

THE IMPRESSIONS OF PRIVATE SEALS

The impressions of private seals on the attached sealings from Seleucia represent a total of one hundred and fifty-six different seals. Of these, one hundred and twenty-nine, or more than eighty per cent, were impressed on sealings found in the archives of the Great House. As groups the impressions from the archives and those from other provenances fail to show distinctions in respect to motif and execution. The former group represents seals which were in use during the third century B.C. and the first half of the second. The attached sealings from other provenances appear to belong to this same period.[1]

The impressions of private seals are of undoubted value for a study of the ethnic relationships of the population and for a determination of the characteristics of the culture that prevailed in the city of Seleucia. Dr. Richter, of the Metropolitan Museum of Art, has written of classical gems that they "reflect faithfully the styles of the various periods to which they belong." Of the choice of a personal seal type she says: "There must often have been a special appropriateness in the chosen device . . . a favorite deity or mythological hero or symbol. . . . Sometimes it commemorated a glorious event in the family."[2] In a general sense, these remarks hold true for the Hellenistic period. One must recognize, however, that the opening of the Orient to Greek domination and settlement as a result of the conquests of Alexander the Great represents a fundamental break with tradition. The trend toward the disappearance of the mutually exclusive concepts of "Greek" and "barbarian," and the stimulation of the imaginative power which must have accompanied this period of Greek emigration to the East, would inevitably develop new tastes in the choice of personal devices. Glyptic art among both Greeks and Orientals must have been affected by the new conditions.

[1] See p. 14.
[2] *Catalogue of Engraved Gems in the Classical Style*, pp. xvii, xx.

The use of the seal impressions as the basis for general deduction imposes caution in other respects. The very fact that we are dealing with impressions rather than with the original gems limits seriously the accuracy of the study in respect to details. Careless impression and the damage wrought by fire, breakage, and exposure tend to destroy certain elements in the types and the clean lines upon which depends an evaluation of the quality of execution. Again, it must be borne in mind that seals represent almost exclusively the masculine element in any population. A reasonably complete picture of social conditions in Seleucia must include a study of other classes of objects, especially the figurines that reflect more faithfully the tastes and the traditions of the women.[3]

Finally, the question must be raised of the place in society occupied by the owners of the seals whose impressions we are considering. The private seals that had been impressed on the sealings found in the archives represent principals and witnesses in wholesale transactions. The principals in these engagements were evidently men of recognized commercial and financial standing.[4] Whether or not witnesses were drawn largely from among other merchants of the same social group or from among the class of clerks as well, cannot be determined. There is no evidence in Seleucid Babylonia pointing to the presence of professional witnesses such as appear to have existed in earlier periods. Under the circumstances it is reasonable to assume in respect to the impressions from Seleucia that they represent both the upper stratum and a less elevated but yet substantial group in the city's commercial life. If the witnesses were not themselves wholesale merchants and bankers, they were men associated with such principals. The impressions as a whole must certainly be connected with this element rather than with the other principal classes, the retail merchants, artisans, and the bureaucracy of government, whether civil or military. Whatever of value, therefore, may be deduced from these impressions can be applied to a limited portion only of the social group within the city.

[3] A volume in this series, *Figurines from Seleucia on the Tigris*, is being prepared by Dr. Wilhelmina van Ingen under the direction of the Institute of Archaeological Research of the University of Michigan. The pottery from the Parthian period recovered at Seleucia has been published by Dr. Neilson C. Debevoise, *Parthian Pottery from Seleucia on the Tigris*, University of Michigan Studies, Volume XXXII of the Humanistic Series.   [4] See pp. 186 and 195.

Notwithstanding the various limitations which impose themselves, the impressions of private seals possess qualifications that establish their value for purposes of study. The very fact that they apply to a single group in the society of Seleucia enhances their value as evidence concerning the character of that group. A study based on the seals themselves is handicapped by the vagueness of their associations. Illicit diggers at ancient sites recognize the value of a gem while they overlook, as a rule, the impressions of seals. The greater part of the ancient seals available for study have passed through the hands of dealers. Their provenances, therefore, must remain questionable. Some doubt indeed must attach to the chronological associations of seals found by scientific excavators. Gems are both durable and attractive; all objects having these characteristics tend to be passed along from one occupation of a site to later occupations. Instead of the seal serving to identify the dates of other classes of material, all too often its find associations must be employed to establish the date of the seal. When this is accomplished doubt may remain as to the place in society occupied by the original user of the seal.

The impressions from Seleucia have as a group definitely established limits both with respect to their dates and to the social organization which they represent. Their number is sufficiently large to permit some generalizations. At the same time they form only a moderate portion of the total number of seal impressions that have been recovered from sites in the Near East.[5] The value possessed by the impressions from Seleucia is threefold. They may aid in fixing the time limits of seals and seal impressions from unknown or doubtful provenances. Studied in relation to impressions from related sites whose associations have been established, they will provide a means for comparing and contrasting the social order in Seleucia with that in other Hellenistic centers. Within the limitations laid down an analysis of the type groups to be found on the impressions will elucidate problems of the racial characteristics, the religious and social concepts, and the aesthetic appreciation of the population of Seleucia.

The terms used in the tables to express the variation in motif,

[5] See M. I. Rostovtzeff, "Seleucid Babylonia: Bullae and Seals of Clay with Greek Inscriptions," *Yale Classical Studies*, 3 (1932), 5–14.

"Greek," "Oriental," and "general," require explanation. By a Greek motif is meant one that represents a culture predominantly Greek. Such a motif would appeal to the Hellenized Syrian or Babylonian as well as to the man of Greek race. It might have within it elements foreign to strictly Greek thought. By Oriental a motif is designated that shows no signs of Greek influence in its concept. The term "general" is applied to motifs that were common to both Greek and Oriental concepts. Under this heading would be included a seal type which represented a concept peculiar to Oriental culture, but which was executed in a Greek style. There is a temptation to pursue the possible transfer of concepts from one culture to the other. As an example one may take the group of impressions that portray Odysseus. It has been suggested that, since the Odyssey and the Babylonian epic regarding Gilgamish may have a common source, this group should be taken to represent a Babylonian concept dressed in Greek forms. Such an analysis lies beyond the scope of this work, and the effort has been made to limit the classification of motifs to that which is fundamental.

In estimating the quality of execution of the seals represented by the impressions the term "good" has been used as roughly equivalent to the quality of the Hellenistic and Graeco-Roman gems illustrated in Furtwängler's *Die antiken Gemmen*. The other terms, "fair," "mediocre," and "crude," are to be contrasted with this standard. It should be emphasized again that a judgment based on impressions rather than on the original seals is of limited value.

By reference to the table it will be seen that of one hundred and fifty-six different impressions one hundred and forty-four have motifs that may be described as Greek, whereas only five are Oriental, five general, and two doubtful. The proportion clearly demonstrates that the class in society represented by these impressions was overwhelmingly Greek in culture. One may proceed a step farther and attempt an estimate of the proportion between the Hellenic and the Hellenized elements within this class. Such an attempt must be based on the assumption that a relation exists between the choice of a seal type and the inherited tradition of an individual as opposed to his environment. In other words, though a Hellenized Oriental might be expected to draw on the general store of Greek concepts for a

An Analysis of the Impressions of Different Private Seals

CLASS AND TYPE	TOTAL	OBSCURE	GREEK	ORIENTAL	GENERAL	GOOD	FAIR	MEDIOCRE	CRUDE
Principal deities									
Apollo	3	..	3	..	..	1	2	..	..
Dionysus	4	2	4	..	..	..	2	..	..
Athena	13	3	13	..	..	2	5	1	2
Artemis	5	..	5	..	..	1	3	1	..
Nike	6	2	6	..	..	1	1	..	2
Tyche	11	3	11	..	..	..	4	3	1
Unidentified deities	4	2	4	..	..	..	1	..	1
Total	46	12	46	..	..	5	18	5	6
Minor deities									
Hermes	2	..	2	..	..	..	1	1	..
Eros	11	..	11	..	..	3	2	3	3
Psyche	6	1	6	..	..	..	2	2	1
Silenus	3	1	3	..	..	..	1	1	..
River god	1	..	1	..	..	..	..	1	..
Total	23	2	23	..	..	3	6	8	4
Acts of religious observance	3	2	..	3	..	..	..	1	..
Heroes									
Hercules	4	..	4	..	..	..	2	2	..
Odysseus	6	..	6	..	..	..	3	3	..
Penelope	1	..	1	..	..	..	1	..	..
Total	11	..	11	..	..	..	6	5	..
Mythological motifs									
Medusa	5	1	5	..	..	..	2	2	..
Opheltes and the dragon	1	..	1	..	..	..	1	..	..
Winged demons	2	1	2	..	..	..	..	1	..
Griffins	4	1	4	..	..	..	..	3	..
Total	12	3	12	..	..	..	3	6	..
Mortals									
Draped women in formal pose	7	1	7	..	..	..	1	3	2
Nude women	6	1	6	..	..	2	1	1	1
Warriors	4	1	4	..	..	..	1	..	2
Men in pastoral scene	1	..	1	..	..	..	1	..	..
Men in convivial scene	1	..	1	..	..	..	..	..	1
Total	19	3	19	..	..	2	4	4	6
Symbols and objects	32	6	28	2	2?	4	12	8	2
Animal life	10	1	5	..	5	..	2	2	5
Totals	156	29	144	5	7?	14	51	39	23

seal motif, the choice within that store displayed by a group of Hellenized individuals would differ from that of a group who were Greek by race. This assumption obviously is subject to attack, and conclusions based on it may not be unduly stressed. On the other hand, a certain body of evidence supports it. The worship of Athena, for instance, never became popular in Syria or in Ptolemaic Egypt. There is little evidence of it in Hellenistic Asia Minor. Yet of the forty-two seal types that represent identified deities, thirteen portray this goddess — more than thirty per cent. In this connection it should be borne in mind that four of the thirteen impressions represent Athena Alkis and thus show Macedonian affinities.[6]

Greek mythology would tend to be less rapidly propagated among Orientals than would the cults of popular deities. The latter were frequently adopted through political motives. In the modern Orient, where tradition is still handed down for the most part orally, folklore passes from mother to child rather than through the father. Presumably, similar conditions held true for the Greek colonies in the Orient established in the Hellenistic period. The Greek settlers in Seleucia, as in other parts of the East, were for the most part soldiers from the more backward districts of European Greece, including Macedonia, or else were traders. The existence of gymnasia and of the various associations in these centers does not evidence a literary taste on the part of the inhabitants, even of the upper commercial class. Rostovtzeff has noted the absence of literary interest in the Zeno letters and other correspondence from Ptolemaic Egypt.[7] The scholars for which Alexandria became noted were not representative. The presence among our impressions of a considerable body of motifs drawn from Greek mythology points to a closer relationship with Greece than would be afforded by environment alone. "Environment" is here used to designate principally the association of Orientals with Greeks in the Greek centers of the East. Hellenization as a product of interracial marriage does not satisfactorily explain the strength of this group of motifs for the reason that the Greek element in these families was due almost exclusively to the male side. So far as the evidence is applicable, it suggests that motifs recalling the wanderings of

[6] See p. 77, No. IIIA1c(1).
[7] "Ptolemaic Egypt," *The Cambridge Ancient History*, VII, 152.

Odysseus, the patience of Penelope, and the stories of Medusa and of Opheltes and the dragon were chosen as seal types by men of Greek stock as well as of Greek cultural inheritance.

Further evidence is afforded by the small proportion of motifs that might be termed bacchanal in character and the entire absence of obscene seal types, both developments a product of the internationalization of Hellenism. This characteristic of our impressions, taken with the large proportion of types that have religious connotations, points to a certain lack of sophistication on the part of the owners of the seals. A reasonable conclusion to be drawn from these conditions supports the assumption that this group in Seleucia was drawn largely from the more backward areas or social classes of old Greece, the logical recruiting ground for Greek colonization in the East.

The slight extent of the evidence for a process of Hellenization of alien elements afforded by the impressions from Seleucia receives independent corroboration from other circumstances. The impressions as a group have been shown to belong to the third century B.C. and the first half of the second. The Greek colonization of Babylonia began only with the opening of the third century about 290 B.C. Social intercourse and intermarriage with the native elements in Babylonia can have been accepted only gradually by the incoming Greeks. There are few grounds, therefore, for an assumption that the process of Hellenization had made an appreciable change in the characteristics of the population by the middle of the second century B.C.

It is unfortunate that so little evidence regarding the Orientals in the population has been revealed by the impressions. It is essential to bear in mind that these impressions are representative of a limited class only in the city. Within the class with which we are now concerned Orientals are represented by five impressions. With the inclusion of those the motif of which is doubtful or which was common to both Greek and Oriental concepts a maximum of twelve impressions might be assigned to this element. Of the five impressions that are definitely Oriental three show Semitic influence, one has characteristics that may be either Anatolian or Syrian, and the fifth represents a concept common to various Oriental cultures.[8] The scanty

[8] See pp. 98–99, Nos. IIIA3a(1)–(3); p. 113, No. IIID1b(1); p. 113, No. IIID1c(1).

nature of our evidence renders it of slight value for purposes of analysis. Of greater interest is the fact that on the bullae found at Warka Oriental motifs form by far the majority. Rostovtzeff has remarked in this connection that astrology was a very important factor in the choice of seal types.[9] Among the impressions from Seleucia only two may possibly have this connotation. No. IIIDıc(1) has as type a star or a sun, and No. IIIE3b(1), a crab or a frog.[10] On the relatively few bullae found at Nippur Greek and Babylonian motifs in seal design are commingled.[11] No exact date may be assigned to these sealings, but they are certainly of the Seleucid period. So far as the evidence is of value in the absence of opportunity for comparative study, it would seem that Greek influence was stronger at Nippur than at Warka. In comparison with that at Seleucia it was, of course, slight.

Of the one hundred and fifty-six impressions of different seals twenty-nine are so obscure that no determination of the quality of execution of the seals may be made. Of the remaining one hundred and twenty-seven fourteen are classed as good, fifty-one fair, thirty-nine mediocre, and twenty-three crude. That is, a trifle over eleven per cent are of good quality, slightly more than eighteen per cent are crude, and the balance are of medial quality, fair, and mediocre. The users of these seals were principals and witnesses in important business transactions and appear to have been largely of Hellenic extraction. If we bear these circumstances in mind, the proportions take on a certain significance. The conclusion already stated, that the commercial class among the Greek settlers in Seleucia was not drawn from the upper strata or the great centers in the older Hellenic countries, appears to receive corroboration from the execution of the seals used by these individuals. Seals of good workmanship were to be had in Seleucia, whether engraved locally or imported we do not, of course, know. There can be no doubt that the principal merchants and bankers of the Greek cities in Asia Minor provided themselves with signets worthy of their position, the work of the better artists of the age. That the

---

[9] "Seleucid Babylonia," p. 21.   [10] See pp. 113 and 126.
[11] L. Legrain, "The Culture of the Babylonians," *University of Pennsylvania, The University Museum, Publications of the Babylonian Section*, XIV(1915), Part I, 356.

same category of individuals in Seleucia, a commercial center of comparable importance, contented itself with seals of an inferior average quality affords reasonable evidence that this class in Seleucia in large measure was not drawn from the social group that controlled the commerce of the older centers in the Aegean area. Individuals may be presumed to have formed an exception; the ten per cent of the impressions represent seals of reasonably good quality. But as a whole the evidence suggests that what one may call the commercial aristocracy of Seleucia did not represent an extension of the trading and banking organizations of the older centers, but rather the local development of new institutions on the part of Hellenic elements drawn from the less sophisticated areas and groups of Greece.

In this regard a justifiable analogy within limits may be drawn between the settlement of Greeks in the East during the Seleucid period and the economic penetration of the Far East by Europeans during the nineteenth century. In this later development fortunes in the European colonies or trading centers were built up by individuals who as a class did not represent established trading, banking, and shipping interests in the home lands. An obvious comparison may be drawn also with the commercial as opposed to the agricultural penetration of the American West during the eighteenth and nineteenth centuries. In this movement the trading and banking institutions and families of the eastern seaboard participated to some degree. But the commercial aristocracy of the new areas was composed largely of men who had forced their way up from a lower station in life.

In this respect the settlement of Greeks in the Seleucid east differed radically from that during the great periods of Greek city colonial expansion from the eighth to the sixth centuries B.C. For the most part that earlier movement comprised an extension of new branches of older commercial institutions dominated by economic interests. In the later expansion we have the military and police requirements of the Seleucid dynasty dominating the emigration of prospective soldiers and traders representing the more depressed portion of the population in Greece and Macedonia.

The variation in the quality of execution of the seals represented by the impressions does not appear to have a relation to the degree of Hellenization of the seal owners. There is no evidence to indicate that the seals of rather crude quality were used in large measure by Orientals or by Hellenized individuals. Of the five impressions already cited which have Oriental motifs two have been obscured to an extent that does not permit of judgment concerning the engraving; of the three remaining one is of good quality, one fair, and one mediocre. The portrayal of men and women in scenes of daily life is characteristic of Greek glyptic art and is almost never found on Oriental seals. Such concepts in art would not be so readily assimilated by Hellenized Orientals as would Greek traditions of deities and heroes. Thus the group of impressions the types of which portray mortals are perhaps more representative of Hellenic as opposed to Hellenized influences at Seleucia than is any other class. Yet of the eighteen impressions two are obscure, two are of good quality, four fair, four mediocre, and six crude.

From whatever angle it may be analyzed the evidence afforded by the impressions of private seals in respect to the ethnic and social characteristics of the upper commercial class in Seleucia points to a preponderant Hellenic racial stock drawn as a whole from a simple and unsophisticated background into a rapidly developed position of domination. Their culture was marked by at least traditional respect for the old Greek deities and hero stories and by a relative freedom from lightness of character. Their aesthetic appreciation, however, was limited.

CHAPTER IX

MISCELLANEA

Token Sealings

IN THE previous chapters I have discussed sealings which had been attached by means of cord to documents or containers. Well known, also, is the variety of sealing that was affixed directly to the surface of a document.[1] We have now to consider another class of sealings from Seleucia that is entirely distinct. It numbers seventy-seven specimens and comprises two forms. The great majority are crude, unfinished lumps of clay shaped by the pressure of thumb and two fingers at the moment of application of the seals. A very few are roughly finished as disks. One bears the impressions of two seals; the others have one each. None show the remains of holes or grooves made by cord, or the imprint left by the fiber of writing or packing material. None could have been employed as stoppers. It must be assumed that these objects had not been associated with documents or containers. Certain other characteristics should be noted. They had no intrinsic or aesthetic value, and they were not durable. In two instances a quantity of sealings similar in form and impressed by a single seal were found together; it follows that they might be used in numbers. They have been found in several different areas of the excavations. Two were recovered from grave structures and nineteen from rooms of the Great House. Finally, it should be noted that two of the sealings bear the impressions of what appear to be official seals.

Of the seventy-seven sealings nine were found on the surface, three in débris, sixty-four in Parthian levels, and one in a Seleucid level. The seal impression on the last has a motif that is characteristic of Sassanian art.[2] The sealing is probably late Par-

---

[1] J. G. Milne, "Clay Sealings from the Fayoum," *The Journal of Hellenic Studies*, 26 (1906), 32–45, and "Ptolemaic Seal Impressions," *ibid.*, 36 (1916), 87–101; C. C. Edgar, "Notes from the Delta," *Annales du Service des antiquités de l'Égypte*, 8 (1907), 154–157.

[2] See p. 238, No. B2e(1).

thian and was intrusive in the earlier level. It should be noted further that in the earliest Parthian stratum, Level III, which came to an end about 43 A.D., the token sealings are rare; they become abundant in Level I, from about 117 A.D. to at least 215 A.D.

Similar sealings have been discovered at Susa, said to have been associated with graves of the Parthian period, and in a grave of the Achemenid period at Ur.[3] The extant evidence suggests that this form of sealing was a local development in the east which probably centered in Parthian Babylonia. Though dissimilar in form from regular tessarae, they may well have served for admission to gatherings, public or private. Borne by a messenger they might have established the authenticity of the message. A further use is suggested by a practice in the present-day Near East. Porters when carrying goods into a general warehouse may drop into a container at the entrance pebbles, twigs, or other small objects previously decided upon by the owner of the goods and the warehouse clerk. These tokens serve to check the number of units entered. A pellet of clay bearing the impression of the owner's seal would obviously constitute a more satisfactory token.

On the basis of the evidence the impressions on these sealings may be taken as representative of certain social strata in Seleucia during the first and second centuries A.D. If the predominant use of the tokens in commerce be granted, the owners of the seals must have been merchants of some standing. The impressions reproduce a total of twenty-four different seals. These seals in turn comprise twenty motifs: one Parthian royal portrait and representations of six deities, five different symbols and objects, and eight forms of animal life. The influence of Greek culture is predominant in the choice of motifs, but these sealings display a larger proportion of Oriental motifs than is true of the attached sealings of the Seleucid period.[4] This Oriental element appears to be more

---

[3] The token sealings from Susa have been briefly described by R. de Mecquenem, "Inventoire de Cachets et Cylindres, Suse 1925–26," *Revue d'Assyriologie*, XXIV (1927), No. 1; those from Ur by Dr. L. Woolley, *Antiquaries Journal*, 12, No. 4 (1932). I was permitted to inspect the latter through the courtesy of Dr. Leon Legrain of the University Museum, University of Pennsylvania.

[4] See Chapter VIII. Cf. N. C. Debevoise, "The Essential Characteristics of Parthian and Sasanian Glyptic Art," *Berytus*, 1 (1934): 1–7

largely Iranian than Mesopotamian. In addition the execution of the motifs that are Greek in concept generally betrays a greater separation from Greek sources than may be remarked in the earlier impressions. The evidence of the token sealings suggests a class of individuals predominantly Oriental in race, yet, through inheritance, Greek in culture. This class, however, was becoming increasingly responsive to the stimulation of that other culture which in a later form was to become known as Sassanian.

In the catalog of the impressions that follows, under the description of the types the terms "Greek," "Oriental," and "general" are in some instances employed to express the relationships of the motifs.[5] After the description of the design there will be found the serial number of each sealing, its characteristic form, and provenance. The terms "finished" and "unfinished" express the distinctions in the form of the sealings noted in the preceding paragraph. The significance of the various provenances has been discussed in the Preface.[6]

Catalog of Impressions

A. OFFICIAL

1. *Having a monogram associated with the type*

a. Having as type the representation of a deity (?)

(1) Oval; 12.5 × 8 mm.; execution fair, conventionalized. Pl. V, Fig. 95.

Type: Head right. The hair is drawn into a knot over the nape of the neck. Above the forehead is an ornament the exact form of which cannot be determined. The execution of the features is reminiscent of archaic representations of Apollo, but the absence of a laurel wreath and the presence of the ornament render this identification impossible. Another impression of a private seal, No. B1c(1), is rather similar in style and execution and shows a head ornament in the same relative position. In this instance the head is accompanied by the representation of a dove and a crescent. These attributes suggest a portrayal of Aphrodite, and on the strength of the relationship between the

---

[5] These terms have been defined on page 224.
[6] See p. vii.

two impressions I tentatively assign the present type to this deity.[7]

Sealing No. BI(1), unfinished. Trial trench 4, Level II, Room 10.

(2) Oval, incompletely impressed; 11 × 8 mm.; execution fair. Type: Design and monogram similar to those on No. (1). The two seals appear to have been the work of a single engraver.

Sealing No. BI(2), unfinished. Great House, Level III, Room 149.

b. Having as type a representation of royalty

(1) Ovoid; 12 × 6 mm.; execution mediocre. Pl. V, Fig. 96. Type: Head left, male, wearing a diadem. There is a short beard, and the hair is dressed in the style common to Parthian coin portraits of the period of Mithradates II.[8] The impression occurs in duplicate on two sealings of similar form. For the value of the monogram see note under No. a(1).

Sealing No. BI(3), unfinished. Surface.

(2) A duplicate of No. (1).

Sealing No. BI(4), unfinished. Surface, found with No. (1).

B. PRIVATE

1. *Deities*

a. Helios

(1) Oval; 14 × 10 mm.; execution crude. Pl. V, Fig. 97. Type: Figure standing facing, male, apparently nude. The head is turned left, and the right foot is advanced. The left arm is extended outward, with the hand raised above the level of the shoulder; a small object may be held in this hand. The right arm appears to be dropped at the side. The head is distinctly radiate. Immediately behind the figure is an object the nature of which I have been unable to determine definitely. It

---

[7] The evidence pointing to the reservation of the use of monograms on seals to a particular class of officials has been discussed in Chapter IV, pp. 151–155. The same argument is assumed in explanation of the monograms that occur on token sealings. They represent some form of controller in the administration of the government. The nature of their functions cannot be determined more exactly.

[8] W. Wroth, *Catalogue of the Coins of Parthia*, Pl. VI.

consists of a framework, apparently of wood, and may possibly represent a plow. It is not a rudder. In any case the motif involves some manifestation of the sun god. Helios heads occur on Parthian coins, and a grafitto from Doura-Europos represents a Semitic form of this deity, a standing figure having a radiate headdress.[9] If, as appears probable, our figure is nude, the concept is in part, at least, Greek. This impression occurs on forty sealings of similar shape. The cache was found by accident just under the surface at a point on the northeastern section of the mounds where no excavations have been undertaken.

Sealing No. BI(16), unfinished.

(2)–(40) Duplicates of No. (1).

Sealings BI(17)–(55), unfinished. Provenance as under No. (1).

b. Dionysus

(1) Nearly circular; 13 × 12 mm.; execution fair, conventional. Pl. V, Fig. 98.

Type: Bust right, male, bearded. A garland encircles the head. The shoulders appear to be draped. This is clearly not a representation of Zeus, but does suggest the bearded Dionysus. The concept is Greek. The same impression occurs on two sealings of different shape.

Sealing No. BII(1), finished, plano-convex. Great House, Level II, Room 83 sub.

(2) A duplicate of No. (1).

Sealing No. BI(5), unfinished. Great House, Level II, Vault 159.

c. Aphrodite

(1) Oval; 11.5 × 6 mm.; execution mediocre.

Type: Head right, female. The hair is done in a small roll at the back of the head. Over the forehead may be discerned an ornament the form of which is obscure. Above the head is a crescent; below, a bird — apparently a dove in flight. The treatment as a whole is sketchy. The presence of the dove and

---

[9] Wroth, *op. cit.*, p. lxxiii; M. I. Rostovtzeff, *Yale University Excavations at Dura*, IV, Pl. XIX, 2.

the crescent lead one to believe that the head represents some form of Aphrodite. This deity is frequently shown with a symbolic ornament over the forehead. On the other hand, the motif of Aphrodite on ancient seals is more frequently expressed by a full figure than a head or bust. Since the attributes, the dove and the crescent, might well be associated with some Mesopotamian form of Artemis, and since this deity is frequently represented by a head, the identification of our type must be considered tentative. The motif is Greek. The impression occurs on ten sealings of a single shape, found together.

Sealing No. BI(6), unfinished. Great House, Level I, Room 219.

(2)–(10)   Duplicates of No. (1).

Sealings Nos. BI(7)–(15), unfinished. Provenance as under No. (1).

d. Artemis

(1) Oval, incompletely impressed; 14 × 9 mm.; execution crude. Pl. V, Fig. 99.

Type: Head right, female. The hair is massed at the back of the head. The neck is of an exaggerated length. This technique was a recognized feature of the art of the Parthian period. It occurs on figurines from Parthian levels at Seleucia and also on Parthian coins.[10] The type of our impression clearly does not represent portraiture but, rather, a deity. The assignment to Artemis is based on the fact that this goddess is frequently portrayed without distinctive headdress or head ornament. Owing to the incomplete character of the impression it is possible that the original seal bore one of the familiar symbols of Artemis, such as the quiver.[11] Temples of Artemis in Parthian towns are frequently mentioned by Isidore of Charax.[12] The motif is Greek, and the particular technique of execution was not limited to the Parthian east.

Sealing No. BI(56), unfinished. Great House, débris, level not established.

---

[10] Wroth, *op. cit.*, Pl. XXXIII, 21, 22.

[11] What appears to be a head of Artemis accompanied by a crescent occurs on a sealing of the Seleucid period (p. 83, No. III A1d(6)).

[12] Parthian Stations (ed. Schoff), Section 1, p. 4; Section 6, p. 6.

e. Nike

(1) Oval, incompletely impressed; 15 × 10 mm.; execution fair. Pl. V, Fig. 100.
Type: Winged figure standing right, female, draped. The right hand holds in front of the breast an object resembling a small wreath. The left hand grasps a leafed branch, not a palm, reversed toward the ground. The motif is, of course, Greek.
Sealing No. BI(57), unfinished. Surface.

f. Eros

(1) Oval; 15 × 11 mm.; execution mediocre.
Type: Winged figure standing right, male, nude. The wings and the form of the body are characteristic of representations of Eros. A kantharos is held in front of the body and a thyrsos rests against the left shoulder. This concept, Eros as Dionysus, is typically Greek. An impression of the same seal occurs on another sealing of similar form.
Sealing No. BII(2), an oval disk finished in a careless manner. Great House, Level II, Room 201, in brickwork of wall.

(2) A duplicate of No. (1).
Sealing No. BII(3), similar to No. (1). Surface.

(3) Oval; 10 × 7 mm.; execution mediocre. Pl. V, Fig. 101.
Type: Winged figure standing right, male, nude. The wings are of the cupid type. The figure has the legs crossed, and the folded arms rest on a knobbed club. One hand holds a wreath, from which are suspended two streamers that have pompons at their extremities. This representation of Eros as Hercules is again Greek in concept.
Sealing No. BI(62), unfinished. Great House, Level II, Room 187 sub.

2. *Symbols and objects*

a. Thunderbolt

(1) Oval, incompletely impressed; 9 × 6 mm.; execution fair.
Type: Winged thunderbolt of usual form. The motif is Greek. The seal has been impressed twice on the one sealing.

Sealing No. BI(58), unfinished. Great House, Level I, Room 244.

b. Wreath

(1) Oval, partly broken; 17 × 11 mm.; execution obscure.
Type: A wreath surrounding some object the nature of which cannot be determined. The motif of the wreath is traditionally Greek.
Sealing No. BI(59), unfinished. Great House, Level I, Room 20, in pavement.

c. Ring

(1) Oval; 11 × 7 mm.; execution fair. Pl. V, Fig. 102.
Type: A signet ring. Within the circle of the ring are two bars. The motif is Greek.
Sealing No. BI(60), unfinished. Surface.

d. Plant

(1) Oval; 12 × 9 mm.; execution mediocre.
Type: The head of a plant with a double row of petals, stamens, and a pistil. The execution is conventionalized. The motif is one found on Greek gems of the Hellenistic and later periods.
Sealing No. BI(61), unfinished, roughly cone-shaped. Great House, Level I, Room 12.

e. Ornamental device

(1) Oval, incompletely impressed; 9 × 7.5 mm.; execution fair.
Type: A device consisting of a circle attached by short bars to two incomplete squares. This motif is characteristic of Oriental art, especially within the Sassanian Empire. The design appears to be accompanied by two lines of legend, apparently some form of Aramaic script. Owing to wear it is very doubtful whether any reading is possible. Seal impressions closely similar in design have been published by C. C. Torrey.[13]
Sealing No. BI(62), unfinished. Trial trench 4, Level IV sub, Z 100.

---

[13] "Pehlevi Seal Inscriptions from Yale Collections," *Journal of the American Oriental Society*, 52 (1932), 201–207.

3. *Representations of animal life*

a. Ram

(1) Oval; 15 × 8.5 mm.; execution fair.

Type: An animal stretched out in a gallop, right. The horns resemble those of a ram. An astrological symbolism may have been intended, but such an interpretation is not required. The motif and execution are both Oriental rather than Greek.

Sealing No. BI(63), unfinished, a rough disk. Surface.

b. Humped bull (?)

(1) Oval; 15 × 10 mm.; execution very crude. Pl. V, Fig. 103.

Type: Quadruped at gallop, left. The lines of the body, the length of the legs, and the form of the tail suggest an antelope. The horns are those of a bull. Rising from the neck rather than from the shoulders is a somewhat formless mass which, although misplaced, must represent either wings or a hump, more probably the latter. The motif of the Indian bull is more characteristically Oriental than Greek.

Sealing No. BI(64), unfinished. Trial trench 23, 2.5 m.

c. Jerboa (?)

(1) Oval; 10.5 × 5 mm.; execution mediocre. Pl. V, Fig. 104.

Type: A quadruped squatting right, in the act of feeding. The fore legs are short, the hind legs, long, in proportion to the body. The tail is long and slender. In these respects the animal resembles a jerboa, or kangaroo rat, found today in Anatolia and Persia. The ears are overly long to support this identification, but none other is equally satisfactory. Animal motifs on seals were more popular in the East than in the West. On the other hand, the representation of the animal in the act of feeding suggests Greek influence.

Sealing No. BI(65), unfinished. Surface.

d. Bullock's head

(1) Circular; diam. 17 mm.; execution mediocre.

Type: The head of a bullock facing. This motif is very characteristic of Parthian and Sassanian areas of culture. It is not, however, foreign to Greek art. It is classed, therefore, as "general."

Sealing No. BII(4), a finished disk with one face plane, the other pinched into a convex form by the pressure of fingers. Great House, Level II, Street 32.

e. Eagle alighting on a bullock's head

(1) Oval; 13 × 10 mm.; execution mediocre.

Type: An eagle with its wings and tail spread in the act of alighting on the horns of a bullock's head, facing. The latter may be a skull. The motif must be classed as "general." See under No. d(1), just above. Impressions from the same seal occur on three other sealings similar in form.

Sealing No. BI(66), unfinished. Great House, surface débris.

(2) A duplicate of No. (1).

Sealing No. BI(67), unfinished. Great House, Level II, Room 32 sub.

(3) A duplicate of No. (1).

Sealing No. BI(68), unfinished. Great House, Level II, room not established.

(4) A duplicate of No. (1).

Sealing No. BI(69), unfinished. Great House, Level III, Room 63.

f. Stork or crane

(1) Oval, incompletely impressed; 9+ × 6 mm.; execution mediocre.

Type: A bird feeding, right, having long legs and a long neck. There is possibly a tuft or crest on the back of the head. The motif must be classed as "general."

Sealing No. BI(70), unfinished. Trial trench 4, débris.

g. Dove and crescent

(1) Oval; 13 × 9 mm.; execution mediocre.

Type: A bird standing, right. The form approximates that of a dove. Behind the bird is a crescent. The association of the dove with the crescent suggests Syrian or Mesopotamian rather than Iranian influence. Since, however, these elements occur on Anatolian and Greek seals the motif must be classed as "general."

Sealing No. BII(5), finished to resemble an elliptical ring set. Surface.

(2) Oval, incompletely impressed; 10 × 6 mm.; execution mediocre.

Type: Similar to that of No. (1). The two seals represented by the impressions were undoubtedly the work of a single hand.

Sealing No. BI(71), unfinished. Great House, Level II, tomb 169.

h. Insect

(1) Oval, incompletely impressed; 9 × 6 mm.; execution mediocre. Pl. V, Fig. 105.

Type: An insect viewed from above, perhaps a bee. This motif occurs more frequently on Greek than on Oriental gems and is certainly more characteristic of Greek taste. It is classed, therefore, as Greek.

Sealing No. BI(60), unfinished. Another impression of a different seal found on this sealing is No. B2c(1), above. Surface.

Models of Seleucid Coins

These objects, numbering nineteen, are irregular disks of unbaked clay both faces of which bear designs that approximate Seleucid coin types. The diameters of the disks average twenty-six millimeters in a range of from twenty-three to thirty-two millimeters. The thickness varies from four to eight millimeters. Some are finished with reasonable care, whereas others are very crude. There appears to be no doubt that the molds in which the disks were cast had themselves been formed on actual coins. On a number the reproduction of the edge of the coin may be discerned, distinct from that of the cast. In one instance both the edge of the flan and a part of the border of dots of the coin reveal themselves. To judge by the size of the casts and the character of the types, the originals were tetradrachms. It will be remarked, however, that the majority of the types do not appear to reproduce in exact detail those of known Seleucid coins. An explanation of this may lie in the fact that the greater part of the issues represented in collections were minted in the western provinces of the empire, whereas the coins from which the models were made may be presumed to have been issued at Seleucia.

Among the nineteen casts occur five pairs of what appear to be duplicates. That is, the two individuals of each pair, though perhaps not the product of a single mold, were apparently cast in molds which had been formed on coins struck from a single die. In no instance was a pair found together, nor are they similar in details of material or over-all form. The series of casts as a whole comes from a number of separated areas of the site. It is difficult to escape the conclusion that, whatever the use to which they were put, these models were abundant and were widely distributed over the various quarters of the city.

It is reasonable to assume that the casts were fabricated and in use contemporaneously with their originals. Subsequent casting could be explained only on the basis of antiquarian interest, which in turn would involve a limited issue of models with more uniformity of material and execution. The evidence that the models were issued in numbers appears to require an assumption that they had a certain official character. The nature of the material of which they were composed and the carelessness of their execution suggest that their life was intended to be limited and that their use was popular. It is perhaps possible that coin casts were made to replace silver currency during times of strife when bullion could not be secured. It can be demonstrated that, within the date limits assigned to each model, there were one or more periods when access to silver mines by the mint at Seleucia may well have been blocked. The lack of care in the preparation of the casts and the numerous issues during the reign of Antiochus I, however, militate against such an assumption. It is more reasonable to suggest that the models represent a form of largesse issued by successive rulers upon special occasions. The distribution of actual coins in celebration of some event was recognized practice. It is entirely possible that from this developed the issue of imitation coins which served the populace as admission tokens to public feasts or games.[14]

---

[14] Clay coin models from Palmyra, essentially similar to those from Seleucia although they are based on bronze coins of Phoenicia, have been recently discussed by

Catalog of Models

(In the text of this catalog several works are referred to by the names of the authors only; the titles of a few others are given in condensed form. Full titles may be found in the Bibliography on pages xv–xvii.)

1. *Seleucus I*

a. Types and name of Alexander, symbol of Seleucus

(1) Diameter 26 mm.; finish good, incompletely impressed; condition good.

Obverse: Head right, male, covered by a lion-skin headdress. The representation is of Hercules. It approximates the obverse type of coins of Alexander and of Seleucus as satrap (Babelon, p. iii, Fig. 1).

Reverse: Zeus seated left on throne, nude from the thighs up. The back of the throne is not shown. The outstretched right hand holds a bird, right; the left raised above the shoulder rests on a long scepter. This general type occurs on coins of Alexander, Seleucus, and Antiochus I. On the field at the left, partly off flan, appears a symbol, either an anchor or the head of a horse, both symbols of Seleucus.

Legend: to the right, down, [᾿Αλε]ξάνδ[ρου].

Because of the use of the name of Alexander as well as of his types the cast is assigned to the first rule of Seleucus as satrap, from 321/20 to 315/14 B.C. Great House, Level II, débris.

J. G. Milne, "Local Currencies of East Syria under the Roman Empire," *Ancient Egypt and the East*, Part I, June, 1934, pp. 25–27. He suggests that these disks replaced the local bronze currency when copper for the mint could not be secured. Though this explanation cannot be ignored in respect to the Palmyra material, it is opposed by fundamental objections which apply to the models from both sites. In the normal course new issues of coins are made when the currency in circulation becomes insufficient or is so badly worn that the public will not accept it. Both these conditions are relative; new issues can be postponed for several years without causing a breakdown in exchange. Recourse to a clay coinage must then have resulted from a prolonged shortage of stocks of the necessary metals — not from a temporary interruption of traffic. I know of no military or political situations in the history of either Palmyra or Seleucia that would account for such a train of circumstances. In the second place, since the clay models were made from coins which had been in general circulation, their counterfeiting would have been comparatively simple and inexpensive. If it had become necessary to issue clay coins, an original design would have better served the purpose.

b. Types of Alexander, name of Seleucus without title

(1) Diameter 28 mm.; finish fair; condition worn.

Obverse: Head right, male, covered by a lion-skin headdress. This representation of Hercules differs in execution from that on No. a(1); it approximates that on a coin of Seleucus as king (Babelon, Pl. I, 6).

Reverse: In general similar to that on No. a(1), but differing in execution. In the field left a horizontal anchor, above, E.

Legend: one line only, to the right, down, [Σε]λ[εύκου].

The position of the lambda in relation to the type figure requires the restoration offered. The use of the name Seleucus without the royal title indicates as a date for the cast the period from 311 to 306/05 B.C. Surface.

(2) Diameter 26 mm.; finish fair; condition worn.

Obverse: Head right, as on No. b(1).

Reverse: Zeus seated left, as on No. b(1). In the field at the left is an obscure symbol, probably an anchor.

Legend: Traces only have been preserved. There appears to have been only one line, at the right. The details of execution demonstrate that this piece is related to No. b(1) rather than to No. a(1), but Nos. b(1) and (2) do not appear to have been cast from a single mold. Trial trench 4, Level II, A3.

x. Types of Alexander, name obscure

(1) Diameter 30 mm.; finish mediocre; condition worn.

Obverse: Head right, as on No. a(1) or No. b(1).

Reverse: Zeus seated left, as on No. a(1) or No. b(1).

Symbol and legend have been entirely effaced. Great House, Level III, Room 193.

(2) Diameter 24 mm.; finish crude; condition worn.

Obverse: Head right, as on No. x(1).

Reverse: Zeus seated left on throne, the left hand supporting a long scepter. In the outstretched right hand is either a bird or a small Nike, probably the former. The legend has been entirely obscured. Surface.

2. Seleucus I and Antiochus I associated

a. Portrait of Seleucus, reverse type and name of Antiochus

(1) Diameter 24 mm.; finish good; condition worn. Pl. VI, Fig. 106.

Obverse: Head right, male, wearing diadem. The portrait is definitely not that of Antiochus I. It does approximate that of Seleucus on certain of his coins (Imhoof-Blumer, *Porträtköpfe*, Pls. I, 3, and II, 8).

Reverse: Apollo seated left on omphalos. The left hand rests on a grounded bow; the right hand is extended over the lap, undoubtedly holding an arrow which has been obscured. The type is very characteristic of coins of Antiochus I (Babelon, Pl. IV, 9–15). No symbol may be distinguished.

Legend: to the right, worn away; to the left, 'Αντ[ιό]χου.

The portrait of Seleucus with the name of Antiochus occurs on a few coins with a different reverse type (Babelon, p. 15, Nos. 100 and 101). Antiochus was associated with his father from about 294 to 280 B.C. Surface.

(2) Diameter 28 mm.; finish mediocre; condition worn.

Obverse: Head right, male. Only the outline of the face has been preserved, but this serves to indicate that the portrait is of Seleucus, as on No. (1).

Reverse: Apollo seated left, as on No. (1). The arrow has been obscured, but the position of the arm identifies the details of the pose.

The legend has been entirely obscured. In view of the nature of the obverse and reverse types there can be little doubt that the legend bore the name and title of Antiochus. Differences in details of execution demonstrate that Nos. a(1) and (2) were not cast in the same mold. Great House, Level III, Room 302 sub.

3. Antiochus I

a. Portrait, reverse type and name of Antiochus

(1) Diameter 25 mm.; finish good; condition good. Pl. VI, Figs. 107–108.

Obverse: Head right, male, wearing diadem. The portrait is of Antiochus and in features most closely approximates that on a gold coin (Babelon, Pl. IV, 8).

Reverse: Apollo seated left on omphalos, nude and with the hair done in a knot. The left hand rests on a bow; the right hand, extended, holds an arrow pointing diagonally down. The general type is that of Nos. 2a(1) and (2), above, and of the six succeeding models. So far as it is possible to determine, these nine reverse types were cast in seven different molds.

Monograms: in the field at the left, ᛗ; at the right, ⊘. The former occurs on bronze coins of Antiochus, one of which bears the types of Alexander; the latter is found on coins of Seleucus I with Antiochus associated and of Antiochus I with his son, Seleucus, associated (Babelon, p. 16, No. 106; p. 22, No. 157; p. 15, No. 100; p. xl, Fig. 8). The monograms suggest, therefore, that the cast should be assigned to the opening years of the reign of Antiochus.

Legend: to the right, βασιλέως; to the left, 'Αντιόχου.

Great House, Level II, Room 50.

(2) Diameter 27 mm.; finish mediocre; condition of obverse good, the reverse obscured by a double impression of the mold. Pl. VI, Figs. 109–110.

Obverse: Head right, as on No. (1), not a duplicate.

Reverse: Apollo, as on No. (1), but with differences in detail. No monogram appears.

Legend: to the right, obscured; to the left, ['Αντι]όχου. Surface.

(3) Diameter 26 mm.; finish fair; condition worn.

Obverse: Head right, probably a duplicate of No. (2).

Reverse: Apollo as on No. (2), probably a duplicate. No monogram occurs.

Legend: to the right, [β]ασιλ[έως]; to the left, ['Α]ντιόχου.

Trial trench 15, 2.5 m.

(4) Diameter 26 mm.; finish mediocre; condition worn.

Obverse: Head of Antiochus, as on Nos. (1) and (2), but with differences in detail. The portrait appears to approximate that on a tetradrachm (Babelon, Pl. IV, 9).

Reverse: Apollo, as on Nos. (1) and (2), but with differences in detail. The reverse type is very close to that of the tetradrachm cited above. No monogram occurs.

Legend: to the right, [β]ασιλ[έως]; to the left, ['Αντ]ιόχο[υ].

Trial trench 4, débris.

(5) Diameter 26 mm.; finish fair; condition worn.

Obverse: Head right, probably a duplicate of No. (4).

Reverse: Apollo, as on No. (4), probably a duplicate.

No monogram can be distinguished. The legend has been obscured. Surface.

(6) Diameter 23 mm.; finish mediocre; condition fair.

Obverse: Head of Antiochus, as on Nos. (1)–(5), but with slight variations. The details do not conform to those of known mint portraits.

Reverse: Apollo as above, but with variations in execution. No monogram can be distinguished.

Legend: to the right, βασιλέως; to the left, ['Αντ]ιόχου.

Trial trench 4, Level V, Y1.

(7) Diameter 25 mm.; finish crude; condition of obverse fair, of reverse worn.

Obverse: Head of Antiochus, as on Nos. (1)–(6), with slight variations.

Reverse: Apollo as above, but with variations in detail.

No monogram can be distinguished. The legend has been obscured. Surface.

4. *Antiochus I, with Seleucus his son associated*

a. Portrait of Antiochus, reverse type and name of Seleucus

(1) Diameter 28 mm.; finish crude; condition worn. Pl. VI, Figs. 111–112.

Obverse: Head of Antiochus right, wearing diadem. The portrait approximates closely that of the elderly Antiochus reproduced on his later coinage (Babelon, Pl. V, 19; Gardner, *The Seleucid Kings of Syria*, Pl. III, 5, 7).

Reverse: Apollo nude, standing left and leaning the left elbow on a tripod. The right hand holds an arrow pointed diagonally down. This type is characteristic of the coinage of Seleucus II, grandson of Antiochus. No monogram can be distinguished.

Legend: to the right, [β]α[σιλ]έως; to the left, [Σ]ελεύκου.

The use of the portrait of Antiochus I as obverse type renders impossible an attribution of this piece to either Seleucus I, his father, or Seleucus II, his grandson. It is assigned, therefore, to a son Seleucus, who died before his father and who is named as co-king with Antiochus in the dating of cuneiform tablets during the period from 280 to 268 B.C.[15] Surface.

(2) Diameter 24 mm.; finish crude; condition worn.

Obverse: Head of Antiochus, as on No. (1); not necessarily a duplicate.

Reverse: Apollo standing, as on No. (1); not necessarily a duplicate. No monogram can be distinguished. The legend has been obscured. The close similarity of the types of No. (2) to those of No. (1) makes reasonable the attribution of this piece to Seleucus, son of Antiochus. Great House, Level III, Room 304.

5. *Antiochus III (?)*

a. Royal portrait, reverse type of Apollo seated, name Antiochus

(1) Diameter 24 mm.; finish fair; condition worn. Pl. VI, Fig. 113.

Obverse: Head right, male, wearing diadem. The features are those of a young man. Owing to the condition of the piece any identification must be considered tentative. There is, however, a definite relationship between this portrait and that on an early coin of Antiochus III (Babelon, Pl. IX, 2). There appears to be no resemblance to mint portraits of the other Antiochi.

[15] To this Seleucus must be assigned certain coins minted in the eastern portion of the Seleucid Empire which bear the legend βασιλέως Σελεύκου Ἀντιόχου. This fact has been remarked by a number of authors, the last of whom is G. Macdonald, "The Hellenic Kingdoms of Syria, Bactria, and Parthia," *The Cambridge History of India*, I, 434. The fact that the coin models mention the young Seleucus as king, unaccompanied by the name of his father, raises the question whether some coins now assigned to Seleucus II, Callinicus, may not rather belong to his little-known uncle.

Further discussion of this cast will be found on pages 213–214.

On the basis of the identification the cast must be assigned to the opening years of the reign of Antiochus III.

Reverse: Apollo seated left on omphalos holding an arrow in the right hand while the left rests on a bow. The details approximate closely those of the reverse type of the coin cited above. No monogram occurs.

Legend: to the right, obscure; to the left, ['A]ντιόχο[υ]. Great House, Level III, Room 18.

6. *Antiochus IV*

a. Royal portrait, reverse type of Apollo seated, name Antiochus

(1) Diameter 26 mm.; finish mediocre; condition, reverse obscured by triple impression of the mold. Pl. VI, Fig. 114.

Obverse: Head right, male, wearing diadem. Border of dots. The features approximate those reproduced on two coins, one assigned to Seleucus IV, the other to Antiochus IV (Babelon, Pl. XI, 13, and XII, 3).

Reverse: Apollo seated left on omphalos. The right hand holds an arrow; the left hand, though obscured, may be presumed to rest on a bow. No monogram may be distinguished.

Legend: to the right, obscured; to the left, ['Αντιό]χ[ου].

On the basis of the accepted attribution of the coins the cast must be assigned to the opening years of the reign of Antiochus IV. Alternatively the portrait may be identified as that of Seleucus IV, and the cast, along with certain coins, assigned to the brief reign of Antiochus, son of Seleucus IV. Great House, Level III, Room 220.

7. *Timarchus*

a. Royal portrait with reverse of Hercules crowning himself

(1) Diameter 32 mm.; finish good; condition fair. Pl. VI, Figs. 115–116.

Obverse: Head right, male, wearing kausia and diadem. The execution is in high relief and of good quality.

Reverse: Figure male, nude, standing facing. The legs are crossed, and the left hand rests on a large knobbed club upon which the figure leans. Hanging from the left arm may be discerned some form of drapery. The right arm is raised over the head, apparently in the act of placing a wreath or crown. This type is unknown in the Seleucid coinage, but is found in the Bactrian (Grose, III, p. 407, No. 9687; p. 410, No. 9705). No monograms occur.

Legend: To the right and the left of the type figure are four lines of what was intended to be legend. Actually, they form a series of marks without meaning. It is doubtful whether a simulation of writing was intended. The quality of execution of the types does not permit an assumption of ignorance on the part of the craftsman involved. It has been noted that a certain carelessness in execution characterizes these casts. It is probable that in the present instance the original coin on which the mold was formed bore a four-line legend in Greek, and that carelessness in the preparation of both mold and cast has obscured the form of the individual letters. The attribution of the cast to Timarchus has been discussed in a preceding chapter (see pp. 214–220). Surface.

Monogram Stamps on Pottery

This class of objects comprises twenty-eight pot handles and five fragments of bowls, each of which bears a stamp in the form of a monogram. To judge from the fragments, the bowls were of varying sizes and weights; two of the five fragments show glaze. A number of the handles retain portions of the rims and bodies to which they were attached. The original pots appear to have had a common form distinguished by rather straight sides and a large mouth with a slight lip. The top of each handle was flush with the lip. The handles were relatively short. All the pots appear to have been of one general quality, rather mediocre and underfired. It is evident from an examination of the handles that all the pots had been completely glazed on the inside, whereas on the exterior the glaze extended for only a short distance below the lip. It had been applied in a careless fashion. The pots evidently were of two or three different sizes. Some idea of their size is afforded by the diameters of the handles, which varied between two and three centimeters.

These characteristics afford some indication of the use to which these vessels were put. That other than these fragments no vessels with monogram stamps have been found, notwithstanding that the pottery from Seleucia is abundant, demonstrates that this class of stamped vessels was limited in numbers. The preservation of the fragments is probably due to the collecting instinct of children who played around the city's rubbish heaps. The mediocre quality and the careless application of the glaze point to local kilns as the source of this ware. Since, however, none of the numerous vessels of local ware that have been recovered bear such stamps, it may not be assumed that the monograms represent potters' marks. The vessels were too small and of too poor a quality to have been employed for storage purposes; the stamps, therefore, do not refer to goods which the vessels were intended to contain. The application of the glaze within the pots and around the outside of the lips suggests that the pots were used for liquids other than water. The absence of discoloration on the fragments of bodies discounts the theory of their use in cooking.

The conditions appear to favor an assumption that the pots were employed as liquid measures for oil, wine, and milk, and that the monograms identified officials responsible for the standards of measure. Similarly, the bowls may have served to measure grain, salt, or other goods of this nature. It is to be presumed that both types were employed by retail merchants. The use in antiquity of official stamps to attest the accuracy of weights is well known.[16] In Constantinople as early as the tenth century A.D. retail sellers of wine were obliged to use only containers that bore the stamp of the prefect.[17]

Of the thirty-three fragments of pots or bowls sixteen were found on the surface of the mounds and seventeen in the various Parthian levels, principally in and around the Great House. The provenances of these objects are of little value for a determination of their dates. That no examples have been found in the Seleucid level is primarily due to the slight extent of the excavations carried on in that level. The fragments recovered may represent vessels which antedate the levels in which they were found as well as those which were contemporary. In like manner the quality of the local ware and the form of the vessels,

[16] Such a weight from Seleucia is described on pages 256–258.

[17] A. E. R. Boak, "The Book of the Prefect," *Journal of Economic and Business History*, I (1929), 597–598.

in so far as this may be determined, fail as criteria of age within the limits of the city's life. They do give the impression that the vessels belonged to a relatively late period, perhaps the first to the third century A.D. However, there are no grounds for an assumption that pottery of this quality and style was not manufactured locally in the first and second centuries B.C.

The thirteen different monograms that constitute the stamps are reproduced below:

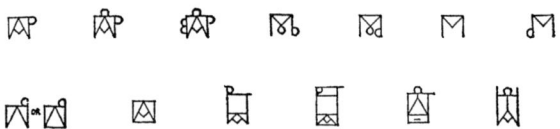

Stamped Jar Handles

These storage jar handles are of ordinary form. Though a larger number have been uncovered in the excavations, only on eleven can the details of the stamps be distinguished. It will be noted that six of the eleven handles were found in trial trench No. 4, a vertical cut to water level. There is evidence that the buildings partly uncovered here formed a part of the temple area in the different levels. To a large extent they appear to have comprised storehouses and factories. The catalog of stamps follows.

1 Two lines of legend in a rectangular stamp.

ἘπÌ Ἀγεστράτου | Ἀρταμιτίου

The personal name occurs in Pape.[18] Trial trench 21, débris.

2 Three lines of legend in a rectangular stamp.

Ἐπί | Κληωνύμου | Καρνήου

The personal name does not occur in Pape or in Preisigke.[19] Surface.

3 Three lines of legend in a rectangular stamp.

Ἐπ Ἱερέως | Ἡραγορα | δάμου

The names Ἡραγόρος and Δᾶμος occur in Pape. The combination as we appear to have it here does not occur. Trial trench 4, Level V, Z 3.

[18] W. Pape, *Wörterbuch der griechischen Eigennamen*³.
[19] Friedrich Preisigke, *Namenbuch* . . . .

4 A facing head of Helios, with two lines of legend in a rectangular stamp.

Ἐπὶ Ἀγε | μάχου

The name occurs in Pape. Trial trench 4, Level IV, débris.

5 Three lines of legend in a rectangular stamp. The first line has been incompletely impressed.

[   ] | [. .]μμαχ[ου] | Δα[.]ίου

I have been unable to make a satisfactory restoration of the names. Surface.

6 Two lines of legend in a rectangular stamp.

Διο[. . ?]ονου | Ἐ[. . . . ?]ιος

A satisfactory restoration has not been found. Trial trench 4, Level II, C 1.

7 One line of legend in a rectangular stamp.

Δωροθέου

The name occurs in Pape. Trial trench 4, Level IV, C 5.

8 One line of legend in a rectangular stamp.

Δωροθέου

The execution of No. 8 differs from that of No. 7. Trial trench 4, débris.

9 One line of legend in a rectangular stamp. It is probable that the legend was accompanied by a design, now obscured.

Ἡφακλείτου

The name does not occur in Pape or Preisigke. Great House, Level III, Room 304 sub.

10 One line of legend accompanied by a wreath with fillets, in a rectangular stamp.

Ἀμύντα

The form appears incomplete, but there is no suggestion of a character after the final alpha. Ἀμύντας occurs in Preisigke. Surface.

11 Circular legend surrounding an obscure design, in a circular stamp.

Δαμοκρατεῦς

Δαμοκράτης (genitive ους) occurs in Pape. Trial trench 4, Level V, E 4.

A Greek Stamp for Bricks

The stamp, of unbaked clay, is 9.8 centimeters square. The face opposite that which bears the legend has been built up toward the center to form a rough knob for grasping. The thickness varies from 1.5 centimeters at the edges to 5.5 centimeters at the center. The stamp is, of course, a negative, and the letters are embossed. It is broken and incomplete. The break has taken the form of cleavage along a plane roughly parallel with the finished face. The lower portion of the detached face is missing. The inner face revealed by the cleavage bears the remains of a legend. Since this face is undulating and distorted one must assume that after the stamp had been prepared, but while the clay was still soft, additional clay was pressed over the original face and legend, and a legend embossed on this new face. As this occurred while the original clay was still soft, the two legends must be strictly contemporary. Though it is possible that the two legends were distinct, the fact that only a matter of minutes separated them in time makes reasonable an assumption that their contents were similar. The superimposition was probably due to a mechanical error in the original execution.

The exterior legend, so far as it has been preserved, consists of three lines:

⊐ ▢ I A И I [.
] ▢ ⋊ I И Ǝ ꟼ Ǝ ⵣ
] A И M Y ⊓

There is a space of 2.2 centimeters between the upper edge of this face and the top of the first row of characters. This space has suffered severe abrasion. The letters of the legend vary in height between 7 and 8 millimeters. It is possible, therefore, that a line of legend occupied the abraded area.

The interior legend has been almost entirely destroyed by the super-imposition of the new face. At the top, directly under the abraded portion of the exterior legend, the single letter alpha may be distinguished at about the center of the line. At the bottom of this face, forming a curved rather than a straight line, occurs the legend ⊐ M ⊐ Y ▢ ⊓ Ǝ. This line lay under that portion of the exterior legend that is now missing.

The complete legend appears to have been composed of five lines reading as follows:

1   ]α[
2 . . . ιναῖος
3 Φερενίκο[υ]
4 Γυμνα[σιάρχος or ης]
5 Ἔτους μς

Lines two and three certainly represent proper names, the former that of the owner of the stamp, the latter perhaps that of his father. Line one is probably a part of the name. Line two was composed of nine letters. The first was almost certainly phi. The second was probably omicron (rectangular) or epsilon, possibly rho (rectangular). The third letter may have been gamma, iota, or rho, possibly tau, but scarcely upsilon. Line four must be presumed to refer to the owner of the stamp, and is completed in the nominative. The date has been calculated on the basis of the Seleucid Era and the Babylonian calendar to read 72/71 B.C. This agrees with the provenance of the stamp, Level III of the Great House, which belongs to the period from about 140 B.C. to about 43 A.D. It is probable that the stamp belonged to the owner of the Great House, who was, therefore, gymnasiarch in that year.

Inscribed Objects for Play

Among the large number of knuckle bones found in the Great House are four which bear roughly incised Greek letters: A, H, ◊, X. Another gives a complete name, Δημητρίου. The last, along with those inscribed with eta and chi, are from Level II, which dates from about 43 A.D. to 115–20 A.D. The bone marked with a theta is of Level I, from 115–20 to some time after 199 A.D. That marked with an alpha is from a late occupation of Level III, which dates from about 140 B.C. to about 43 A.D.

A circular clay disk, twenty-five millimeters in diameter and pierced through the center, bears on each side the name Καλλιμεδόντος. The letters have been roughly scratched. The name is listed in Pape. The disk was found in trial trench 4, Level V, Room 2. This level is definitely Seleucid, but a more exact date cannot be determined.

An Inscribed Weight

There was found a rectangular object of bronze weighing 29.5 grams and having dimensions of 20 × 19 × 10 millimeters. On one face is incised the monogram ⏧; on the other, the letters ΧΗ. Around the four edges runs the legend: Πατρο | φίλου | Ἔτους | ΕΠΤ. On the basis of the Seleucid Era and the Babylonian calendar the date corresponds to 74/75 A.D.

A weight found near the ruins of Babylon and dated in the first century B.C. bears the name and the title of the agoranomus. This was probably a public standard kept in the market place.[20] A weight in the British Museum records a proper name and the title παραφύλαξ. It has been suggested that this official was a "warden of weights."[21] The inscription on the weight from Seleucia appears to be the work of two different hands. The alpha of the monogram has a straight cross bar; that of the name, a V-shaped bar. The execution of the name and the date is noticeably more crude than that of the lettering on the two faces. If the monogram and the name referred to the same individual, there would have been no point in inscribing both on the one weight. It has been argued elsewhere in this volume that monograms were essentially official symbols and appear to represent controllers.[22] The weight seems to afford a clear instance of such a use. The monogram can be explained satisfactorily only on the assumption that it represents an official who, through the inscription of his monogram, attested the accuracy of the weight. Patrophilus, however, must be presumed to have been the owner of the weight.

The weight from Seleucia, unlike that from Babylon, was not a public standard. To which classification belongs the weight in the British Museum is not clear. Numbers of uninscribed weights have been found at Seleucia, principally of low denominations. The rarity of a privately owned weight which bore an official stamp is not unnatural. Until recently in the modern Orient for each finished and stamped weight in the market there were several stones or pieces of metal which appeared to satisfy

---

[20] Albert Dumont, "Poids grec trouvé à Babylone," *Revue archéologique*, N. Sér. 20 (1869), 191.

[21] F. H. Marshall, "Recent Acquisitions of the British Museum," *The Journal of Hellenic Studies*, 29 (1909), 160.   [22] See pp. 151–155.

both buyers and sellers. Commonly accepted weight standards were of course available as checks.

The characters XH on one face must be read as the unit of weight with the number of units. The former was employed to denote the chalkos as a unit of weight.[23] Our bronze, therefore, represents eight chalkoi (one obol). On the basis of the effective weight of the bronze the chalkos involved was one of 3.69 grams. This is four times the weight of the Attic chalkos as listed by Hultsch, 0.091 gram.[24] The weight found at Babylon is of 17 grams and bears in part the legend χρυσοί δύο. Dumont, taking the Attic drachm as 4.25 grams and the χρυσοῦς στατήρ as 8.50 grams, finds in this weight the exact equivalent of an Attic double stater of gold. He concludes that in the period in which the weight is dated, the first century B.C., the pure Attic standard was in use at Babylon.[25] The two weights from Babylon and Seleucia afford, however, an inadequate basis for broad conclusions concerning a system of weights in general use in Parthian Babylonia. It is a well-known fact that in the ancient, as in the modern, East a given term in respect to weights and measures might vary in value according to the period and the locality. In a single city a term might have more than one value, depending on the commodity involved.

It is noteworthy that the most common Parthian bronze coin found at Seleucia has an average weight very close to that of the chalkos established by our weight, 3.69 grams. This is approximately equivalent to the weight of the Attic half-chalkos coin. Babelon has pointed out that bronze coins of a given monetary unit frequently decreased in weight progressively over a number of years. He cites a complete series of bronze coins from Chios of the Roman period which reveal a decrease amounting to about 50 per cent.[26] It is very possible, therefore, that the type of coin from Seleucia just noted was actually the current chalkos. The hypothesis is supported by the proportions in which it occurs. The equivalence suggested between the weight of a bronze coin and that of the weight bearing the same name is not true of the Attic standards. Since, however, such an interrelation in respect to silver and gold was traditional, its occurrence in bronze units is not unnatural.

[23] Friedrich Hultsch, *Griechische und römische Metrologie*², p. 142, note 4.
[24] *Op. cit.*, p. 705, Table XII, A.   [25] *Op. cit.*, p. 199.   [26] *Op. cit.*, p. clxxxv.

OBJECTS FROM SELEUCIA

The weight was found in a room of Level I of the Great House. Patrophilus was perhaps a household slave who was engaged in retail trade. Since, however, Level I was first occupied only about 115–120 A.D., the relationship of the weight to the Great House may not be stressed.

STELE FRAGMENTS

The excavations have produced very little in the way of inscriptions. This may well be due to the fact that work has been confined largely to a private dwelling and to Parthian levels. Three fragments of inscribed stone have been recovered.

The largest fragment is of limestone and has a height of 25.2 centimeters, a width that varies between 20 and 16 centimeters, and a thickness of from 10 to 12 centimeters. The top, bottom, and right edges of the stele are intact. Parts of the inscribed surface have been badly abraded. The face opposite that which bears the inscription is unfinished. The fragment was built into a subsurface wall of a Parthian structure in trial trench 4. The provenance is of little importance for a determination of the date.

The inscription consisted of six lines. The letters have an average height of 15 millimeters, and the execution is of fair quality. The spacing of the characters is not entirely consistent. On line three, which ends in an incomplete word, a margin of 41 millimeters separates the last word and the edge of the face. On line four, however, although a word ends just 20 millimeters from the edge, the initial letter of a new word has been inserted in this space. Line six shows a right-hand margin of 43 millimeters. In lines one, two, and five abrasion has rendered impossible a determination of the margin. At the top of the inscription the margin measures 16 millimeters; at the bottom, 86 millimeters. The incomplete inscription reads as follows:

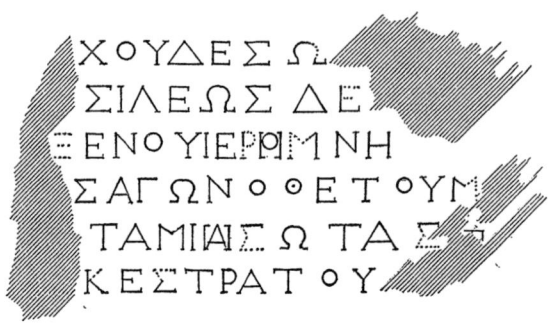

It is clear that in lines one and two we have the remains of a list naming both deified and living kings. The use of the particle δέ rather than καί in such a list is, I believe, unique. The group 'Αντιόχου | δὲ | Σωτῆρος must have been preceded by the name and a title indicative of the deified Seleucus I. The first part of line two can have contained only the name and the title of Antiochus II, and the group βα]σιλέως δὲ of this line must have been followed by the name of Seleucus II. The question arises whether Antiochus II was included as a deified king and the inscription dated in the reign of Seleucus II, or whether the stele belongs to the reign of Antiochus II with his son Seleucus associated as joint king. No inscriptions or cuneiform tablets are known that associate this particular pair, but the practice was, of course, normal in time of strife. The second hypothesis would assign the inscription to the period of war with Egypt before the second marriage of Antiochus and the consequent struggle between the queens Laodice and Berenice. Such a restoration of the list of royal names — to comprise two groups, one of two deified kings, the other of two living kings — might serve to explain the use of the particle δέ.

The third line bears the final letters of a name in the genitive case, together with the beginning of an official title; the fourth line gives another title completed in the same case. It would appear that the ἱερομνήμων and the ἀγωνοθέτης are named in the inscription as eponymous magistrates. In the fifth line we find a title, ταμίας, and a name, 'Ωτᾶς, both in the nominative.[27] It is probable that the title was associated with a preceding name. The two individuals were among the dedicators of the inscription. Line six ends in a proper noun in the genitive case, probably the name of the father of the last dedicator. Though the occurrence of the three titles in the inscription is important, it simply confirms the presence of social organisms the existence of which would necessarily be assumed for Seleucia in the third century B.C.

The second fragment is of a fair quality of marble and has a height of 8.3 centimeters, a length of 7.2 centimeters, and a thickness of 2.4 centimeters. The letters are well formed and have a height of 9 millimeters. The face of the fragment is complete only at the top. There is a margin of 31 millimeters

[27] The name occurs in Preisigke, *Namenbuch* . . . .

between the edge and the first line of inscription. Parts of three lines have been preserved:

The fragment was found in Room 130 of Level III of the Great House. The occupation of this level extended from about 140 B.C. to about 43 A.D.

The third fragment is of a poor quality of marble. It has a height of 7.5 centimeters, a length of 12.2 centimeters, and a thickness that averages 5.4 centimeters. The top and the left edge are complete. Owing to chipping, characters can be distinguished only on the left portion of the fragment. The letters are crudely formed and have an average height of about 5 millimeters. The margin at the left was of 10 to 12 millimeters, but that at the top appears to have been of not more than 6 millimeters. There is little spacing between lines and the individual letters. The initial characters of seven lines of inscription have been preserved:

The final surviving letters on lines one and two are definitely lambda, not alpha. It would appear that on both lines we have some form of the stem Ἑλλην–. On line three the final character may be either iota or an upright stroke of another letter. On line five the character after the iota may be kappa. On line seven the reading of the third and fourth letters is tentative. The fragment was found in the Great House in Room 200, assigned to Level I. A possibility exists that the suite to which this room belongs was constructed as a part of Level II and survived intact the construction of Level I. It is not possible, therefore, to state to which period the stele belonged. Occupation of Level II extended from about 43 A.D. to 115–20 A.D.; occupation of Level I ceased some time after 199 A.D.

Apart from the quality of their execution there is only one difference in form to be noted in respect to the characters common to the three stelae. On fragments one and two alpha has a straight cross bar; on fragment three, a V-shaped bar.

CHAPTER X

CONCLUSION

The attached sealings discussed in Chapters I–VIII belong to the period from about 294 to about 141 B.C. These sealings had been associated with documents or containers concerned with commercial transactions, largely, perhaps entirely, of a wholesale character. The impressions of official seals which occur on the sealings represent offices and functions of the royal government, varied in character but all having to do with the administrative and fiscal organization of Seleucid Babylonia. Although many of these offices and functions cannot be identified by means of the impressions alone, of a number we now possess through this means a more or less comprehensive idea.

The bybliophylax had previously been recognized as an official concerned with the registration of the royal lands in the various parts of the empire. It now becomes apparent that he in addition possessed some measure of control over the managers of the royal estates, especially in regard to the sale of their produce. By analogy with the use of the Seleucid anchor as the emblem of the royal treasury the presence of the equally significant tripod on the seal of the bybliophylax suggests that this official was attached to a principal department of state, identified by the tripod, which was responsible for the estates and the private revenues of the royal family.

The chreophylax, although originally a municipal official, became under the Seleucid kings a part of the royal administration. In some areas he may well have retained both fiscal and juridical functions. In Seleucia, however, owing probably to the great size of the city and to the consequent greater complexity of organization, the chreophylax appears to have had only one function, the notarization of important documents for the protection of the principals concerned.

One impression represents a form of registration of slaves, perhaps an appraisal of value for tax purposes in connection with their sale. Another form of registration, the katagraphe, is well known through the use of the term in documents from Ptolemaic Egypt. There is some difference of opinion concerning the exact value of the word as employed in the papyri, but in Seleucia it unquestionably represented a function of the government, a registration required in connection with the levy of a sales tax. It is probable that slaves were a commodity subject to this act and to the sales tax. The katagraphe was in use in Seleucia as early as about 280 B.C. This antedates the earliest record of the term in Egypt for which a definite date can be established.

The material provides evidence pointing to the existence of a class of officials, somewhat analogous to that of controllers of the mint, who were responsible for the accuracy of the established weights and measures. The seals of these officials were characterized by the use of their monograms as the type or as an element in the design. The evidence includes material from the period of Parthian control of Babylonia, after 141 B.C.

In addition to the tax on the sale of slaves, the existence of which is implied in the act of katagraphe as it occurs on the impressions, there is direct evidence of a tax on imported slaves. There appears to have been, indeed, a well-organized regulation of the slave trade in Seleucid Babylonia, a condition which favors an assumption that this trade was an important factor in the fiscal organization of the state.

A form of salt tax was of equal, perhaps greater, importance. There was no monopoly in the production of salt or in its wholesale trade. A tax, however, was collected from the purchaser upon the first-handling of this commodity, that is, upon its sale by the producer or, possibly, by the importer. Royal stewards were frequently the vendors, and one may assume that the royal estates in Babylonia included important beds of deposit salt such as are found in that area today. The evidence points to a condition of open competition in the sale of produce between the royal stewards and private individuals. The fiscal importance of the salt tax is indicated by the practice, apparently developed as early as the reign of Seleucus II, of employing the tax as a means of securing cash advances to the government. The evidence afforded by a series of impressions suggests the use of this means to finance, at least in part, the second campaign of Antiochus III into Iran. Besides the various royal taxes mentioned the impressions reveal the existence of a special levy by and for the port of Seleucia. This was of course distinct from general taxes that may have been collected on goods entering the port.

The administrative and fiscal organization of Seleucid Babylonia was fully developed early in the third century B.C. Impressions attesting the satisfaction of the salt tax occur dated in the reigns of Seleucus I and Seleucus II. As has been stated, the act of katagraphe was functioning in the opening years of the reign of Antiochus I. To the same period can be dated a sealing which bears the impress of the seals of three royal officials in addition to that of the chreophylax. That is, the transaction of which the sealing is the partial record required certification by four distinct offices of the government. The highly developed system of administration revealed by the new evidence from Seleucia was probably the work of Antiochus I, or of his advisers, during the years when he reigned as co-king with his father. Throughout this period Seleucus was involved in war and intrigue with his rivals in the west. In the east, however, Antiochus enjoyed the tranquillity necessary for the development of the forms of civil administration and, in addition, the visible evidence of the achievements in this field of his Achemenid predecessors.

The impressions throw some interesting light on the relationship of the cities in Babylonia to the royal government. The capital city, Seleucia, enjoyed less autonomy than did the neighboring city of Orchoi. In the collection of the royal taxes the city was the fiscal unit. Although direct evidence is lacking, it is probable that, with the exception of the estates of the royal family and, possibly, of temples, all arable lands were attached to the cities, and the produce of the country was taxed as it entered the city.

The material affords some little evidence for the study of the political history of the Seleucid Empire. The rather shadowy personality of Seleucus, the elder son of Antiochus I, is further defined by the appearance of his portrait as the type of an official seal and by the presence of his name with the title of king on models of coins. The revolt of Timarchus is given new significance by the Bactrian characteristics of seal impressions and a coin model which bear his portrait.

The impressions of private seals on the attached sealings may be considered representative of the upper commercial class in Seleucia. The motifs and style of these impressions demonstrate that this class was overwhelmingly Hellenic, with but little evidence of Hellenized native elements. Iranian influence as well as Babylonian, however, is found. The impressions indicate that the commercial aristocracy possessed no great degree of refinement. It appears to have been closely akin to the stock that furnished the bulk of the colonists planted throughout Asia by the Seleucid kings, people from the more backward social strata of Greece and Macedonia. It can have had little in common with the aristocracy of the older Greek cities in the western part of the empire. This orientation of the governing class in Seleucia is of real significance for the interpretation of the political history of the city in its relations with the Seleucids, the Arsacids, and Rome.

The miscellaneous material discussed in Chapter IX belongs in part to the Seleucid period, in part to the Parthian. The latter extended from about 141 B.C. to well into the third century A.D. A fragment of a stele can be assigned to the reign of Antiochus II or to that of Seleucus II. It gives us three titles which hitherto have not been found in records from the eastern part of the empire: hieromnemon, agonothetes, and tamias. A stamp that is dated in 72/71 B.C. bears a Greek name (incomplete) and the title gymnasiarch. Greek names occur on a bronze weight dated in 74/75 A.D. and on objects for play. Knuckle bones, one bearing a Greek name, the others, single letters, were found in levels that belong to the first and second centuries A.D. A large group of token sealings of this same period bear impressions which are in large measure Greek in motif and style. Here, however, the evidence for the Hellenization of native stocks is stronger. Designs characteristically Iranian become more common.

It must be borne in mind that the material treated in this volume comes largely from a single area of the excavations, the residence of a wealthy family in each of the periods of the city's life. Unsupported by the results of further research and excavation it cannot be accepted as representative of the cultures prevalent throughout Seleucia.

GREEK INDEX

I. TERMS

ἀγωνοθέτης, 258
ἀλικῆς, 50–64
ἀνδραποδικῆς, 41, 42, 64
ἀτελῶν, 55–64
βασιλέως, 246–248, 258
βυβλιοφυλακικός, 39
γυμνασιάρχος or -ης, 255
εἰσαγωγικῶν, 64
ἐπιτελῶν, 50–55

[ἐ]πιμη[[ἐ]πιφη[, 41
ἔτους, 255, 256
ἱερομνήμων, 258
ἱερέως, 252
καταγραφῆς, 42
λιμένος, 64
σωτῆρος, 258
ταμίας, 258
χρεοφυλάκων, 40

II. PROPER NAMES

A. Complete

Ἀγεμάχου, 253
Ἀγεστράτου, 252
Ἀλεξάνδρου, 243
Ἀμύντα, 253
Ἀντιόχου, 245–247, 249, 258
Ἀρταμιτίου, 252
Δαμοκρατεῦς, 253
Δημητρίου, 255
Δωροθέου, 253
Ἡραγοραδάμου, 252
Ἡφακλείτου, 253
Καλλιμεδόντος, 255
Καρνήου, 252
Κληωνύμου, 252

Πατροφίλου, 256
Σελευκείας, 50–64
Σελεύκου, 244, 248
Φερενίκου, 255
Ὠτᾶς, 258

B. Fragmentary

Δα[.]ιου, 253
Διο[. .?]ονου, 253
Ἑλλ[, 260
Ἐ[. . . .?]ιος, 253
[. . .]ιναιος, 255
]κεστρατου, 258
]μμαχου, 253
]ξενου, 258

GENERAL INDEX

Abstracts, 4, 9, 133
Administration, Seleucid in Babylonia, viii, 4, 5, 9, 25, 150, 151, 153, 158, 171, 189, 262, 264; Babylonian influence on, 6; and Antiochus I, 6, 34, 138, 179
Agents, private of royalty, 65, 129, 130, 191, 199, 201, 206, 207, 262
Agonothetes, 259, 265
Agoranomus, 146, 256
Agriculture, 204
Alexander Bala, 5, 13, 64, 68, 147, 169, 216; *see* Portraits
Alexander the Great, 243
Amphora, 118
Anchor, 30, 33, 34, 41, 43, 127, 128, 138, 158, 161, 243, 244; half-anchor, 33, 50, 158, 159, 162, 190
Antioch, 131
Antiochus I, 6, 13, 30, 51, 137, 146, 160, 179, 198, 203, 205, 206, 213, 245, 248, 264; *see* Portraits
Antiochus II, 128, 202, 206, 215, 259
Antiochus, son of Seleucus III, 13, 66; *see* Portraits
Antiochus III, 13, 52, 53, 54, 55, 64, 66, 132, 168, 178, 182, 193, 194, 263; *see* Portraits
Antiochus, son of Seleucus IV, 249
Antiochus IV, 13, 59, 60, 61, 67, 117, 163, 216, 249; *see* Portraits
Aphrodite, 233, 236
Apollo, 30, 31, 32, 47, 48, 74, 90, 148, 149, 245, 246, 247, 248, 249; Citharoedus, 31; *see* Helios
Apotheosis: of Seleucus I, 211, 212; of the Seleucid dynasty, 212
Aramaic, script, 238
Archives, of Great House, 7, 11, 143, 149, 182, 183, 190, 191, 192, 194

Aristocracy, of Seleucia, 219, 229, 230, 265
Arrow, 47, 74, 75, 81, 246, 249
Artabanus III, 167
Artemis, 33, 48, 81, 82, 83, 113, 148, 149, 236; Ephesian, 90, 113
Astrology, 126, 228, 239
Athena: Alkis, 77, 78, 79, 226; Nike, 80; Nikephore, 80; Promachos, 79, 80, 81
Autonomy, of Seleucia, 6, 166, 167, 168, 170, 171, 172, 173
Avroman, parchments, 3, 12, 187

Babylon, 146, 160, 168, 203, 205, 206, 256
Bactria, 67, 218, 219, 220
Bankers, 194, 195
Bee, 241
Bird, 94; *see* Dove, Eagle, Peacock, Pheasant, Stork
Bow, 47, 81, 245, 246, 249
Branch, 237; *see* Palm
Bullae, 1, 2, 5, 7, 9, 12; classes of, 15; Sassanian, 5
Bull, humped, 239
Bullock, head of, 124, 239
Bybliophylax, 39, 128, 129, 130, 131, 262

Caduceus, 60, 113, 163
Calendars, 157, 158, 159, 160, 161
Camel, 124
Chair, 110
Chlamys, 75, 78, 80
Chreophylax, 32, 40, 129, 131, 136, 137, 145, 149, 150, 165, 169, 170, 171, 262
Cities, relationship of, to royal administration, 264; *see* Polis

268

City goddess, *see* Tyche
Cloak, 98
Club, 99, 100, 218, 237, 249
Column, 87, 89, 91, 106, 107, 109, 113, 120
Congius, 138
Constantinople, 251
Contracts, 6, 7, 131, 150, 186, 187
Controllers, 49, 130, 151, 153, 154, 234, 256, 263
Cornucopiae, 85, 86, 87, 88, 89, 90
Countermarks; *see* Thumb nail
Crab, 126, 228
Crane, 240
Crescent, 83, 90, 113, 115, 138, 235, 240

Dates, on seals, 156, 157, 158; *see* Calendars
Deities, representations of, 74; as seal types, 30; *see* the individual names
Demeter, 87
Demetrius I, 13, 62, 63, 64, 181, 197, 216; *see* Portraits
Demetrius II, 13, 68, 132, 169, 182, 201; *see* Portraits
Demons, 104, 105
Device, Sassanian, 231, 238
Diala River, 184
Didyma, 128
Dioiketai, 131
Dionysus, 49, 75, 76, 235, 237
Dolphin, 94
Doura-Europos, 98, 134, 187, 235
Dove, 125, 235, 240
Dragon, 104

Eagle, 125, 240
Envelopes, 2, 8, 9
Environment, 224, 226
Episema, 111
Eponion, 142; *see* Tax
Era, Seleucid, 157, 161; *see* Calendars
Eros, 92, 93, 94, 237
Estates, royal, 129, 131, 201, 202, 203, 205, 262, 263

Ethnikon, 165, 166, 168, 169
Eucratides, of Bactria, 218
Exemption, from tax, 55 ff; *see* Tax, Salt

Figurines, from Seleucia, 222, 236
Fiscal area, 172, 173; *see* Registration
Flowers, 107
Frog, 126, 228
Fruit, 122

Gilgamish, 224
Great House, at Seleucia, vii, 11, 182, 184, 255, 258; fire in, 13, 182, 183, 191, 192, 194, 221
Griffins, 105, 106
Gymnasiarch, 255, 265

Hand, clasping object, 121
Hassock, 110
Hats, 98, 112; *see* Kausia, Petasos, Pylos
Helios, 51, 163, 164, 234, 235, 253
Hellenism, 225, 226
Hellenization, 225, 226, 227, 230, 232, 233, 265
Helmet, 77, 79, 80, 81, 110
Heracleides, 214, 216; *see* Portraits
Hercules, 99, 100, 218, 237, 243, 244, 249
Herm, 81, 91, 115
Hermes, 92
Hieromnemon, 259, 265
Hillah, 146
Horse, head of, 30, 43, 127, 243

Impressions; *see* Seal Impressions
Insect, 126, 241

Jerboa, 239

Kalathos, 87, 89, 91
Kantharos, 75, 77, 237
Katagraphe, 42, 141, 143, 144, 145, 148, 149, 262

Kausia, 46, 67, 215, 217, 218, 249
Kerykeion, 92
Knuckle bones, 255, 265

Label, 4, 5, 8
Ladder, 121, 122
Lamp, ceremonial, 114
Laodice, wife of Antiochus II, 202, 205
Laodice, wife of Seleucus IV, 71; see Portraits
Levels, of occupation, vii
Lion, 123
Lyre, 74, 104, 105, 107, 108

Mace, 99
Masks, 97; comic, 115, 116, 117; tragic, 117; multiple, 117
Measures, 251
Media Atropatene, 184
Medusa, 103, 227
Men: warriors, 110, 111; in pastoral scene, 112; in convivial scene, 112
Mithradates I, 219
Mithradates III, 167
Models, of coins, 241
Monograms, 26, 27, 31, 32, 34, 49, 50, 138, 139, 151, 153, 154, 233, 234, 251, 252, 256, 263; on coins, 27, 152, 154, 246; on weights, 27, 152, 256; on pottery, 27, 152, 250, 251, 252
Monopoly, in salt, 179, 184, 186, 187, 188, 189, 190, 195, 202
Motifs, of private seals, 224, 225
Mounds, of Seleucia, vii
Mythology, Greek, 226

Nike, 52, 80, 83, 84, 90, 163, 164, 237; see Athena
Nippur, 228

Octroi, 177, 188, 189, 196
Odysseus, 100, 101, 102, 224, 227
Oikonomoi, 131

Omphalos, 74, 90, 245, 246, 249
Opheltes, 104, 227
Opis, 160
Orchoi, viii, 7, 25, 33, 128, 129, 131, 140, 149, 157, 165, 168, 172, 175, 181, 194, 264
Orodes I, 167

Palm, branch, 85, 106, 107; tree, 121, 122
Palmyra, 181, 189, 242
Parthian, occupation of Seleucia, 6, 167
Peacock, 125
Penelope, 102, 227
Petasos, 92; see Hat
Pheasant, 125
Pilei, 119
Pillar, 113; see Column
Plant, 238
Play, objects for, 255
Plow, 235
Polis, 165, 167, 170, 171, 172; see Cities
Port: of Seleucia, 174, 177, 264; dues, 64, 173, 174
Portraits: private, 30; royal, 26, 29, 32, 34, 132, 148, 172, 199, 201, 207, 232, 234; of Seleucus I, 44, 65, 151, 209, 210, 245; of Antiochus I, 40, 41, 151, 211, 245, 246, 247, 248; of Seleucus, son of Antiochus I, 45, 211, 213; of Seleucus III, 45; of Antiochus, son of Seleucus III, 66; of the queen of Seleucus III, 71; of Antiochus III, 66, 248; of Seleucus IV, 66; of Laodice, queen of Seleucus IV, 71; of Antiochus IV, 45, 67, 249; of Timarchus, 46, 67, 214, 216, 217, 249; of Heracleides, brother of Timarchus, 46, 214; of Demetrius I, 49, 69; of Alexander Bala with Cleopatra Thea, 68; of Demetrius II, 13, 68; with Cleopatra Thea, 69
Pottery, from Seleucia, 222
Priests, 98

Principals, to contracts, 4, 6, 7, 8, 9, 143, 150, 186, 222
Psyche, 95, 96
Pylos, 100, 101, 102; *see* Hats

Ram, 239
Registers, 134; *see* Abstracts
Registration: offices of, 4, 7, 134; acts of, 7, 8, 33, 137, 139, 146, 148, 150, 151, 156, 197, 198, 262; notarial, juridical, and fiscal, 135, 137; of slaves, 33, 139, 143, 146, 147, 162, 175, 177, 178, 263; of slaves for assessment, 41, 138, 140, 147, 262; of slaves for sale, 42; *see* Chreophylax, Katagraphe
Ring, 238
River god, 97

Salt, 143, 181, 184, 187, 194, 200, 202; merchants, 194, 196; *see* Monopoly, Tax
Sardis, 131
Scepter, 85, 86, 88, 89, 91, 92
Sea horse, 94
Seal engravers, 29
Seal impressions: characteristics of, 25; condition of, 36, 222; synopsis of, 36 ff; of private seals, 186, 221, 222, 223, 264
Sealings: definition of, 1; attached, 1, 14, 262; table of, 15 ff.; appended, 1, 3, 9; convex, 3, 4, 5, 9; container, 10; token, 1, 231, 232, 265
Seals: definitions of, 1; purpose of, 25; design of, 28; types of, 29, 156; of state, 34; official, shape of, 26, 156; official, size of, 26, 200; official, other characteristics of, 31, 35, 156; private, 28
Seleucia, vii, 5, 25, 27, 33, 120, 130, 146, 150, 158, 159, 160, 165, 166, 167, 168, 171, 172, 177, 191, 193, 195, 201, 203, 204, 205, 206, 216, 219, 221, 232, 242, 264, 265; Greeks in, 221, 222, 226, 227, 228, 230; Orientals in, 227, 230, 232, 233
Seleucus I, 5, 13, 30, 51, 65, 160, 182, 198, 201, 203, 204, 206, 209, 243, 244, 245, 259; *see* Portraits
Seleucus, son of Antiochus I, 213, 248, 264; *see* Portraits
Seleucus II, 13, 52, 164, 182, 194, 248, 259, 263
Seleucus IV, 56, 57, 58, 66, 249; *see* Portraits
Settlement, of Greeks in Orient, 221, 229
Shield, 77, 78, 79, 80, 110, 111
Silenus, 97
Slaves; *see* Registration, Tax
Snake knot, 103
Spear, 79, 80, 91, 110, 111
Staff, 91, 100, 101, 102, 112
Stamps: definition of, 1; on jar handles, 252; for bricks, 254
Stand, 109
Standard, ceremonial, 114
Standards, 139, 140, 154, 251, 257
Star, 60, 61, 113, 138, 163, 228
Stelae, 258, 259, 260
Stewards, royal; *see* Agents
Stork, 240
Sun, 113, 228
Surface, objects from, viii
Susa, 232
Sword, 100, 102

Tamias, 259, 265
Tax, sales, 140, 142, 186, 188, 195, 197; salt, 50, 142, 162, 179, 181, 184, 185, 193, 194, 195, 197, 263; on imported slaves, 64, 162, 175, 177, 263; *see* Octroi, Port dues
Tax collectors, 7, 50, 128, 143, 150, 156, 163, 165, 169, 170, 186, 191
Temple, 26, 75, 132, 133, 202, 205, 206, 252; archives, 6
Tessarae, 232
Throne, 91
Thumb nail, impression of, on sealings, 10

Thunderbolt, 114, 237
Thymiaterion, 49, 109
Thyrsos, 75, 77, 237
Timarchus, 61, 67, 163, 214, 215, 218, 219, 220, 264; *see* Portraits
Tiridates II, of Parthia, 164
Titles, at Seleucia, 259
Token sealings; *see* Sealings
Torch, 86, 87, 88, 89, 90
Trade: transit, 174; routes, 219; control of, 6, 150, 174
Treasury, royal, 34, 43, 127, 128, 140, 161, 162, 170, 171, 190, 193, 194
Trial trenches, vii
Tripod, 31, 39, 74, 75, 98, 112, 128, 248, 262
Tunic, 81, 112
Turreted crown, 87, 88
Tyche, 85, 86, 87, 88, 89, 90, 91

Ur, 232

Vase, 33, 41, 138
Versions, exterior and interior, 4, 5
Vessel, 49, 98, 112, 118, 119, 120; *see* Amphora, Congius, Vase

Weights, 146, 153, 256, 257, 265
Wheat, 123
Wig, 99
Wind instrument, 109
Witnesses, to a contract, 6, 7, 9, 143, 155, 186, 187, 191, 202, 222
Women: dancers, 109; draped, 106, 107; nude, 108, 109; posed informally, 109, 110
Worshipers, 98
Wreath, 49, 75, 76, 83, 84, 91, 92, 93, 94, 97, 108, 114, 120, 235, 237, 238, 249, 253
Writing material, 12

Zeta, reversed, 56, 61
Zeus, 32, 210, 243, 244

PLATES

PLATE I

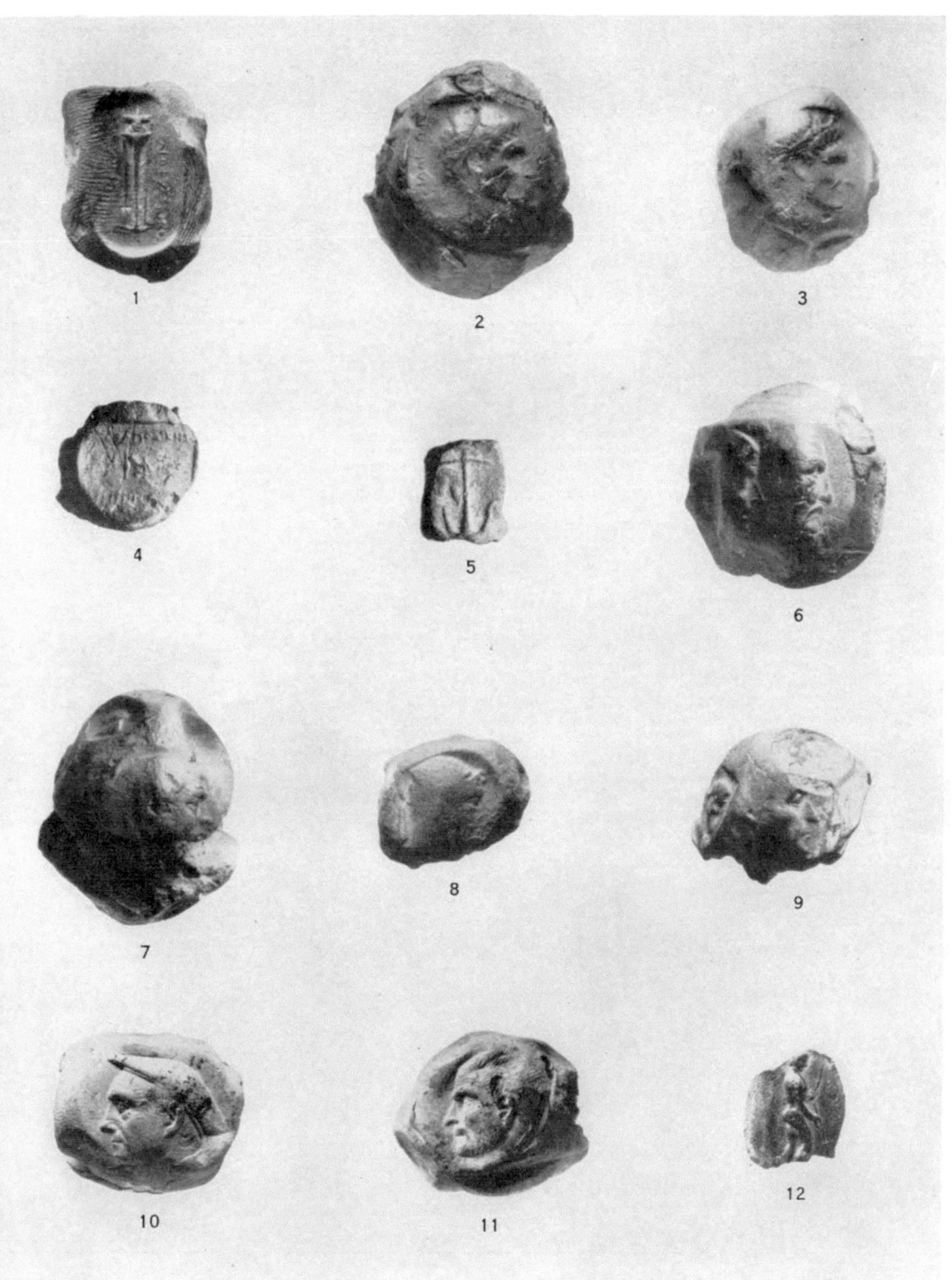

Official seals

PLATE II

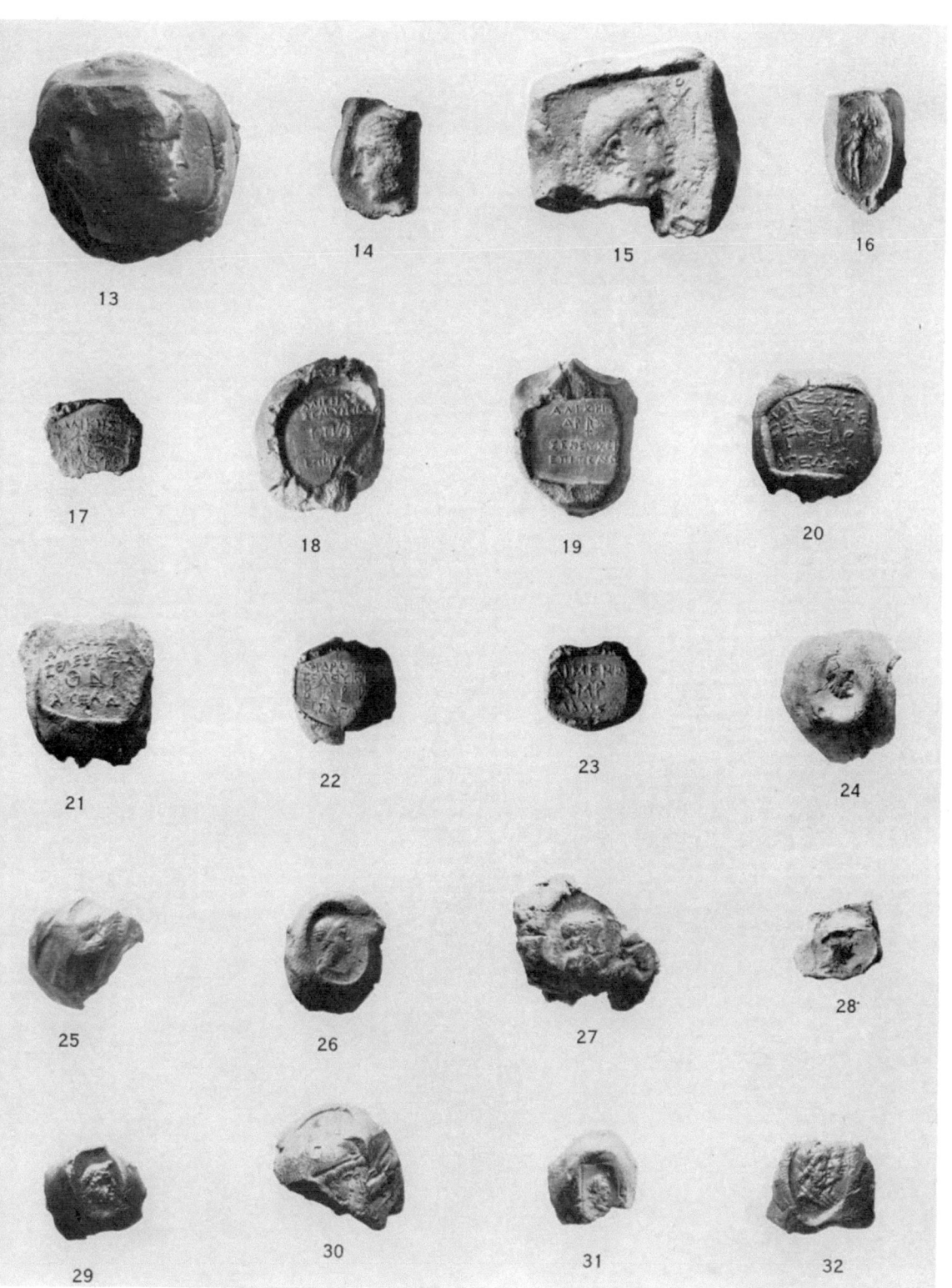

Official seals, 13–23; seals of private agents of royalty, 24–32

PLATE III

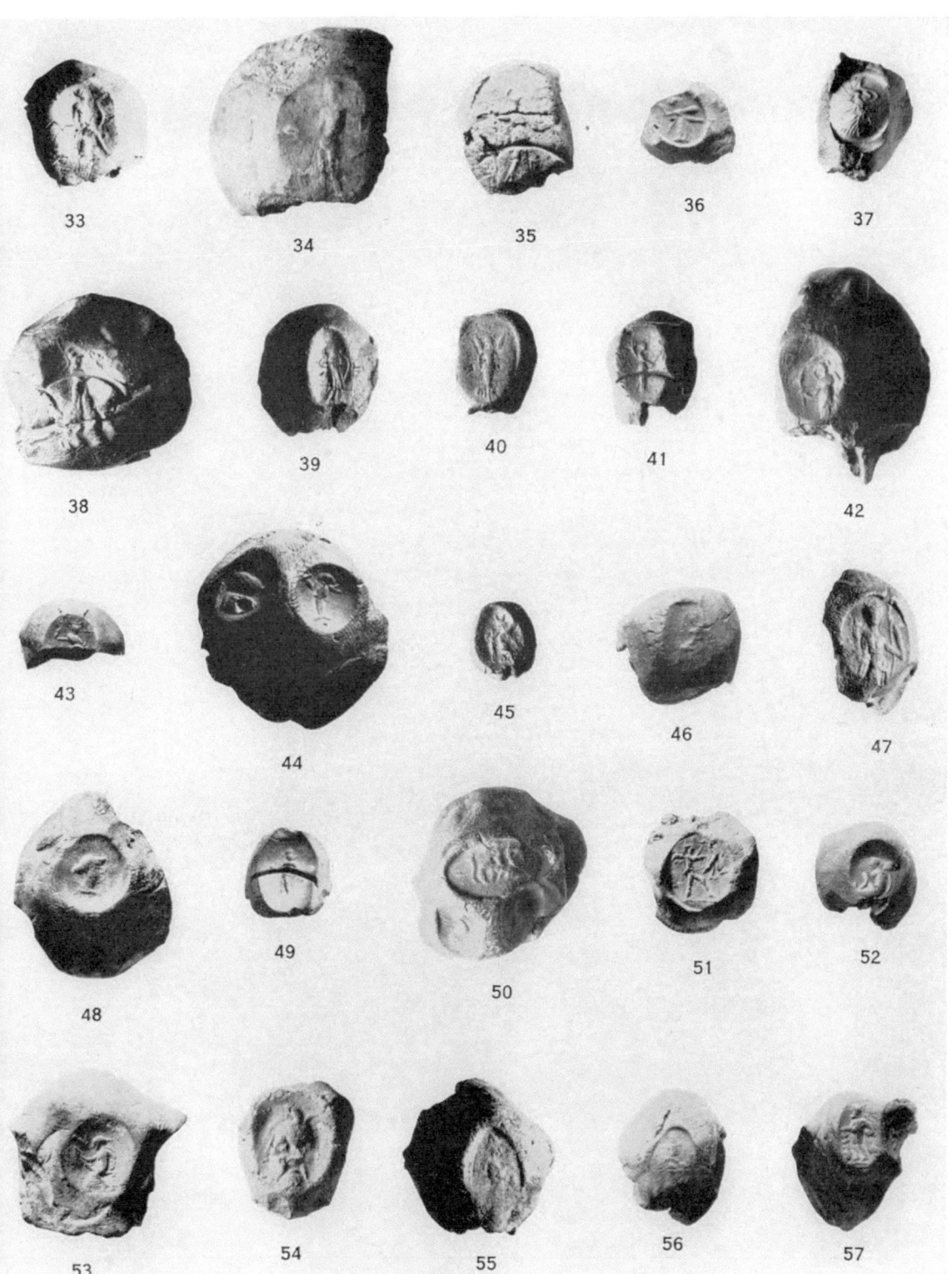

Private seals

PLATE IV

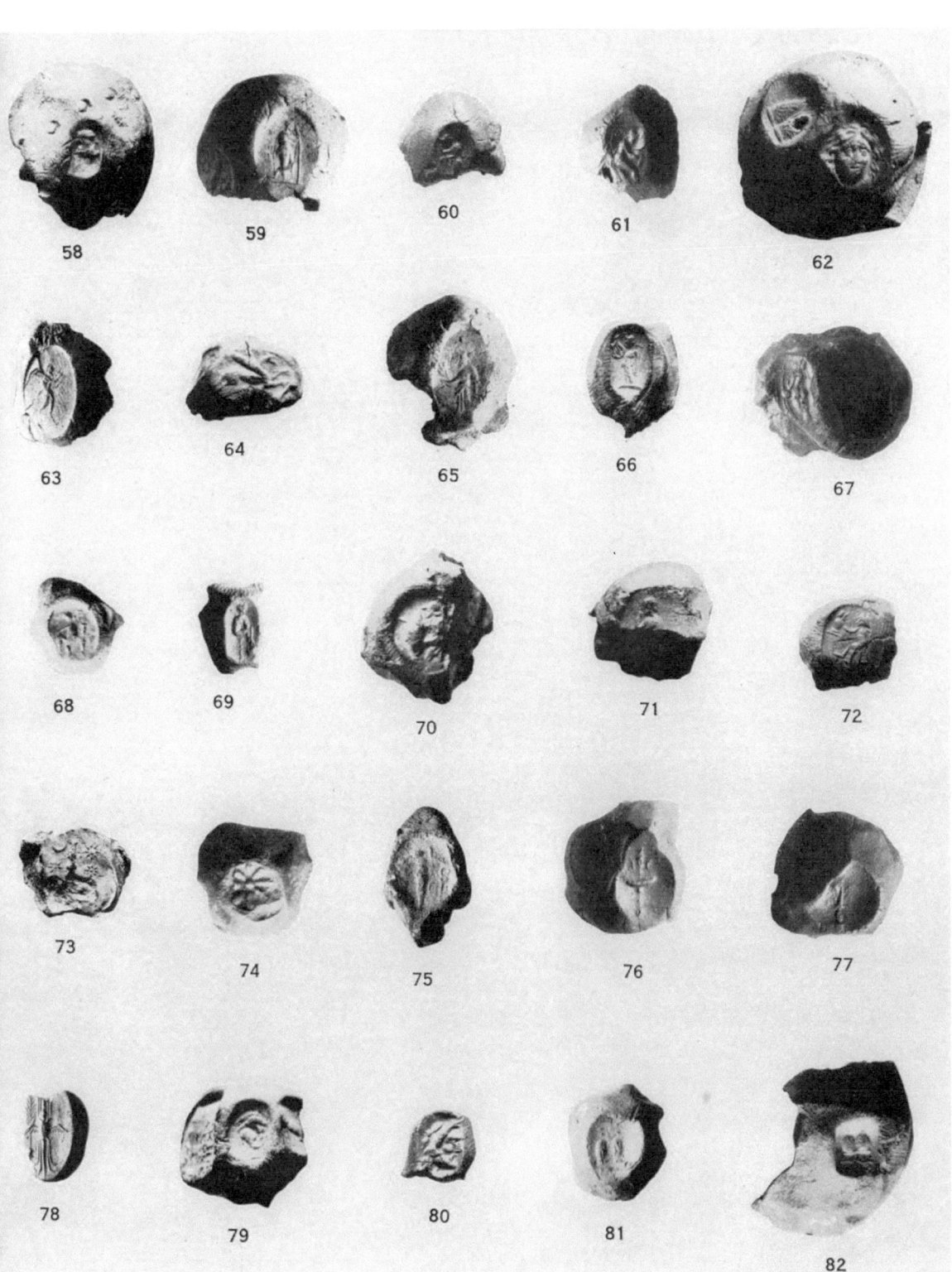

Private seals

PLATE V

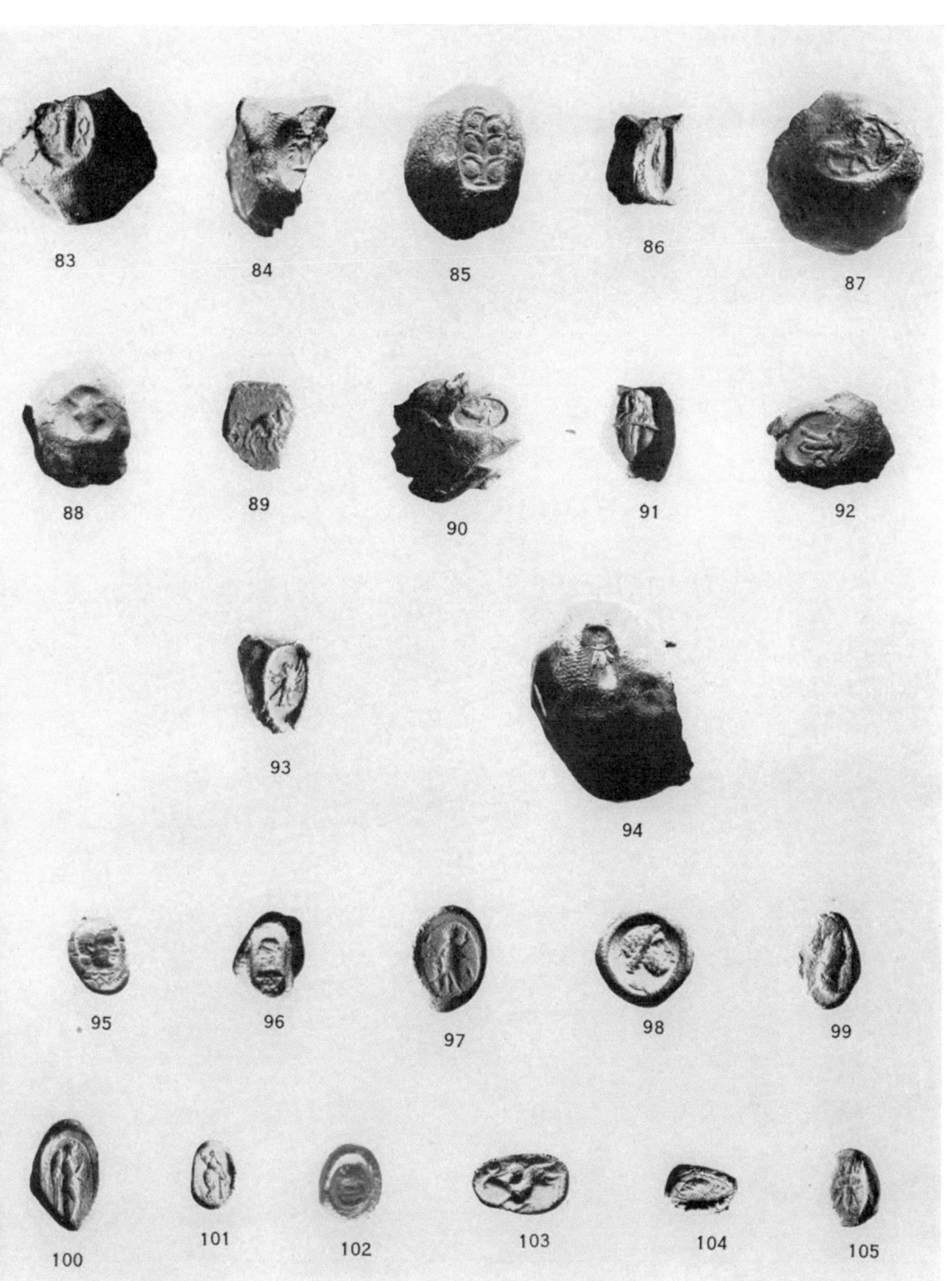

Private seals, 83-94; token sealings, 95-105

PLATE VI

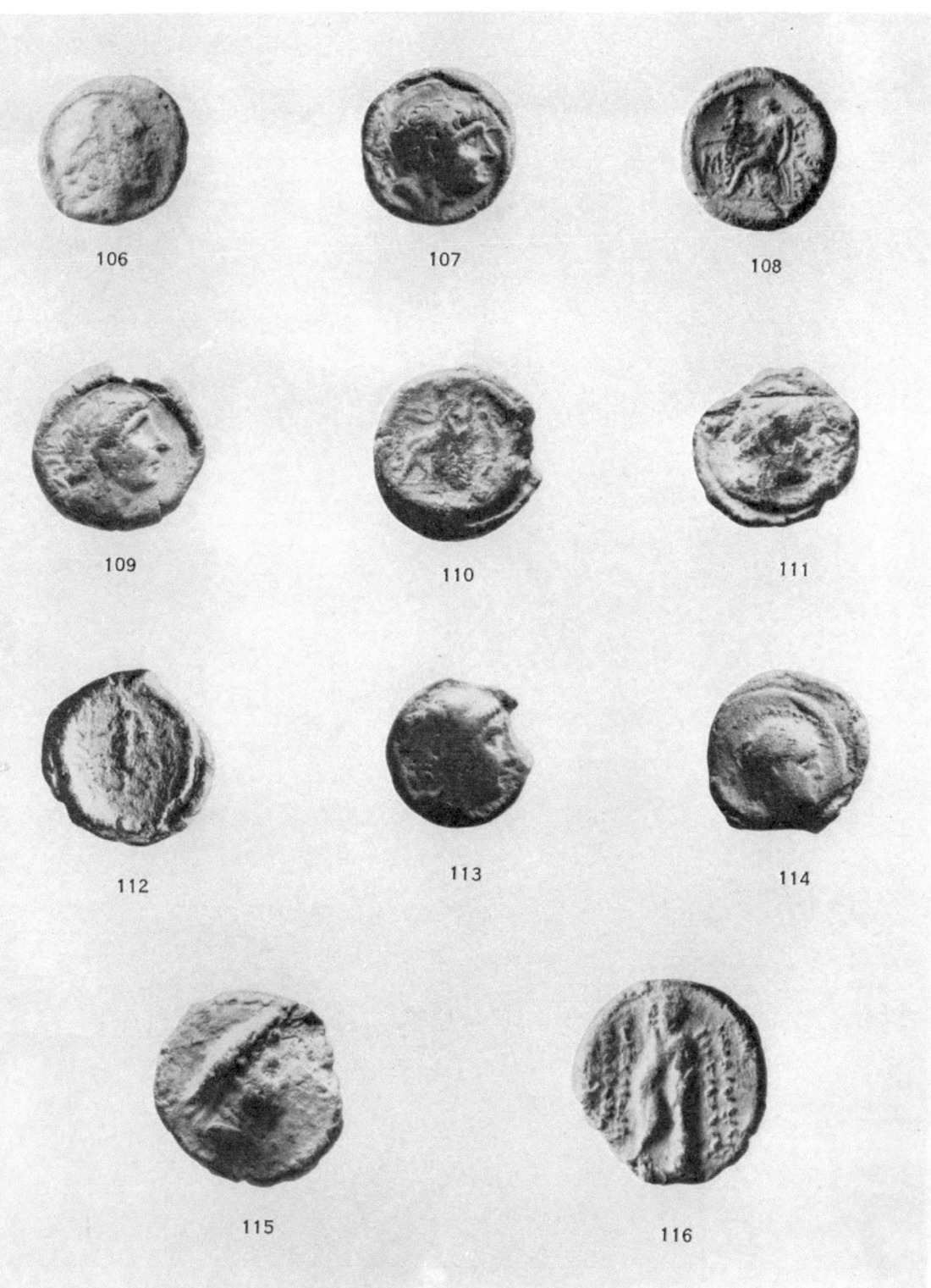

Models of Seleucid coins

University of Michigan Studies

HUMANISTIC SERIES

General Editors: JOHN G. WINTER, HENRY A. SANDERS, and EUGENE S. McCARTNEY

Size, 22.7 × 15.2 cm. 8°. Bound in cloth.

Vol. I. ROMAN HISTORICAL SOURCES AND INSTITUTIONS. Edited by Henry A. Sanders. (*Out of print.*)

Vol. II. WORD FORMATION IN PROVENCAL. By Edward L. Adams. Pp. xvii + 607. $4.00.

Vol. III. LATIN PHILOLOGY. Edited by C. L. Meader. (*Out of print.*)

Parts I, II Available in Paper Covers

Part I. THE USE OF IDEM, IPSE, AND WORDS OF RELATED MEANING. By C. L. Meader. Pp. 1–112. $0.75.

Part II. A STUDY IN LATIN ABSTRACT SUBSTANTIVES. By M. A. Stewart. Pp. 113–78. $0.40.

Vol. IV. ROMAN HISTORY AND MYTHOLOGY. Edited by Henry A. Sanders. (*Out of print.*)

Parts I, III Available in Paper Covers

Part I. STUDIES IN THE LIFE OF HELIOGABALUS. By Orma Fitch Butler. Pp. 1–169. $1.25.

Part III. ROMAN LAW STUDIES IN LIVY. By Alvin E. Evans. Pp. 275–354. $0.40.

Vol. V. SOURCES OF THE SYNOPTIC GOSPELS. By C. S. Patton. Pp. xiii + 263. $1.30.

Size, 28 × 18.5 cm. 4to.

Vol. VI. ATHENIAN LEKYTHOI WITH OUTLINE DRAWING IN GLAZE VARNISH ON A WHITE GROUND. By Arthur Fairbanks. With 15 plates, and 57 illustrations in the text. Pp. viii + 371. $4.00.

Vol. VII. ATHENIAN LEKYTHOI WITH OUTLINE DRAWING IN MATT COLOR ON A WHITE GROUND, AND AN APPENDIX: ADDITIONAL LEKYTHOI WITH OUTLINE IN GLAZE VARNISH ON A WHITE GROUND. By Arthur Fairbanks. With 41 plates. Pp. x + 275. $3.50.

Vol. VIII. THE OLD TESTAMENT MANUSCRIPTS IN THE FREER COLLECTION. By Henry A. Sanders. With 9 plates showing pages of the Manuscripts in facsimile. Pp. x + 323. $3.50.

Parts Sold Separately in Paper Covers

Part I. THE WASHINGTON MANUSCRIPT OF DEUTERONOMY AND JOSHUA. With 3 folding plates. Pp. vi + 104. $1.25.

Orders should be addressed to The Librarian, University of Michigan, Ann Arbor, Michigan.

Part II. THE WASHINGTON MANUSCRIPT OF THE PSALMS. With 1 single plate and 5 folding plates. Pp. viii + 105–357. $2.00.

VOL. IX. THE NEW TESTAMENT MANUSCRIPTS IN THE FREER COLLECTION. By Henry A. Sanders. With 8 plates showing pages of the Manuscripts in facsimile. Pp. x + 323. $3.50.

Parts Sold Separately in Paper Covers

Part I. THE WASHINGTON MANUSCRIPT OF THE FOUR GOSPELS. With 5 plates. Pp. vii + 247. $2.00.

Part II. THE WASHINGTON MANUSCRIPT OF THE EPISTLES OF PAUL. With 3 plates. Pp. vii, 249–315. $1.25.

VOL. X. THE COPTIC MANUSCRIPTS IN THE FREER COLLECTION. By William H. Worrell. With 12 plates. Pp. xxvi + 396. $4.75.

Parts Sold Separately in Paper Covers

Part I. THE COPTIC PSALTER. The Coptic Text in the Sahidic Dialect, with an Introduction, and with 6 plates showing pages of the Manuscript and Fragments in Facsimile. Pp. xxvi + 112. $2.00.

Part II. A HOMILY ON THE ARCHANGEL GABRIEL BY CELESTINUS, ARCHBISHOP OF ROME, AND A HOMILY ON THE VIRGIN BY THEOPHILUS, ARCHBISHOP OF ALEXANDRIA, FROM MANUSCRIPT FRAGMENTS IN THE FREER COLLECTION AND THE BRITISH MUSEUM. The Coptic Text, with an Introduction and Translation, and with 6 plates showing pages of the Manuscript in Facsimile. Pp. 113–396. $2.50.

VOL. XI. CONTRIBUTIONS TO THE HISTORY OF SCIENCE. By Louis C. Karpinski and John G. Winter. With 11 plates. Pp. xi + 283. $3.50.

Parts Sold Separately

Part. I. ROBERT OF CHESTER'S LATIN TRANSLATION OF THE ALGEBRA OF AL-KHOWARIZMI. With an Introduction, Critical Notes, and an English Version. By Louis C. Karpinski. With 4 plates showing pages of manuscripts in facsimile, and 25 diagrams in the text. Pp. vii + 164. $2.00.

Part II. THE PRODROMUS OF NICOLAUS STENO'S LATIN DISSERTATION ON A SOLID BODY ENCLOSED BY PROCESS OF NATURE WITHIN A SOLID. Translated into English by John G. Winter, with a Foreword by William H. Hobbs. With 7 plates. Pp. vii + 169–283. $1.30.

VOL. XII. STUDIES IN EAST CHRISTIAN AND ROMAN ART. By Charles Morey and Walter Dennison. (*Out of print.*)

VOL. XIII. FRAGMENTS FROM THE CAIRO GENIZAH IN THE FREER COLLECTION. By Richard Gottheil, and William H. Worrell. Text, with Translation, Notes and an Introduction. With 52 plates showing the different styles of writing in facsimile. Pp. xxxi + 273. $4.00.

Orders should be addressed to The Librarian, University of Michigan, Ann Arbor, Michigan.

University of Michigan Studies

Vol. XIV. Two Studies in Later Roman and Byzantine Administration. By Arthur E. R. Boak and James E. Dunlap. Pp. x + 324. $2.25.

Part II Available in Paper Cover

Part II. The Office of the Grand Chamberlain in the Later Roman and Byzantine Empires. By James E. Dunlap. Pp. 161–324. $1.00 net.

Vol. XV. Greek Themes in Modern Musical Settings. By Albert A. Stanley. (*Out of print.*)

Parts Sold Separately in Paper Covers

Part I. Incidental Music to Percy Mackaye's Drama of Sappho and Phaon. Pp. 1–68. $0.90.

Part II. Music to the Alcestis of Euripides with English Text. Pp. 71–120. $0.80.

Part III. Music for the Iphigenia among the Taurians by Euripides, with Greek Text. Pp. 123–214. $0.75.

Part IV. Two Fragments of Ancient Greek Music. Pp. 217–225. $0.30.

Part V. Music to Cantica of the Menaechmi of Plautus. Pp. 229–263. $0.50.

Part VI. Attis: A Symphonic Poem. Pp. 265–384. $1.00.

Vol. XVI. Nicomachus of Gerasa: Introduction to Arithmetic. Translated into English by Martin Luther D'Ooge, with Studies in Greek Arithmetic by Frank Egleston Robbins and Louis C. Karpinski. (*Out of print.*)

Vols. XVII–XX. Royal Correspondence of the Assyrian Empire. Translated into English with a Transliteration of the Text and a Commentary. By Leroy Waterman.

Vol. XVII. Translation and Transliteration. Pp. x + 492. $4.50.

Vol. XVIII. Translation and Transliteration. Pp. iv + 524. $4.50.

Vol. XIX. Commentary. Pp. x + 377. $4.00.

Vol. XX. Supplement and Indexes. (*In preparation.*)

Vol. XXI. The Minor Prophets in the Freer Collection and the Berlin Fragment of Genesis. By Henry A. Sanders and Carl Schmidt. With 7 plates. Pp. xii + 436. $3.50.

Vol. XXII. A Papyrus Codex of the Shepherd of Hermas, with a Fragment of the Mandates. By Campbell Bonner. Pp. x + 137. With 5 plates. $3.00.

Vol. XXIII. The Complete Commentary of Oecumenius on the Apocalypse: Now printed for the first time from Manuscripts at Messina, Rome, Salonika and Athos. By H. C. Hoskier. Pp. viii + 260. $4.00.

Orders should be addressed to The Librarian, University of Michigan, Ann Arbor, Michigan.

University of Michigan Studies

Vol. XXIV. Zenon Papyri in the University of Michigan Collection (= Michigan Papyri, Vol. I). By C. C. Edgar. Pp. xiv + 211. With 6 plates. $3.50.

Vol. XXV. Karanis: Topographical and Architectural Report of Excavations during the Seasons 1924–28. By A. E. R. Boak and E. Peterson. Pp. viii + 69. With 42 plates, 19 plans, and 1 map. $2.00.

Vol. XXVI. Coptic Sounds. By William H. Worrell. With an Appendix by Hide Shohara. Pp. xviii + 186. $3.00.

Vol. XXVII. Athenian Financial Documents of the Fifth Century. By B. D. Meritt. Pp. xiv + 192. $3.50.

Vols. XXVIII–XXIX (= Michigan Papyri, Vols. II–III). Papyri from Tebtunis. By A. E. R. Boak.
Vol. XXVIII (= Michigan Papyri, Vol. II). Pp. xvi + 259. With 4 plates. $3.50.
Vol. XXIX. (*In preparation.*)

Vol. XXX. Karanis: The Temples, Coin Hoards, Botanical and Zoölogical Reports, Seasons 1924–1931. Edited by A. E. R. Boak. Pp. xii + 93. With 37 plates, 16 plans, and 4 diagrams. $2.50.

Vol. XXXI. Ancient Textiles from Egypt in the University of Michigan Collection. By Lillian M. Wilson. Pp. x + 77. With 23 plates. $2.50.

Vol. XXXII. Parthian Pottery from Seleucia on the Tigris. By Neilson C. Debevoise. Pp. xiv + 132. With 14 plates. $3.00.

Vol. XXXIII. The Athenian Assessment of 425 b.c. By B. D. Meritt and A. B. West. Pp. xiv + 112. With 2 plates and 17 figures. $2.50.

Vols. XXXIV–XXXV. Greek Ostraca in the University of Michigan Collection. By Leiv Amundsen.
Vol. XXXIV. Part I, Text. Pp. xiv + 232. $3.50.
Vol. XXXV. Part II, Commentary. (*In preparation.*)

Vol. XXXVI. Stamped and Inscribed Objects from Seleucia on the Tigris. By R. H. McDowell. Pp. xviii + 272. $3.50.

Vol. XXXVII. Coins from Seleucia on the Tigris. By R. H. McDowell. (*In preparation.*)

FACSIMILES OF MANUSCRIPTS

Facsimile of the Washington Manuscript of Deuteronomy and Joshua in the Freer Collection. With an Introduction by Henry A. Sanders. Pp. x; 201 heliotype plates.

Orders should be addressed to The Librarian, University of Michigan, Ann Arbor, Michigan.

Limited edition, distributed only to libraries, under certain conditions. A list of libraries containing this Facsimile is printed in *University of Michigan Studies, Humanistic Series*, Volume VIII, pp. 351–353.

FACSIMILE OF THE WASHINGTON MANUSCRIPT OF THE FOUR GOSPELS IN THE FREER COLLECTION. With an Introduction by Henry A. Sanders. Pp. x; 372 heliotype plates and 2 colored plates.

Limited edition, distributed only to libraries, under certain conditions. A list of libraries containing this Facsimile is printed in *University of Michigan Studies, Humanistic Series*, Volume IX, pp. 317–320.

FACSIMILE OF THE WASHINGTON MANUSCRIPT OF THE MINOR PROPHETS IN THE FREER COLLECTION AND THE BERLIN FRAGMENT OF GENESIS. With an Introduction by Henry A. Sanders. With 130 plates.

Limited edition, distributed only to libraries, under certain conditions. A list of libraries containing this Facsimile is printed in *University of Michigan Studies, Humanistic Series*, Volume XXI, pp. 431–434.

THE JEROME LECTURES

LIFE AND LETTERS IN THE PAPYRI. By John G. Winter. Pp. viii + 308. $3.50.

SCIENTIFIC SERIES

Size, 28 × 18.5 cm. 4°. Bound in cloth.

VOL. I. THE CIRCULATION AND SLEEP. By John F. Shepard. Pp. ix + 83, with an Atlas of 63 plates, bound separately. Text and Atlas. $2.50.

VOL. II. STUDIES ON DIVERGENT SERIES AND SUMMABILITY. By Walter B. Ford. Pp. xi + 194. $2.50.

Size, 23.5 × 15.5 cm.

VOL. III. THE GEOLOGY OF THE NETHERLANDS EAST INDIES. By H. A. Brouwer. With 18 plates and 17 text figures. Pp. xii + 160. $3.00.

VOL. IV. THE GLACIAL ANTICYCLONES: THE POLES OF THE ATMOSPHERIC CIRCULATION. By William Herbert Hobbs. With 3 plates and 53 figures. Pp. xxiv + 198. $2.75.

VOLS. V–VIII. REPORTS OF THE GREENLAND EXPEDITIONS OF THE UNIVERSITY OF MICHIGAN (1926–31). W. H. Hobbs, Director.

VOL. V. AËROLOGY, EXPEDITIONS OF 1926 AND 1927–29. With 23 plates and 30 text figures. Pp. x + 262. $6.00.
VOL. VI. AËROLOGY, EXPEDITIONS OF 1930–31. (*In preparation.*)

VOL. VII. METEOROLOGY. (*In preparation.*)
VOL. VIII. GEOLOGY, GLACIOLOGY, BOTANY, ETC. (*In preparation.*)

Orders should be addressed to The Librarian, University of Michigan, Ann Arbor, Michigan.

Vol. IX. THE GENUS DIAPORTHE NITSCHKE AND ITS SEGREGATES. By Lewis E. Wehmeyer. Pp. xii + 349. With 18 plates. $3.50.

Vol. X. THE DISTRIBUTION OF THE CURRENTS OF ACTION AND OF INJURY DISPLAYED BY HEART MUSCLE AND OTHER EXCITABLE TISSUES. By F. N. Wilson, A. G. Macleod, and P. S. Barker. Pp. viii + 59. $1.50.

University of Michigan Publications

General Editor: EUGENE S. McCARTNEY

HUMANISTIC PAPERS

Size, 22.7 × 15.2 cm. 8°. Bound in cloth.

THE LIFE AND WORK OF GEORGE SYLVESTER MORRIS: A CHAPTER IN THE HISTORY OF AMERICAN THOUGHT IN THE NINETEENTH CENTURY. By Robert M. Wenley. Pp. xv + 332. $1.50.

HENRY PHILIP TAPPAN: PHILOSOPHER AND UNIVERSITY PRESIDENT. By Charles M. Perry. Pp. xii + 475. $3.25.

LATIN AND GREEK IN AMERICAN EDUCATION, WITH SYMPOSIA ON THE VALUE OF HUMANISTIC STUDIES. Revised edition. Edited by Francis W. Kelsey. Pp. xiii + 360. $2.00.

Size, 18 × 12 cm.

THE MENAECHMI OF PLAUTUS. The Latin Text, with a Translation by Joseph H. Drake, University of Michigan. Pp. xi + 129. $0.60.

LANGUAGE AND LITERATURE

Vol. I. STUDIES IN SHAKESPEARE, MILTON AND DONNE. By Members of the English Department of the University of Michigan. Pp. viii + 232. $2.50.

Vol. II. ELIZABETHAN PROVERB LORE IN LYLY'S 'EUPHUES' AND IN PETTIE'S 'PETITE PALLACE,' WITH PARALLELS FROM SHAKESPEARE. By Morris P. Tilley. Pp. x + 461. $3.50.

Vol. III. THE SOCIAL MODE OF RESTORATION COMEDY. By Kathleen M. Lynch. Pp. x + 242. $2.50.

Vol. IV. STUART POLITICS IN CHAPMAN'S 'TRAGEDY OF CHABOT.' By Norma D. Solve. Pp. x + 176. $2.50.

Vol. V. EL LIBRO DEL CAUALLERO ZIFAR: Part I, Text. By C. P. Wagner. Pp. xvii + 532, with 9 plates. $5.00.

Orders should be addressed to The Librarian, University of Michigan, Ann Arbor, Michigan.

Vol. VI. El Libro del Cauallero Zifar: Part II, Commentary. By C. P. Wagner. (*In preparation.*)

Vol. VII. Strindberg's Dramatic Expressionism. By C. E. W. L. Dahlström. Pp. xii + 242. $2.50.

Vol. VIII. Essays and Studies in English and Comparative Literature. By Members of the English Department of the University of Michigan. Pp. viii + 231. $2.50.

Vol. IX. Toward the Understanding of Shelley. By Bennett Weaver. Pp. xii + 258. $2.50.

Vol. X. Essays and Studies in English and Comparative Literature. By Members of the English Department of the University of Michigan. Pp. vi + 278. $2.50.

Vol. XI. French Modal Syntax in the Sixteenth Century. By Newton S. Bement. Pp. x + 168. $2.50.

Vol. XII. The Intellectual Milieu of John Dryden. By Louis I. Bredvold. Pp. viii + 189. $2.50.

Three Centuries of French Poetic Theory (1328–1630). By W. F. Patterson. (*In press.*)

HISTORY AND POLITICAL SCIENCE

The first three volumes of this series were published as "Historical Studies" under the direction of the Department of History. Volumes IV and V were published without numbers.

Vol. I. A History of the President's Cabinet. By Mary Louise Hinsdale. (*Out of print.*)

Vol. II. English Rule in Gascony, 1199–1259, with Special Reference to the Towns. By Frank Burr Marsh. Pp. xi + 178. $1.25.

Vol. III. The Color Line in Ohio; A History of Race Prejudice in a Typical Northern State. By Frank Uriah Quillan. (*Out of print.*)

Vol. IV. The Senate and Treaties, 1789–1817. The Development of the Treaty-Making Functions of the United States Senate during Their Formative Period. By Ralston Hayden. Pp. xvi + 237. $1.50.

Vol. V. William Plumer's Memorandum of Proceedings in the United States Senate, 1803–1807. Edited by Everett Somerville Brown. Pp. xi + 873. $3.50.

Vol. VI. The Grain Supply of England during the Napoleonic Period. By W. F. Galpin. Pp. xi + 305. $3.00.

Orders should be addressed to The Librarian, University of Michigan, Ann Arbor, Michigan.

Vol. VII. Eighteenth Century Documents relating to the Royal Forests, the Sheriffs and Smuggling: Selected from the Shelburne Manuscripts in the William L. Clements Library. By Arthur Lyon Cross. With 4 plates. Pp. x + 328. $3.00.

Vol. VIII. The Low Countries and the Hundred Years' War, 1326–1347. By Henry S. Lucas. Pp. xiv + 696. $4.00.

Vol. IX. The Anglo-French Treaty of Commerce of 1860 and the Progress of the Industrial Revolution in France. By A. L. Dunham. Pp. xiv + 409. $3.50.

Vol. X. The Youth of Erasmus. By A. Hyma. Pp. xii + 350. With 8 plates and 2 maps. $3.00.

CONTRIBUTIONS FROM THE MUSEUM OF PALEONTOLOGY

Vol. I. The Stratigraphy and Fauna of the Hackberry Stage of the Upper Devonian. By Carroll Lane Fenton and Mildred Adams Fenton. With 45 plates, 9 text figures, and 1 map. Pp. xi + 260. $2.75.

Vol. II. Consisting of 14 miscellaneous papers. With 41 plates, 39 text figures, and 1 map. Pages ix + 240. $3.00.

Vol. III. Consisting of 13 miscellaneous papers. With 64 plates, 49 text figures, and 1 map. Pp. viii + 275. $3.50.

Vol. IV. Consisting of miscellaneous papers. (*In progress.*)

ARCHAEOLOGICAL REPORTS

Preliminary Report upon the Excavations at Tel Umar, Iraq, Conducted by the University of Michigan and the Toledo Museum of Art. Leroy Waterman, Director. With 13 plates and 7 text figures. Pp. x + 62. $1.50. Bound in paper.

Second Preliminary Report upon the Excavations at Tel Umar, Iraq, Conducted by the University of Michigan, the Toledo Museum of Art, and the Cleveland Museum of Art. Leroy Waterman, Director. With 26 plates and 12 text figures. Pp. xii + 78. $1.50. Bound in paper.

PAPERS OF THE MICHIGAN ACADEMY OF SCIENCE, ARTS AND LETTERS

(Containing papers submitted at annual meetings)
Editors: EUGENE S. McCARTNEY and ALFRED H. STOCKARD
Size, 24.2 × 16.5 cm. 8°. Bound in cloth.

Vol. I (1921). Pp. xi + 424. $2.00.

Vol. II (1922). Pp. xi + 226. $2.00. Bound in paper, $1.50.

Orders should be addressed to The Librarian, University of Michigan, Ann Arbor, Michigan.

University of Michigan Publications

VOL. III (1923). Pp. xii + 473. $3.00. Bound in paper, $2.25.

VOL. IV (1924), Part I. Pp. xii + 631. $3.00. Bound in paper, $2.25.

VOL. IV (1924), PART II. A KEY TO THE SNAKES OF THE UNITED STATES AND LOWER CALIFORNIA. By Frank N. Blanchard. Pp. xiii + 65. Cloth. $1.75.

VOL. V (1925). Pp. xii + 479. $3.00. Bound in paper, $2.25.

VOL. VI (1926). (Papers in botany only.) Pp. xii + 406. $3.00. Bound in paper, $2.25.

VOL. VII (1926). (No papers in botany.) Pp. xii + 435. $3.00. Bound in paper, $2.25.

VOL. VIII (1927). Pp. xiv + 456. $3.00. Bound in paper, $2.25.

VOL. IX (1928). (Papers in botany and forestry only.) Pp. xiv + 597. $4.00. Bound in paper, $2.25.

VOL. X (1928). (No papers in botany or forestry.) Pp. xiv + 620. $4.00. Bound in paper, $2.25.

VOL. XI (1929). (Papers in botany and zoölogy only.) Pp. xii + 494. $3.50. Bound in paper, $2.25.

VOL. XII (1929). (No papers in botany or zoölogy.) Pp. xii + 348. $3.00. Bound in paper, $2.25.

VOL. XIII (1930). (Papers in botany and zoölogy only.) Pp. xii + 603. $4.00. Bound in paper, $2.25.

VOL. XIV (1930). (No papers in botany or zoölogy.) Pp. xv + 650. $4.00. Bound in paper, $2.25.

VOL. XV (1931). (Papers in botany, forestry, and zoölogy only.) Pp. x + 511. $3.50. Bound in paper, $2.25.

VOL. XVI (1931). (No papers in botany, forestry, or zoölogy.) Pp. x + 521. $3.50. Bound in paper, $2.25.

VOL. XVII (1932). (Papers in botany, forestry, and zoölogy only.) Pp. x + 738. $4.00. Bound in paper, $2.25.

VOL. XVIII (1932). (No papers in botany, forestry, or zoölogy.) Pp. x + 623. $4.00. Bound in paper, $2.25.

VOL. XIX (1933). Pp. xii + 662. $4.00. Bound in cloth, $2.25.

VOL. XX (1934). (*In press.*)

Orders should be addressed to The Librarian, University of Michigan, Ann Arbor, Michigan.